DATE DUE

DEMCO 38-296

WELFARE OR WELFARE STATE?

Also by David Marsland

SOCIOLOGICAL EXPLORATIONS IN THE SERVICE OF YOUTH
(1978)
BREAKING THE SPELL OF THE WELFARE STATE (1981)
NEGLECT AND BETRAYAL (1985)
EDUCATION AND YOUTH (1987)
UNDERSTANDING YOUTH (*editor*) (1987)
SEEDS OF BANKRUPTCY (1988)
CRADLE TO GRAVE (*with Ralph Segalman*) (1989)
THE END OF THE WELFARE STATE (*with Eamonn Butler,
    Madsen Pirie and Michael Bell*) (1994)
WORK AND EMPLOYMENT IN LIBERAL DEMOCRATIC
    SOCIETIES (*editor*) (1994)
SELF-RELIANCE: Reforming Welfare in Advanced Studies (*editor*)
(1995)

Welfare or Welfare State?

Contradictions and Dilemmas in Social Policy

David Marsland

Professor of Social Sciences
Director of the Centre for Evaluation Research
Brunel University College
London

Foreword by Baroness Thatcher

St. Martin's Press
New York

WELFARE OR WELFARE STATE?
Copyright © 1996 by David Marsland
Foreword copyright © 1996 by Baroness Thatcher
All rights reserved. No part of this book may be used or reproduced in any manner whatsoever without written permission except in the case of brief quotations embodied in critical articles or reviews. For information, address:

St. Martin's Press, Scholarly and Reference Division, 175 Fifth Avenue, New York, N.Y. 10010

First published in the United States of America in 1996

Printed in Great Britain

ISBN 0–312–12920–3 (cloth)
ISBN 0–312–12921–1 (paper)

Library of Congress Cataloging-in-Publication Data
Marsland, David.
Welfare or welfare state? : contradictions and dilemmas in social policy / David Marsland.
p.   cm.
Includes bibliographical references (p.   ) and index.
ISBN 0–312–12920–3 (cloth). — ISBN 0–312–12921–1 (paper)
1. Great Britain—Social policy.   2. Public welfare—Great Britain.   3. Welfare state.   I. Title.
HN385.5.M363   1996
361.6 ' 5 ' 0941—dc20   95–33088
                                                                              CIP

This book is dedicated to Professor Ralph Segalman, a pioneer in the analysis of the damage done to free people by state welfare

I am the master of my fate:
I am the captain of my soul.

W. E. Henley

Contents

Foreword

It has been evident for many years now that the Welfare State is not working well. Its extravagant demands on public expenditure are crippling the real economy. It has consistently failed to provide effective help for those in real need. It undermines the spirit of enterprising self-reliance without which the freedom we so much treasure in Britain cannot be assured.

For all these reasons I set in train from the beginning of my first administration in 1979 a whole programme of reforms of the welfare system. We corrected some of the worst deficiencies of the Welfare State we inherited, and prevented others which the collectivist ideology of the Labour Party and its allies would otherwise have encouraged. Welfare reform has been continued along these lines by John Major and his Ministers, with beneficial effects in education, health care and social security.

Now even the Opposition Parties, who resisted it tooth and nail, acknowledge that this reform programme was essential. Even socialists admit that there can be no going back to the irresponsible spending and glib multiplication of rights which characterized the three decades after 1945. Suddenly everyone claims to be in the business of welfare reform.

In this context, Professor Marsland's new book is an invaluable guide. On the basis of thorough research and careful scholarship he charts the failings of state welfare and the damage it has done to the British people. I am glad to see that he emphasizes particularly the destructive effects on character and social behaviour of welfare dependency. The underclass life created by misconceived state welfare poses a grave threat to freedom and civility throughout Britain – and not least to those who are most disadvantaged.

Not content with systematic diagnosis of the problems of the Welfare State, Professor Marsland also provides, in the second half of this book, a comprehensive and radical plan for continuing welfare reform. I would not agree with every aspect of his reform proposals, and no doubt they will be keenly debated. Their general thrust, however, certainly seems to me to be correct. He urges greater self-reliance all round. The majority of the population should be encouraged to provide for themselves, through market and mutual agencies, for the whole range of their welfare needs. The minority who are temporarily unable to fend for themselves and their families should be helped back to self-reliance by subtler and more realistic measures than the Welfare State has ever managed to provide.

In the next five years I expect we shall see a wide-ranging debate in Parliament and in the media about the scale and nature of welfare reform required to secure progress and prosperity in Britain. I commend *Welfare or Welfare State?* as an honest, intelligent and thoughtful contribution to that debate.

MARGARET THATCHER

Introduction

Laurence Marks's devastating, and devastatingly accurate, obituary of the Soviet Communist Party concludes as follows (*Observer*, 25 August 1991):

The Communist Party of the Soviet Union will be remembered for the cruelty, corruption, mendacity, and administrative incompetence of its leaders, for the credulity and cynicism of its western apologists, for its repression of ethnic minorities and religion, for its silencing and destruction of the greatest flowering of twentieth century Russian literature and art, for its obscurantist persecution of scientists, and for the dark night of the soul it inflicted on three generations of the Soviet people.

Now of course the Welfare States of democratic societies cannot remotely be compared with communism in terms of criminal savagery or even perverse incompetence. The damage they have done and are doing – despite democracy – is none the less enormous. Moreover, the source of their destructiveness is identical with what made communism such a fearful enemy of humanity and progress – *its commitment to a specious form of equality and to institutionalized envy*. Again, in both cases the strategy adopted to secure this so-called equality is identical – *subversion of supposedly bourgeois, actually human, values, and expropriation of private property and the market*.

How *dare* we in Britain chide the peoples of the former communist empire for their dilatory movement towards the condition of a market society and democratic freedom when we ourselves continue to exclude from the market the whole of the welfare sphere – one-half at least of economic transactions, involving many of the most important services people need? The necessity of rolling back the state and liberating individual initiative is at least as imperative in Britain or the United States or France as it is in Russia or Romania or Khazakstan.

There, as here, there are many influential collectivists who claim not only that a free market in the industrial sphere is compatible with a powerful central state apparatus controlling planning and welfare, but that it actually necessitates it. Reluctantly and late in the day, collectivists East and West now concede that the market may serve the population well as an instrument of economic efficiency and dynamism. From Mr Blair to

Mr Deng, from Scandinavian social democrats to the ANC leadership in South Africa, socialists worldwide have all unblushingly retracted their virulent denunciations of competition and profit in the industrial marketplace.

As far as freedom and human dignity are concerned, however, and the whole sphere of what has come to be defined as welfare, they remain dogmatic collectivists. Outside the sphere of industry narrowly defined, they persist in their antique conviction that the market is at best irrelevant and at worst a grave impediment to progress. They continue to insist that, as far as welfare is concerned, political mechanisms – including ownership, control and bureaucratic regulation by the state – are necessary to protect the interests of the population.

The conclusion I reach in this book is that they are gravely mistaken. Their views are the product of what Herbert Spencer called 'the shaping of ignorance into the semblance of knowledge'. The market is a precondition both of freedom and of human dignity. Only a market can guarantee people a real choice in relation to those most fundamental aspects of their lives which currently fall under the control of the Welfare State – education, health care, housing, and protection against misfortune. Where people cannot choose freely in the arena of liberty which the marketplace provides, they have little hope of securing or maintaining freedom more broadly.

Moreover, by requiring – indeed constraining – individual choice, the market schools us to prudent consideration, careful judgement, autonomy and self-reliance (Novak, 1991). It is thus the seedbed of human dignity as much as it is the foundation of freedom.

Where the free market is outlawed, the people are serfs. Where the market is substantially restricted, as it is in Britain and in other Welfare State societies, the people are half-free, half-slave. The argument which justifies markets as the antidote to socialist dictatorship in Eastern and Central Europe is *at the same time and by the same token* an argument for the disestablishment of the Welfare State in the democracies. If it is valid there, it is valid here.

In *Parliament of Whores*, P. J. O'Rourke characterizes the welfare-induced poverty of a contemporary New Jersey housing project – 'all squalor and stench' – as worse than conditions in Beirut and Manila:

> What we managed to escape in 1966 in Squaresville, Ohio, was not poverty. We had that. What we managed to escape was help.

The phoney help on offer from the Welfare State is no help at all. It is a lethal threat to our freedom. We should get rid of it once and for all, and replace it in its entirety with social policies more appropriate to free men and free women in a free society. We cannot rely securely on the state – on any state – for our welfare. Real welfare is produced by the effort, initiative and moral choice of individual men and women. With the state off our backs – and only thus – we could do it.

Addressing the Independent Seminar of the Open Society in 1993, I spoke to the title 'Welfare Farewell', intending two distinct but complementary messages. First, a warning. So long as we allow education, health care, pensions, housing, unemployment insurance, and the rest to be monopolistically dominated by the state, the people's real welfare will be in jeopardy. Goodbye to real welfare so long as the Welfare State is allowed to survive. Second, a rallying-call for radical reform – Welfare Farewell meaning let us cut the Welfare State down to size forthwith. Goodbye Welfare State.

I am no anarchist. The state is an indispensable instrument of social functioning and of humanity's progress. Some states more than others, admittedly, but *all* states have essential tasks to perform: defence in the face of external enemies; international diplomacy; the maintenance of internal law and order; and securing the monetary foundations of the economy.

Alas, for many decades our state has fulfilled these essential tasks a good deal less adequately than the British people need and deserve. These failures, this dereliction of the state's essential duties, is due in no small part to the distraction of the state into a continuously expanding role in the sphere of welfare, where it has no essential or proper role at all. The Welfare State has grown and grown like Topsy, as it were – or more accurately, like a cancer sucking the life-blood out of the people. Yet extraordinarily there are people, even among those who are not avowed socialists or self-confessed collectivists, who seek to defend it, and some even who apparently want to see it expanded still further. I spoke at a conference on welfare in 1993 organized by the 21st Century Trust. The programme outline, which I have in front of me now, begins as follows:

> The term welfare state is synonymous with postwar western societies. It describes not only a set of policies and institutions but also a philosophy, even an attitude of mind. With its basic ideals of full employment and universal state services, the welfare state is generally regarded as one of the great achievements of advanced capitalist societies.

What nonsense it is! And there is worse. For even in going on to raise apparently open and critical questions about the role of the Welfare State in the future, the document quite extraordinarily poses the question, 'Will the Welfare State grow or contract?'

How could *anyone* at this time so much as contemplate, even hypothetically, the possibility of further expansion of an institution which is already
so bloated that it threatens to invade and overwhelm and stifle the whole
of the natural, healthy, spontaneous cultural and institutional life which a
free society depends on absolutely – above all the family, the local
community, the voluntary agencies of civil society, and the market?

What the free societies need is not an expansion of state welfare but
systematic contraction. Rapid movement out of the state welfare monopoly cocoon is, as I seek to show in this book, entirely feasible in practical
terms. It is also, in moral and political terms alike, essential. For the
Welfare State is a contradiction in terms: a nation devoted to universal
state welfare provision inevitably destroys the people's real welfare.

Real welfare can only be secured by free people acting individually and
on behalf of their own families out of their own resources as they severally
freely choose. Genuine and sustainable welfare in human society is a
product of individual choice, initiative, effort and self-reliance. A Welfare
State system subverts and suppresses all these elements of freedom almost
as effectively as does socialism. The Welfare State is an enemy of real
welfare.

Welfare in the United States

I hope this book may prove useful not only in Britain, but also elsewhere
in the English-speaking world, and in particular in the United States. If
this is to be achieved, I need to indicate my view of the American welfare
situation.

It is commonly assumed in Europe that the United States remains a
haven (or hell) of liberal capitalism, that the work ethic and the ideology
of self-reliance have survived intact in the land of opportunity, and that in
consequence America has been spared our problems with state welfare.
These Panglossian and erroneous opinions are sometimes, more dangerously, expressed even in the United States itself. Nothing could be further
from the truth, as Aaron Wildavsky (1987) and Lawrence Mead (1986 and
1992) have both shown.

Of course, the extent of domination by state welfare is less than it is in
Europe (Drover and Hokenstad, 1994; Gordon and Winter, 1989). How
could it be otherwise when the United States has been spared two of its
main progenitors – an organized trade union movement and a successful
socialist party? Moreover, the ideology of individualism and self-reliance
has long been more strongly entrenched in America than anywhere else in
the world. None the less, even in the United States the Welfare State is

flourishing – and doing its usual damage to economic progress and to liberty.

Thus, quite contrary to the general image of American health care as a free-market system, almost half of the total health-care budget is already actually carried by the Federal Government, and this seems likely to increase still further in coming years. The monopoly of the state in education – admittedly local, but none the less political – is as complete as anywhere in Europe, and apparently taken for granted even by self-styled conservatives. In consequence, standards are so patchy and inadequate that employers are obliged to examine high-school ratings thoroughly before they can safely take on a new employee.

Again, right across the face of the States, in every one of its great cities, there are huge swathes of project housing like the Taylor Homes in Chicago, planned by agents of state power and paid for out of taxes, which provide for their wretched inhabitants out of wasted Federal funds an environment as destructive of self-confidence, self-reliance, and enterprising initiative as their openly socialist equivalents in Moscow, Minsk or Bratislava.

On the pensions front, the problem is less grave than in Britain, owing to the much greater involvement, over a longer period, of employers, public and private, in pensions provision. Even so, demographic change is occasioning similar problems to those manifest in Europe, and for the large number of Americans whose main source of retirement income is Social Security or SSI (Supplementary Security Income), the problem is even worse. In the sphere of welfare more narrowly defined, the extent of involvement by the state is large and currently still increasing, producing all the problems of disincentive effects and dependency so graphically analysed by Charles Murray in *Losing Ground* (1984), and described even earlier by Ralph Segalman and Asoke Basu in *Poverty in America* (1981).

What with AFDC (Aid to Families with Dependent Children), funded 75 per cent by the Federal purse, and its extension to the families of the unemployed (AFDCU); what with special versions of SSI for the disabled; and what with General Assistance for the unemployed at local community level – with all of this and other Byzantine systems beside, the scale of involvement by the state in welfare is huge and the extent of consequent damage to the fabric of the family and to the character of the free people of the United States is nothing less than enormous (Douglas, 1990).

Compared with the situation in Britain and Scandinavia, or even in Continental Europe, the United States at least seems to have the advantage that these extensive provisions by the state have not yet been so firmly entrenched in the popular psyche as unchallengeable rights. The countervailing force of popular commitment to the ideology of self-reliance remains much stronger than we have dared to expect on this side of the Atlantic since the 1950s or even the 1930s. However, the bigger the system grows, the more people get used to taking it for granted, the more welfare workers there are with a vested interest in defending it and extending it further, and the more academics and politicians there are whose sole expertise is in finding plausible justifications for moving further and further in the direction of a fully elaborated American Welfare State.

Thus this book, written by a European in part for Americans, is not a work of exotic anthropology reporting strange and alien ways of life to an enlightened and civilized people whose advanced standards provide a protection against the barbarous customs of distant, primitive cultures. It is rather an analysis of an advanced state of a disease with which the United States, like Britain, is already infected. It reports on those progressive stages of the welfare disease which we can confidently expect to strike soon with similar severity in the United States, unless radical reform is entered on boldly and urgently. It proposes innovative remedies for the disease which may, like other earlier British inventions, prove useful with suitable modification for the American context.

Americans might reasonably counter this claim by reminding me that the President has made welfare reform a priority, that he has already made a number of public and official statements condemning abuses of welfare which are bolder and more honest than we have ever heard from any Western leader, and that reform legislation was already on the stocks at an early stage of the presidency. I quote Mr Clinton with approbation in the body of this book, and in my BBC2 film *Let's Kill Nanny* (shown on 4 August 1994) on welfare reform, a clip of the President addressing Congress courageously and intelligently about workfare and about the responsibilities of lone parents figures powerfully.

However, without wishing to take anything away from the courage of the President's commitments on welfare, I have to insist that his plans seem unlikely to be sufficient to reverse the tide of collectivist state welfare sweeping – under administrations of all political colours – over American society (Carlson, 1994). Ronald Reagan presented some excellent plans as Governor of California as long ago as 1971, in 'Meeting the Challenge: a Responsible Program for Welfare and Medical Reform', but little was achieved in practice. Only a revivified commitment to self-reliance and detailed practical planning for genuinely independent welfare programmes will be strong enough to resist the combined pressures of the political gravy-train, radical feminism, socialist social scientists, and the liberal media.

Mr Gingrich and the new Republican majorities might, one hopes, succeed, capitalizing on the 75 per cent of Americans agreeing at a November 1994 exit poll that the Welfare State 'had on balance made things worse by causing able-bodied people to be too dependent on government' (Macrae, 1995). Unless they adhere closely, however, to systematic radical analysis, and commit themselves unwaveringly to a programme of fundamental reconstruction, they will certainly fail. The extent of the problem was exposed in the recent report of the Bipartisan Commission on Entitlement and Tax Reform. Solutions will require considerable courage and intelligence.

Welfare Reform

State welfare is causing grave damage in the United Kingdom, in the United States, and elsewhere throughout the free world. It is impeding the dynamism of global economic competition, and thus slowing world economic growth. Through the bureaucratic centralization and the underclass dependency which it inevitably creates, it poses a serious long-term threat to liberty and to the stability of democracy.

This book argues for a return to that spirit of self-reliance which quite recently in Britain and even more recently in the United States was at the very centre of the value system of our two societies (Smiles, 1986). That enterprising spirit has indeed been the foundational creative element of the culture of all the free societies. Without it, or restricted to the attenuated form of it which is all that welfare state ideology can tolerate, we shall find that our liberty is at peril. It is time now to plan urgently and radically for excision of most of the swollen state welfare which we have foolishly allowed to grow up since the 1940s.

No one in recent years has analysed more accurately the deficiencies of the Welfare State, or done more to encourage the discovery of sensible alternatives, than Madsen Pirie. In two short paragraphs which Secretaries of State for Social Security (of whatever political party) might usefully have inscribed on vellum and hung above their desks, he pinpoints the problems and spells out the solution (Bell *et al.*, 1994, pp. 25 and 26):

> the system itself is fraudulent. It talks glibly of insurance and a social security fund, but there is none. It is run as a straight transfer system. Money from today's contributors goes straight into the pockets of today's claimants.... As long as there are enough fit workers to fund it, the obligations can be met. As the population ages the number of burdens will rise faster than the number of shoulders. The morality of

Social Security is that of the chain letter. You only benefit if people in the future are even bigger mugs than you were.

For the foreseeable future, and perhaps always, there will be a need to transfer wealth from those who are young, fit and in work to those who are elderly, sick or unemployed. Welfare reform has to be based on the simple principle that the best person to support someone who is elderly, sick or unemployed is that same person when young, fit and in work. In other words, where we today transfer across society from some groups to others, an efficient welfare system would transfer within a group across time. People would pay in provision when they were able to do so, and draw upon those provisions when circumstances made it necessary. They would be supporting themselves.

This is the same radical yet practical conclusion at which I arrive in this book. If it seems to some readers a little immoderate, they might consider an analysis of the Welfare State's prospects provided by Martin Jacques (1994), not, as the former editor of *Marxism Today*, a noted Thatcherite:

Three common themes are evident. One is a greater emphasis on ensuring that social security systems do not impede the reduction in unemployment. Lower benefits, requiring the unemployed to undergo training, and workfare policies based on work in return for benefits are all intended to boost employment levels. Secondly, there is growing pressure for people to provide their own welfare. This is already the case in the Anglo-Saxon world, but pressures to reduce benefit levels, including premiums, will have a similar effect elsewhere. Thirdly, there is the widening of the funding basis for the welfare state, with tax-based systems looking to contributions from employers and employees and vice-versa for contribution-based systems. It should be noted here that so far there is little evidence of any major extension of the welfare state: all the pressures at the moment seem to be towards a diminution in its role.

Acknowledgements

My analysis goes beyond Jacques's in positively commending the changes which he merely acknowledges as likely trends. Our current welfare arrangements are not only ineffective: they are wholly misconceived, based as they are on mistaken concepts of security and misunderstandings of the nature of risk (Wildavsky, 1987; Adams, 1995). It seems to me that we should move away from collectivist state welfare and towards independent self-reliance as quickly as can be managed.

Such explicit and outright opposition to the Welfare State is still regarded, in Britain particularly, as an outlandishly heretical view, representing an almost blasphemous challenge to the fundamental values of civilization. Apparently a problem has to reach a condition of near insolubility before any attention is paid to those who have provided warnings about it for years. Inattention to the destructive effects of state welfare is close to reaching the scandalous level of neglect by the British establishment in the 1930s of the threat to peace and democracy posed by Nazism. In relation to this even more massive problem, the writer William Shirer, writing after his return to the free world after years of providing futile, unread reports of the truth about what was happening in Germany, said: 'We could tell our story now to a world too afraid not to listen.'

I am fortunate, therefore, in my work over several years on this book, to have had the support of several of the most distinguished and most expert of my fellow welfare-dissidents. I wish to thank: Professor Ralph Segalman, to whom the book is humbly dedicated; Dr Digby Anderson, Director of the Social Affairs Unit; Dr Madsen Pirie and Dr Eamonn Butler of the Adam Smith Institute; Ralph (Lord) Harris, Arthur Seldon, Dr David Green, and John Blundell of the Institute of Economic Affairs; Professor Roger Scruton; Charles Murray; Professor Patrick Minford; Michael Ivens; Dr Dennis O'Keeffe; Professor Antony Flew; Norman Dennis; Professor Peter Saunders; Dr Tim Evans; Professor Irving Louis Horowitz; Dr Nigel Ashford; Michael Bell; and Dr Errol Mathura.

Others to whom I owe a considerable debt of gratitude include Professor Donald MacRae, Professor Julius Gould, Professor David Martin, Dr Chris Badcock, John Spiers, Chris Tame, Brian Micklethwaite, Sue Douglas, and Paul Norcross.

In writing *Welfare or Welfare State?* I have made much use of work of mine published or broadcast during the past five years. I must acknowledge the support and encouragement provided by BBC Television, BBC Radio, Macmillan, the Claridge Press, Transaction Books, Paragon House Press, *Social Policy and Administration* (particularly Professor Bob Leaper), the *Salisbury Review* (especially Merrie Cave), *Modern Management, Parliamentary Brief*, the Radical Society, the Adam Smith Institute, the Libertarian Alliance, the *Daily Mail*, and the *Sunday Times*.

I must also thank Professor John Kane, Murie Robertson, Beryl Wakeman-Reynolds, David Anderson-Ford, Conor Gissane, Geoffrey Matthews, and other supportive colleagues at the West London Institute of Higher Education (now Brunel University College), where I have worked during the period of writing this book. I am very grateful to my students, undergraduate and postgraduate, for continuing stimulus and challenge.

In the political sphere – with which, through the nature of the issues addressed here, I am inevitably intermeshed – I should thank: Lady Thatcher, Lord Tebbitt, Peter Lilley, Michael Portillo, Peter Thurnham MP, Ralph Howell MP, and Frank Field MP, whose well-known courtesy extended even as far as tolerating me as a Specialist Advisor to the Social Security Committee.

Most of all I must thank Dr Athena Leoussi of Reading University for the caring support and intellectual stimulus she manages with complete reliability to provide.

I will conclude this Introduction by flagging up my intentions for my next book. It will follow up the clues provided here by Michael Bell (1994, p. 37):

> In summary, privatization of the state pensions scheme...could probably make the Government a once for all profit of many tens of billions of pounds, and give it a substantial continuing income on the same scale, while transmuting what is effectively an income tax into private pension contributions. The public finances will benefit in every imaginable way, and a notable step forward will have been taken in the process of dismantling an intrusive state which limits opportunity.

In the chapters of this book I examine the deficiencies of state welfare and propose the development of a more efficient and more equitable alternative. It is, I hope, a realistic and practical book, but it is concerned primarily with ideas, arguments, and principles. My next book will focus explicitly on the practicalities of welfare reform. It will examine first the enormous financial gains likely to accrue to any government with the courage to initiate radical reform; and secondly the information which the new consumers of privatized welfare will need to access if they are to choose wisely and well in education, health care, pensions, and insurance.

The advantages, for Britain as a nation and for individuals and families throughout the free world, which the market in welfare will offer are ours for the taking, provided that a critical analysis of the welfare status quo such as that set out in the following pages finds open-minded readers. I live in hope. There are, after all, only four grounds of resistance to reform (Marsland, 1992) – *political expediency, ideology, vested interest*, and *habit*. These are tougher monsters to crush than the Giant Evils targeted by Lord Beveridge, but they are not invincible. Even the left-inclined think-tank Demos has insisted (in an open letter to the Leader of the Labour Party, *Guardian*, 27 September 1994) that: 'A state absorbing 40 per cent of the national wealth is quite large enough already... The key test of public spending should be quality and effectiveness, not quantity.' We must act decisively on the implications of this manifest truth.

1 Paradise Mislaid: The Welfare State as a Failed Utopia

Malcolm Wicks (1987) begins the concluding chapter of his nostalgic apologia for the Welfare State with a story about an old lady he had met in the course of his research. Her flat, he tells us, was cold and expensive to heat. The sitting-room had 'a high ceiling and a very large window'. The fitted electric heater was very expensive to run. She used her own heater in order to reduce fuel costs, and often sat in the hall instead of the sitting-room to reduce her expenses further. Wicks describes her experience of public housing provision as follows:

> She claims that when she visited this flat with an official from the Housing Department, she only saw it from the front door, as the workmen were in. If she had seen the big window in the main room, she would never have taken it. She now wanted to move to a smaller and warmer flat. She had asked the Council... but all to no avail. Her local doctor had written to the Council on her behalf, she said, but he had not been hopeful – 'they screw it up and throw it in the bin'.

Bureaucratic neglect of a citizen's legitimate pleas for assistance and of a doctor's recommendations on behalf of an elderly lady is bad enough. Even more extraordinary is that she had to 'choose' her home without even ever seeing it! She was allowed no chance at all to apply her own evidently competent judgement in a matter in which she was quite capable of making the relevant rational calculations and which was patently the opposite of trivial. There is precious little chance of *caveat emptor* if you are expected to 'buy' blind.

This absurd but not untypical instance of forced choice for consumers of public housing is complemented perfectly on the other side of the state housing supply/demand equation by the extraordinary cases described by Norman Dennis in his carefully researched studies of local authority planning (1970 and 1972). It appears that the planning professionals of the North East (and no doubt elsewhere similarly) were in the habit of making their decisions about which houses to spare and which to demolish – from a moving car!

No doubt Wicks – now a Labour Member of Parliament, who incidentally says not a word about the moral obligations of the old lady's children to help her – would take these and similar cases as decisive evidence of the need to spend even more on public housing, to 'democratize' local politics, to introduce schemes of consumer evaluation and quality assurance, and to bring professionals and bureaucrats under 'popular' control. It seems to me rather more plausible to conclude, on the basis of these and countless similar cases from every sphere of welfare provision, that instead, we should move urgently in quite the opposite direction.

Rather than shore up the decaying system of state welfare with ever more elaborate and expensive bureaucratic apparatus, we should cut it ruthlessly down to size and restrict its operations to modest, essential tasks which it can handle reasonably efficiently.

There is considerable evidence that collective provision of welfare services by the state is at least as ineffective and counter-productive in other spheres as in housing (Savas, 1982 and 1990; Seldon, 1990). Why not, therefore, take privatization seriously, in the welfare sphere as much as in the industrial sector, by disestablishing the whole of state welfare, and turning it over to a real market of genuine producers and consumers? Why not, in short, enter on radical, root and branch reform of the Welfare State?

Reforming Welfare

Even in the old heartlands of socialism in Russia and China, the past decade has seen a reluctant recognition that all-enveloping state provision of cradle-to-grave services is inefficient and morally damaging. In Britain and the United States (as in the rest of the free world), which have been havens of freedom and democracy from time immemorial, we should not have needed to learn this lesson at all – since it is a self-evident corollary of freedom and an unchallengeable axiom of democracy.

For, while democracy can restore freedom to a people who have been robbed of it, freedom and democracy can neither grow spontaneously nor survive successfully except and unless men behave as free men must – that is freely, independently, and with brave self-reliance. The Welfare State has inhibited such free, independent and self-reliant action even in the free world. Hence we too have had to learn the same hard lesson as the Russians and the Chinese: *excessive state power means slavery.*

The ideology and apparatus of state welfare, with whatever benevolent intentions it may be established, inevitably stifles the responsible, adaptive behaviour which freedom requires of those who would claim its precious benefits. Its bureaucratic structures strangle the natural, spontaneously developing co-operative institutions on which freedom depends – the family, the market, the legal system, and the local community foremost among them. Its tangled web of rules and obligations destroys the capacity of free men and women to choose freely for themselves and to pursue their individual interests rationally. Its piratical seizure of moral control abandons the people to purposeless drifting, subservient dependency, and aimless incapacity to choose and act for themselves responsibly and freely (Segalman and Marsland, 1989).

Socialism has failed, and is being replaced. The Welfare State has failed at least as badly. We must set about replacing it with institutions more appropriate to a free people. We must liberate welfare from the shackles of the state, and provide for ourselves a system of welfare which liberates from the cramping oppression of the Nanny State our natural capacity for responsible autonomy.

The process of welfare reform has of course begun, in Britain as elsewhere. In Britain, there are some who view the Government's record on welfare since 1979 as a disappointing failure. From this critical perspective, years which have seen a revolution in other spheres – in improvements in economic management, in privatization, in tax reform, and in controlling illegitmate trade union power – have brought nothing more than organizational tinkering, administrative fine-tuning, and bureaucratic blundering in welfare.

Even in housing, where personal home-ownership has been massively expanded by active sales of public housing stock to tenants, the tied-cottage system of socialism which state tenancy comprises remains none the less much larger in scale than in some Eastern European states even before the collapse of communism. Reforms of social security, health, and education have left the state monopoly system largely intact, while exposing the Government to accusations of uncaring mean-mindedness and hard-hearted cost-cutting for its own sake.

I see the sense of such criticisms, but I am not persuaded of their validity. After all, the Welfare State is deeply entrenched in the British psyche. Its ideological power rests not only on the post-war 'Butskellite' consensus, but also beyond that on nearly a century of cross-party tolerance of state welfare. Beyond that again, its stifling grip on social policy derives from politicized distortions of Christian ethical principles going back deep into the nineteenth century.

In this historical context, welfare reform had to be cautious and gradual, and much has been achieved. Since 1979 the Government has begun to reform the major sectors of the welfare system – education, housing and health care in particular. This is to the Government's credit and to the people's advantage. Ministers deserve support in their efforts to implement reform in the face of concerted resistance by vested interests, ideological collectivists, and the massed ranks of *soi-disant* social affairs experts in the media and among academics (Marsland, 1992).

In the 1970s, extraordinary as it now seems, social policy academics were still arguing, on the grounds of 'balance', that private home-ownership should be actually *reduced* to the meagre levels of private provision in health and education. Now even left-socialists dare not speak out against home-ownership, and council housing is generally regarded as residual provision for the elderly and for other special categories. The Housing Act of 1980, and related legislation, by enshrining the right to buy, has had a powerfully beneficial effect.

Reform of education has proved much more difficult than was envisaged by radicals in the 1970s. Union power is more powerfully entrenched in the schools than in the steel industry or even in coal-mining. Educational ideas remain firmly controlled by egalitarians and play-way theorists. The institutions of reform themselves are still largely in the hands of unreconstructed collectivists (Marsland and Seaton, 1993; Marsland, 1992 [3]).

None the less, the Education Reform Act of 1988 has at least shaken up the system. Competition and choice have been injected into it as a vaccination against bureaucratic inertia. Devolved management of schools is in place. The worst excesses of the politicized curriculum of the 1960s and 1970s have been challenged and limited by the initiation of a national framework. A beginning has even been made – *mirabile dictu* – on assessing the effectiveness of teaching and learning. Parental choice of schools is assured.

In health care, a genuine and courageous start has been made on fundamental re-structuring as a result of the 1989 White Paper and the National Health Service and Community Care Act of 1990. Reform is being fiercely resisted by those who stand to benefit from vested interests in the inertia of status quo bureaucracy and state monopoly. The media and the Labour Party are making the most, and more, out of every heartrending story about supposed cuts, dying children, underpaid nurses and decrepit hospitals.

But the die is cast. Reform is in place (Marsland, 1993). Independent hospitals are managing themselves. The internal market is bypassing the bureaucratic sclerosis of the biggest organization in Europe except the Red Army. Doctors are waking up to costs and the advantages of competition.

Patients are being initiated into the novel privilege of choice. Even the public are beginning to realize that most of the scare stories are nothing but middle-class trade unionists crying 'wolf' (Marsland, 1992).

Again, in relation to social security and the benefit system, some real, if modest, progress has been made through an almost continuous programme of legislation. The essence of the several reforms in this sphere since 1979, including the shift in the mid-1980s from the concept of Supplementary Benefits to Income Support, has been to improve the coherence of the system and to focus targeting more effectively.

The more radical right may scoff at the feasibility of thus rationalizing an over-blown hand-out culture which apparently reproduces and multiplies itself automatically. And it has to be admitted that, despite a decade and a half of Conservative administrations committed to cutting the system down to size, the social security apparatus and its budget have continued to expand inexorably.

But continuing modest reforms have at least put the whole crazy system under question. Even the Labour Party and the professional poverty lobby have become more circumspect than of old with their promises of minimum wages, improved benefit levels, and further extensions of rights to state support. Even socialists, it seems, have recognized that the level of income and the standard of living of the least well-off are shaped more by the health of the economy than by egalitarian sloganizing. If only our television pundits and our sentimentalizing bishops were vouchsafed the same modest level of understanding of economic realities!

Thus, in most of the major spheres of welfare – housing, education, health care and social security, to which one should add pensions and local government – the Government has managed to call a halt, or at least a decisive pause, to collectivist mischief which had previously been entirely taken for granted for decades. It has made at least a start on turning the tide away from the straitjacket of state welfare towards freedom, choice and self-reliance.

The Welfare State as a No-go Area for Radical Reform

Even if these commendable initiatives are successful, however, partial reform leaves entirely unchallenged the underlying concept of the Welfare State, and the outmoded collectivist values which it enshrines. Fundamental challenge to the whole concept remains apparently unacceptable in polite circles. It seems to be assumed that the curious combination of high taxes, state control, and rights without responsibilities which the Welfare State essentially comprises represents the pinnacle of human civilization. We seem to have got ourselves stuck in a posture of neurotic obeisance to the Nanny Totem of the Welfare State.

Thus even after a decade and a half of Thatcherism in government, it seems we remain for the most part smugly content to conceive of our society as a 'Welfare State', and staunch in defence of whatever this fundamentally incoherent notion stands for.

To disapprove of the Welfare State *in principle* is still widely regarded, even by critics of socialism and avowed supporters of individualism and enterprise, as evidence of philistine incivility at best, and at worst as symptomatic of blimpish obscurantism. To argue not merely that the Welfare State is wasteful of resources and inefficient in practice, but beyond this that the values underlying it and the institutions it legitimates are incompatible with liberty and inimical to democracy, is viewed by the British intelligentsia as scarcely less foolish and reprehensible than Anaxagoras' claim – for which he was exiled – that the sun and the moon are not gods but stones.

Indeed, even beyond the massed ranks of social science academics, television presenters, quality press journalists, worldly priests and arts administrators who comprise what passes for the intelligentsia of modern Britain – even, that is to say, among ordinary people and the general population – the Welfare State remains sacred territory, protected by impregnable taboos from rational analysis and honest criticism. If Margaret Thatcher had failed, as Prime Minister, to insist that the National Health Service – the corner-stone of the whole crumbling edifice of the Welfare State – was 'safe in her hands', she would, no doubt, have been arraigned by the media for secular impiety, and impeached by a committee of the great and the good as an enemy of the people's security and happiness.

Thus, as Digby Anderson (1981) suggested not long after Lady Thatcher first became Prime Minister, the influence of the Welfare State is eerily powerful. It reaches far beyond the level of rationality to constitute something close to a magic spell to which we are all to some degree in thrall. To break the spell, while subject to superstitious belief in its magical powers, is almost impossible. The scale of its power is indicated in a letter I received in 1994 from a company director living somewhere in the greenest part of the Home Counties, written in response to an article of mine:

> it has been most noticeable to me as a non-academic that the wider effect of the socialist bias in parts of our education system has reached and almost engulfed, it seems, the natural supporters of liberal conduct. I find that all of my friends in the area in which I live, quite naturally and, when challenged, vehemently defend the Welfare State, the

National Health Service, and almost all other types of interventionist social policy – many of which, of course, they benefit from, completely unnecessarily, themselves. I have found this very difficult to explain....

Critique and Reform

Despite these barriers to rational criticism of state welfare, the damage which the Welfare State is doing to Britain and the British people is such that a serious attempt at challenging its influence is essential. Hence this book.

It is not, of course, the first such critique of the Welfare State. From Herbert Spencer's percipient analysis of the destructive impact of state welfare on nineteenth-century enterprise and prudence (Spencer, 1908; Offer, 1993), through the faltering opposition by a minority of Conservatives and Liberals to emboldened socialism between the two World Wars, to the Institute of Economic Affairs' solitary, courageous resistance to what had become by the 1950s an established welfare orthodoxy (Harris and Seldon, 1977), the damaging threat posed by collectivist benevolence has been regularly identified and challenged. More recently there has been a whole series of systematic investigations of the excessive costs, dubious benefits, and harmful consequences of state welfare, notably by Arthur Seldon (1981 and 1990), Digby Anderson (1981 and 1992), David Green (1984, 1990, and 1993), Madsen Pirie (Bell, 1994), and Charles Murray (1984 and 1990). Criticism has come almost as much from the left (LeGrand, 1982; Plant *et al.*, 1980) as from the right (M. and R. Friedman, 1980), and scarcely less from social scientists associated with no particular political or value inclination (Hasenfeld and Zald, 1985; Spiro and Yaar, 1983).

Yet even in Thatcherite Britain, even indeed in prototypically free-market America, critical analysis of collectivist welfare provision has had remarkably little effect in practice. In both countries, as elsewhere in the free world, expenditure on state welfare continues to expand year in year out, despite ample evidence that it damages the family, generates dependency, and augments the crime-wave (Segalman and Marsland, 1989). Although standards of living have improved out of all recognition, the proportion of the population resorting to state welfare assistance grows bigger all the time. Ignoring entirely the manifest disincentive effects of state over-protection, legislatures are endlessly, tirelessly establishing yet more 'rights' for ever broader circles of the population. With blind disregard for the evidence provided by the headlong collapse of communist regimes in the East that socialism corrupts absolutely the capacity for self-reliance and enterprising initiative, M. Delors and his welfare commissars have been busily engaged in expanding and strengthening state control still further. The British Labour Party, for all its supposed new moderation, springs unthinkingly to the defence of even the most unsavoury aspects of the Welfare State in the face of proposed reforms however modest, and expenditure savings however slight and sensible.

Nor is there any shortage of new intellectual apologias for the Welfare State. Marxist and other left-socialists who during the 1960s and 1970s savaged state welfare unmercifully for its oppressive paternalism and as a supposed instrument of exploitative capitalist control, have reacted to liberal critique of the Welfare State by conveniently rediscovering its positive role as a primary defence of the 'working class' (Walker and Walker, 1987; Loney, 1988; George and Wilding, 1994). Mainline socialists and orthodox ideologues of state welfare have been encouraged by the growing-pains of Britain's infant enterprise culture to produce ambitious new accounts of the economic, social, cultural, and moral grounds for defending the Welfare State and extending its scope even further (Plant in Plant and Barry, 1990; Deakin, 1994; Sullivan, 1994; Cahill, 1994). The publishers' documentation for Cahill's book, *The New Social Policy*, boasts in all innocence that 'Each chapter focuses on the theme of inequality in the examination of social change and social life: the old inequalities which persist and the new inequalities which have been produced.'

As for the British media, which were never in any case better than half-hearted about capitalism and enterprise, they have joined in this reactionary chorus vigorously, with sentimental exposés of the supposedly scandalous sufferings of the poor due to alleged cuts in state expenditure on benefits, housing, health care and education. That old 1960s 'weepy' about the homeless – *Cathy Come Home* – has been ceremonially re-run, and champions of state welfare can be as confident as ever of unlimited opportunities to propagate their dubious vision of a welfare paradise in the press and on the television screen – as if its promise had gone unfulfilled simply and solely because of malicious sabotage by a hard-hearted Government.

The Contexts of Reform

Any decision to move systematically on radical welfare reform will be taken in proper constitutional form by the elected Government and by the British people. I would expect such a decision to be taken very cautiously, and with irrelevant pressures and mistaken arguments carefully discounted. If their irrelevance and error is to be established, systematic analysis of the contexts of reform which these pressures and arguments comprise is essential. It seems to me that there are three crucial contexts: the policies of the Opposition parties in Britain, European initiatives, and the influence of British intellectuals.

The Labour Party and the Liberal Democrats need not detain us long. For, whatever occasional acknowledgements their spokesmen may guardedly make about deficiencies in state welfare and the need for a more considered policy than simply increasing the welfare budget, in the last resort they are blindly – and indistinguishably – committed to the status quo. The Welfare State is to be defended at all costs, and every effort at modernization is to be resisted. Even the Labour Party's celebrated 'Commission on Justice' has turned out, in a context of unavoidable compromise with the collectivist pressure groups on which the Party depends for funding and activist support, to be more or less of a damp squib (Marsland, 1994 [6]).

It seems to me likely that the public will see straight through the blinkered dishonesty of the Parliamentary Opposition's defensive obscurantism. People understand that welfare expenditure is excessive. They do not want higher taxes. They are aware of fraud in the benefit system, and angry about it. They know only too well that the quality of education, health care, and other state services has not improved in parallel with standards in other aspects of their lives which they provide for out of their own pockets in the private sector. They are beginning to understand that self-reliance is a more dependable source of real welfare than the blundering bureaucracy of the state (Saunders and Harris, 1989 and 1990).

The proper reaction of those who favour radical welfare reform to the chauvinist obfuscation of the Opposition parties (and some Conservatives) is thus obvious. The unthinking conservatism of their arguments should be exposed mercilessly, and the case for reform should be pressed unapologetically.

The extent of the European Community's power in Britain in the next five years is likely, fortunately, to be modest. Its influence, however, may be considerable, even supposing that our opt-out from the Social Chapter is successfully protected. This influence will need to be addressed explicitly and countered decisively by welfare reformers (see for example Schmahl, 1991, and more dangerously Kleinman and Piachaud, 1993).

The general tendency of Euro-policy on welfare is accurately reflected in the Commission's Green Paper *European Social Policy* (1993) – a document which, despite its polite rubbishing by key politicians in Germany, France and Britain, is likely to be gradually and quietly influential in the welfare debate. It does at least have the merit of admitting, if somewhat reluctantly, that the Welfare State as traditionally established is less than perfect and stands in need of some measure of reform. This said, however, its overall thrust is transparently collectivist. Its proposals would inhibit the development of independent provision of welfare by the market, and in the long run produce an even more bloated Welfare State right across Europe. One could imagine no surer guarantee of defeat in the face of American and Japanese economic competition.

Despite authorship attributed to an Irishman (Padraig Flynn, the Commissioner for Social Affairs and Employment), it speaks throughout in the alien discourse of continental socialism. For example, people on low incomes, the unemployed, lone parents and others are said to be suffering from 'social exclusion'. The theory underlying this curious concept, of which Mr Flynn is no doubt innocently unaware, is that capitalism (disguised as 'the market') inevitably and deliberately ejects surplus population from normal social intercourse, deprives them of the necessary means of re-entry, and erects barriers to keep them out as viciously unjust as those of apartheid. The nonsensical corollary of this absurd axiom is, unsurprisingly, the need for active intervention by the state to rescue the outcast and to restore to them their natural rights as citizens. Nothing could be better guaranteed than this antiquated socialist theorizing to produce precisely the social conditions it pretends to criticize – a permanent and expanding underclass of European untouchables.

On the basis of this collectivist philosophy, the Green Paper proposes two levels of social policy initiatives, at the national and the continental level, linked by the aspiration of harmonizing national social policy in a new European synthesis. It specifies the 'Primary Issues Common to Member States' as follows: 'Improving the employment situation' – focusing largely on action to address what it construes as structural barriers to job creation; 'Accelerating progress towards a quality-based production system' – which emphasizes working conditions and workers' rights; and 'Stimulating solidarity and integration'. This latter is full of empty echoes of socialist social policies from the 1960s and 1970s, with all their utopian over-emphasis on rights and all their exaggerated attention to piously correct political attitudes.

Not content with proposing continent-wide harmonization on all these aspects of social policy, the Green Paper also spells out separately and in addition a long list of 'Main Policy Objectives at the European Level'. These are in part platitudinous, and thus relatively harmless, but over and above this there is a cautiously but firmly argued plea for harmonizing levels of social security provision and for equalizing other aspects of social protection. If this were implemented, the whole Community would be bankrupted.

There is also an impassioned demand for 'Reinforcing the Social Dialogue' (which seems to be Euro-speak for avoiding difficult decisions at all costs), a proposal for movement towards 'Pan-European Collective Bargaining', and an argument for introducing a transparently corporatist industrial relations strategy right across Europe. As if all this were not enough, a final absurd flourish is reserved, as the last item in their catalogue of nine 'Main Policy Objectives at the European Level', for *'Democratizing the process of social change and constructing a people's Europe'*! One might imagine this had been retrieved from some long-lost manuscript of National Socialist social policy from the 1930s.

Thus, it looks as if we should expect more, and more effective, resistance to welfare reform from Europe than from our home-grown political collectivists. Supporters of reform will need to attend carefully to traps and impediments originating in Brussels (Cousins, 1993). We should also seek to prevent well-intentioned plans for the development of Central and Eastern Europe serving as a second continental back-door to expansion of state welfare. That there is at least some degree of risk on this score is indicated by Barr's (1994) report on a Council of Europe scheme for a 'modified Beveridge' in the former communist countries.

Preconception and Prejudice among the Intellectuals

However, the third context of welfare reform which requires analysis provides more than sufficient evidence of powerful British resistance to modernization – not so much among Opposition politicians, as from our intellectuals. Most of our social scientific academics, most social policy researchers, and a large proportion of social affairs correspondents in the media remain collectivist, egalitarian, anti-capitalist and enamoured of state welfare.

The debate about welfare reform which is just now getting under way concerns one of the most important general policy decisions of the century. Its outcome will affect for good or ill the whole future of the British people. In this crucial debate, the intellectuals are – *sensu stricto* – prejudiced. Their commitment to state welfare is pre-ordained and irreversible, entirely regardless of evidence about its effectiveness or its impacts.

The intellectuals are also influential. Sadly this proposition is not one which is readily believed by ministers, by politicians other than left-wingers, by businessmen, or by most decent, ordinary men and women. None the less, it is true. *Public understanding of welfare in Britain is largely defined and controlled by nonsensical theories given currency by academics and other intellectuals.* From the universities, these mistaken ideas are passed on to the media, and on again from the media to the politicians, and hence to the public.

This vicious process, which magnifies error, multiplies misunderstanding, and perpetuates folly, cannot be reversed simply by ignoring it in the hope that nonsense – about welfare, as about the market, the family, crime and punishment, the nation state, and much else besides – will vanish of its own accord. Its powerful and damaging influence will continue unless and until shoddy thinking is replaced by better thinking, utopian dreams by realistic analysis, wish-fulfilment by honest facts, and incoherent notions by lucid concepts.

Fortunately, the counter-attack, in relation to theories of welfare as on other fronts, is now well under way. From the Institute of Economic Affairs, the Adam Smith Institute, and the Social Affairs Unit, and from individual social scientists such as David Green, Peter Saunders, Dennis O'Keeffe, Digby Anderson and Nigel Ashford in Britain, and Charles Murray, Ralph Segalman, and Irving Louis Horowitz (1993) in the United States, an alternative analysis of welfare is being produced.

Over the past ten years I have endeavoured to make my own contributions to criticism of the prejudiced welfare orthodoxy, and to the development of a practical alternative which allows a proper role to individual choice, competition, and the market (Marsland, 1988 and 1994). Consider just one example from this larger analysis – a perfect illustration of the gross one-sidedness of British intellectuals' approach to welfare which demonstrates the difficulties of those who are committed to radical reform of the Welfare State in the face of hegemonic control of concepts and theories of welfare by the left and by collectivists.

Joan Higgins's book *The Business of Medicine* (1988) is regularly cited by other writers and by teachers as an authoritative source on independent health care. Published by Macmillan, and written by the Director of a university institute of health policy studies who has previously written other well-received books on poverty and welfare, it is a serious and influential volume. Its tone is established unambiguously from the start by Higgins's definition of the object of her analysis as 'the growth of profit-seeking in medicine'. This reminds me of nothing so much as the *Pocket Oxford Dictionary*'s entry on profit which reads 'pecuniary gain, excess of returns over outlay', and exemplifies it with the phrase 'the profits are enormous'! From the same domain of naïve assumptions as Higgins and Oxford, my Macmillan home encyclopaedia manages to include an entry on profit-sharing – and none on profit itself.

In this one-sided vein, Higgins pursues her analysis from the 1940s through to the 1980s, remorselessly hunting down every sign, however modest, of challenge (or, as she would see it, of threat) to the sacred foundational principles of the NHS by the wicked intrusion of anti-socialist (and particularly American) 'profit-seekers'. Commenting on changes in health care elsewhere in Europe, she suggests that 'the real debate... is whether Britain has become "less socialist" as other countries... have become "more socialist" and – many critics might add – whether the NHS is now "socialist" enough.'

In a series of patently rhetorical questions, she asks:

Has the increasing emphasis on profits in medicine and the re-birth of the 'wallet-conscious' doctor meant that the NHS patient has been neglected or kept waiting? Has the private sector drawn resources away from the NHS or has it added to the total pool of available resources? Has the business ethic in medicine led to the abandonment of a commitment to equality of access and fairness in the distribution of health services?

These might all be sensible research questions, provided that parallel queries were raised about the impact of NHS bureaucracy on the efficiency of health care, or about the extent to which the freezing-out of competition had slowed up the development of innovative treatments. They might provide an acceptable framework of analysis, provided we could be confident that her predictably state welfarist answers had not been decided even before she raised the questions. That we cannot safely place our confidence in her impartiality is demonstrated throughout the book, and especially in its concluding chapter.

There she examines, wholly critically in each case, the growth of independent health care, the expansion of 'American influence', the development of independent health care into 'a business', and the widening spread of health care financed by employers. She admits somewhat reluctantly that these trends have so far been very modest in scope, and that there are lessons which the NHS can learn as a result, particularly about responding better to patients as individuals and as consumers. She none the less laments each of these trends, proposes tighter regulation of the independent sector, and condemns on moral grounds any dilution, however slight, of socialist purity in health care. 'For many observers', she says at page 237, without much evidence of excluding herself from this multitude, 'the ultimate test of the private market is not its cost-effectiveness or its effects on NHS waiting lists but its success or failure in meeting certain moral criteria about justice, fairness, and equity.' Translated from welfare-speak, this seems to mean that the possibility that state provision might be extravagantly expensive, or that independent provision might improve the efficiency of services for clients and customers, is to count for nothing. All that matters, apparently, in adjudicating between independent and state provision, is the extent to which they answer a number of opaque and arbitrarily selected criteria, each of them defined in sectarian socialist terms.

'The conclusion must be', she claims, 'that the growth of for-profit medicine in Britain has weakened the commitment to equal access to health services for all, irrespective of age, gender, race, class, or ability to pay. It has challenged the notion that "health is different" and rejected the claim that the distribution of health services should take place beyond the play of the market.' This tendentious judgement glibly muddles errors of fact (there never has been a commitment to equal access, or private medicine would have been outlawed), mistaken analysis (markets exclude only on grounds of ability to pay, not on ascriptive criteria), and value prejudices (*she* may believe that the special characteristics of health and health care are incompatible with market provision, and she is entitled to, but many others may not).

Little wonder, given the preconceptions demonstrated in this judgement, and confirmed in a long passage of authority-seeking reference to Raymond Plant's rather hazy understanding of the nature of markets, that she concludes the whole book with this rankly prejudiced verdict on the market and its role in health care:

> It is not governed by morality or notions of social justice. It provides a choice to those who are not inhibited or constrained by the egalitarianism of the NHS, but in doing so it widens the gulf between the rich and the poor and between the healthy and the sick. The price of further expansion in the market will be increasing inequality and social divisiveness. Many would argue that it is too high a price to pay.

Just such transparently erroneous and prejudiced assumptions govern the thinking of most British intellectuals working as university teachers and researchers in the field of social policy and social welfare. Their shallow arguments have been answered more than adequately by Gilder (1981), Seldon (1990), and O'Keeffe (1995) among others. Their baleful influence persists none the less. They represent an influential elite of preconception and ignorance which will have to be challenged and defeated comprehensively if essential reforms of the whole welfare system are to be undertaken successfully.

A Framework of Analysis

In a context of renewed apologia for the Welfare State, nostalgic yearning for the free rein allowed to its cancerous growth until 1979, and continuing expansion of state welfare even since then, further critical analysis is essential. In the following chapters I attempt several tasks:

- To examine the incoherence of the concept of the Welfare State, and the contradictory policies it necessarily entails in practice (Chapter 2).
- To challenge the need for the Welfare State, given high and improving standards of living (Chapter 3).
- To assess the damaging economic consequences of the Welfare State (Chapter 4).
- To examine the social inefficiencies of state monopoly provision of welfare which result from centralization, bureaucracy, large-scale organization, and absence of market disciplines and consumer choice (Chapter 5).
- To survey the damaging moral consequences of the Welfare State which result from its weakening of the family, the local community and voluntary associations. Specifically, to examine the growing problem of welfare dependency (Chapter 6).
- To demonstrate the general advantages of market provision of welfare by comparison with state collectivist provision (Chapter 7).
- To suggest a programme of disestablishment of the Welfare State, relating to housing, health care, education, pensions and income support – with all these services delivered by normal market mechanisms backed by private insurance (Chapter 8).
- To examine the scope for radical reform of provision by the state of social assistance to the very small numbers of people in temporary special need and incapable of finding their own way without help back to normal self-reliant social life (Chapter 9).
- To consider the economic, social and moral benefits of self-reliance as a source of real welfare in a genuinely free society, by comparison with the all-round ill-fare produced by Welfare States (Chapter 10).

Proponents of the Welfare State have sought, by nationalizing charity and out-lawing self-reliance, to create an egalitarian paradise. Given their naïve assumptions about human nature, their enmity towards the family, their perverse faith in the state, and their lack of confidence in the capacity of democratic capitalism to improve standards of living and quality of life all round – given all this, the abject failure of their project is hardly surprising. Thoroughgoing socialists are at least acknowledging, if rather late

in the day, that *their* god has failed. How long before the champions of the
more modest, more genteel paradise promised by the Welfare State
acknowledge as honestly that they too have lost their way, that their dream
of effortless brotherly prosperity has turned out to be a nightmare of
envious squalor?

Reflecting, from a 'free radical' perspective, as it were, on Gosta
Esping-Andersen's penetrating, if flawed, social democratic analysis of
state welfare (1990), Martin Jacques (1994) draws for us a portrait in
miniature of variant types of the species *Welfare State*:

> In this context, while modern welfare states clearly have fundamental
> characteristics in common – social provision for old age, health and
> education, redistributive goals, etcetera – there are also important differ-
> ences between them. Gosta Esping-Andersen has identified three basic
> types of welfare state. First, there is the 'liberal' welfare state in which
> means-tested assistance, modest transfers, or limited social-insurance
> arrangements predominate. Benefits are targeted mainly at low income
> dependents. Entitlement rules are strict and benefits modest. And the
> state encourages the market to partipate, either by only guaranteeing a
> minimum level of payment or provision, or by subsidising private
> welfare schemes. As Esping-Andersen puts it: 'In this model, the
> progress of social reform has been severely circumscribed by tradi-
> tional, liberal work-ethic norms: it is one where the the limits of welfare
> equal the marginal propensity to opt for welfare instead of work'.
> Typical examples are the United States, Australia, and Canada.
>
> The second model is 'corporatist'. This originally evolved on the ini-
> tiative of the state as a means of binding society together, helping to
> generate a sense of nation, and limiting the influence of the labour
> movement. Bismarck's reforms are a well-known example. Typically it
> rests on a contributory system involving employers and employees. It
> thereby also tends to exclude those who do not work, for example non-
> working mothers. The church has generally been a key actor in shaping
> such systems and the family plays a pivotal role in them. The state is
> seen in a different, and more benevolent, light than in the liberal case.
> Classical examples of this model are Germany, Italy, and France.
>
> Finally there is the social-democratic model. This is based on a uni-
> versal system of generous standards and provision. Services have to be
> of sufficiently high quality to attract the better off who might otherwise
> buy-in private provision. All groups are covered by one universal insur-
> ance system, but benefits are graduated according to earnings. Such a
> system is by far the most expensive and requires a commitment to full

employment in order to contain costs. The classical statement of this social-democratic model was the Beveridge Report in the UK in 1944 which projected a concept of welfare from 'the cradle to the grave', but in practice the archetypal models are Scandinavian, with the Swedish of course being the most famous.

Despite the – exaggerated in my view – differences indicated in the three-way model, Jacques concludes, as does Esping-Andersen, that the Welfare State is in trouble:

> Each of these three models is now facing serious difficulties. For example, Australia, Germany, and Sweden respectively are all now desperately seeking ways of containing the cost of their welfare states. Each model, in other words, is facing similar problems, even though the eventual outcomes may vary for each case.

In the following chapters I examine both the various problems and the potential remedies which might, in any modern context, provide a lasting solution and a distinct alternative to the Welfare State in any of its forms.

2 The Contradictions of State Welfare: Philosophical and Theoretical Incoherence

Every year, according to the Prime Minister's efficiency adviser, Sir Peter Levene, at least £5 billion – one-tenth of the whole of the current public deficit – is lost in benefit fraud (Henessy, 1993). This 'revelation' should occasion anger, perhaps, but none of the surprise with which it has been greeted in many quarters.

What else could be expected from a system which is corrupt and corrupting in its essential nature? Despite the innocently benevolent intentions of its founders and most of its contemporary supporters, the 'welfare state' is a fraudulent concept which has from the beginning systematically deceived the people into expecting something for nothing as of right (Hayek, 1988). Anger is an insufficient response to this latest exposé of the Welfare State's deficiencies. Instead of occasional spasms of irritation and *ad hoc* tinkering, we need principled debate, coherent analysis and a comprehensive programme of radical reform (Segalman and Marsland, 1989).

Nor is such radical reform an impractical dream. For, despite claims to the contrary by Opposition politicians and their acolytes in the media and the universities, our coy British compunction about radical reform of welfare is not shared by our allies and partners abroad. In France, in Holland, in Germany, and even in Sweden the financial, psychological and social costs of excessive and inappropriate state welfare have been acknowledged by conservatives, liberals, and socialists alike. Wide-ranging programmes of retrenchment and fundamental reform have been initiated (Stein, 1990; *The Times*, 1993). In the United States, President Clinton insists that 'We have to end welfare as a way of life.' He is unapologetically proposing 'tough love' as an essential alternative to irresponsible hand-outs to the unemployed and to single mothers. Mr Gingrich is seeking to trump him. In New Zealand, too, radical reform of the whole welfare system is under way (Walker, 1994).

Here too one might expect by now to be hearing, from Ministers and from Opposition spokesmen alike, clear, uncoded proposals for movement towards an alternative and better welfare future, more suited than our antiquated Welfare State to a free and prosperous society. What is there, after all, except habit and cowardice, to prevent a concerted assault on this last remaining bastion of unreconstructed collectivism (Goldsmith, 1994)? There are more than sufficient reasons for believing that radical reform of the Welfare State is essential:

First, the whole concept is confused to the point of incoherence. Some regard it as a safety-net designed to help the temporarily unfortunate back into normal self-reliance. For others it is a transition stage on the way towards a glorious socialist future. For others again it comprises in and of itself a New Model Society which synthesises and transcends the best elements of capitalism and socialism. These three models are mutually incompatible. Incoherent oscillation between one and another confuses consumers and producers of welfare alike, and guarantees chaotic inefficiency (Barry, 1990; Seldon, 1990).

Second, we don't need it anyway. The early stages of state welfare provision in the period up to 1920 made some limited sense, given the persisting poverty and social disruption arising out of industrialization and urbanization. Even the elaboration and bureaucratic institutionalization of the Welfare State in the 1940s could be made to seem at least half-way plausible in the context of postwar reconstruction and the innocently utopian idealism it generated (Marsland, 1992 [2]). Since then, however, the standard of living and the quality of life of the whole population have been improved out of all recognition by straightforward economic progress. There is far less need for welfare than earlier, yet we consistently spend more and more on its provision (Hill, 1989).

Third, we can't afford it. If economic progress is to be continued, direct and indirect taxes alike will have to be reduced substantially, particularly for those on lower incomes, to provide incentives for productive effort. Combine this with the anticipated multiplier effects of demographic change on the state's already extravagant expenditure on health care and pensions, and with the crucial importance of keeping relative wage costs to the minimum in competitive global markets, and the necessity for a real and radical reduction in the scale and cost of the Welfare State is palpable (Pliatzky, 1982).

Next, in any case it doesn't work. However generously it is resourced, the Welfare State does not and cannot produce its intended outcomes. A large proportion of the taxes extracted expensively from the prosperous majority is re-cycled even more expensively to the same people. The more street-wise among the self-sufficient majority cunningly syphon-off still more money into their own pockets from resources intended for the

disadvantaged minority. Those who really need help very often don't get it
at all, or get too little, or have it provided in tawdry, demeaning conditions
and in ways which turn them into dependent caricatures of their
potentially creative, self-reliant selves (Marsland, 1988).

Finally, and worst of all, the Welfare State inflicts damaging levels of
moral and psychological harm on its supposed beneficiaries. It has
seduced the British people away from their natural independence of spirit
and their traditional commitment to hard work, honesty and high
standards. It has transformed much of the population into deferential conformists with an irrational inclination to spasmodic rebellion and a cynical
eye to the main chance. It has made of its primary clients – perfectly
normal, capable men and women before the state got to work on them – a
festering underclass of welfare dependants fit for nothing better than
passive consumption of an ever-expanding diet of 'bread and circuses'. It
is rapidly destroying the family – the main arena of genuine welfare in a
free society, and thereby crippling children for life more reliably than
'dark Satanic mills' ever did. It is turning estates and neighbourhoods right
across Britain into factories of crime and arbitrary violence fuelled by an
increasing flow of drugs and alcohol (Murray, 1984 and 1990; Dennis,
1993; Segalman & Marsland, 1989).

In the following chapters, each of these several failings of the Welfare
State is examined in turn systematically. I begin with the root cause of all
of its other deficiencies: the philosophical and theoretical incoherence of
the concept of a 'Welfare State'.

Welfare Contradictions

It is folly to expect any theory relating to human behaviour to be
absolutely coherent and logically water-tight to the last detail. It is even
more foolish to pursue the utopian will-o'-the-wisp of comprehensive social policies designed to apply supposedly rational principles
systematically to the infinite variability and constant changeability of
people and situations. Just such utopian rationalism is one of the most dangerous political threats posed by welfare state thinking, and a primary
source of its consistent failure in practice. I examine these problems in
detail in Chapter 5 below, together with the antidotes to them offered
by the more modest, diverse, and flexible operations of the market
(Oakeshott, 1991; Flew, 1981 and 1991).

Ironically, however, for all its rigidity in practice, the concept of the
Welfare State is extraordinarily incoherent in logical and philosophical
terms. While the policies it seeks to justify comprise a Procrustean strait-

jacket which has clamped social welfare in hopelessly ineffectual systems of organization and delivery, they are also characterized by fundamental contradictions which inhibit sensible developments by pushing the whole system towards multiple and mutually exclusive goals. As Norman Barry (1990, p. viii) has it: 'in the area of practical politics, the intractability of the concept [of welfare] has generated insoluble policy problems.'

The main lines of the Welfare State's incoherence and self-contradiction are as follows:

- Between equity and equality.
- Between needs and rights.
- Between extravagance and austerity.
- Between permissive licence and authoritarian control.
- Between solving practical problems and a vision of a new society.

Equity or Equality?

The Welfare State grew up in part – and not just in Bismarck's Germany – as an alternative to socialism, and as a mechanism for avoiding the supposed, but actually fanciful, threat of revolution. In consequence, a good deal of socialist theory and ideological baggage is muddled up in welfare state thinking. In particular, the Welfare State is torn between the contradictory objectives of equity – which commits the state fairly modestly to rectifying gross inequalities and to providing assistance for the most desperately disadvantaged in the population – and equality, which entails antagonism towards the more prosperous, envious intolerance of social differences of all sorts, and zealous insistence on egalitarian redistribution.

The more activist proponents of the Welfare State have consistently traded on this contradiction to bid up their demands progressively, dragging more moderate and more reluctant supporters of welfare state concepts, including many liberals and conservatives, in a determinedly socialist direction. The installation of the National Health Service, the inauguration of comprehensive schooling, the credibility foolishly allowed even by intelligent commentators to the Poverty Lobby's nonsensical ideas about levelling incomes, and the Labour Party's long-standing prejudice against home-ownership are prime examples of the effect of this fundamental contradiction between equity and equality.

There was no good reason in equity to overturn the whole established system of health care simply because a small number of poorer families could not afford adequate treatment (Green, 1985 and 1993). It was reprehensible folly, justifiable only in the most primitive of egalitarian terms, to destroy the meritocratic grammar school tradition and the developing technical schools, when all that was really needed was modest, gradual improvement in the resources and staffing of secondary modern schools (Shaw, 1983).

To punish the prosperous majority by excessive taxation in order to offer to those on lower incomes short-term gains was a typically foolish policy strategy of the 1960s and 1970s arising from welfare state confusion between equity and equality. It had typically damaging consequences, too, since it actually reduced the real standard of living of its presumed beneficiaries as a result of the inflation it predictably produced.

Again, to seek, as the Labour Party did for decades until it became an undeniable electoral liability, to prevent the spread of home-ownership to the mass of ordinary people was an absurd example of this persistent contradiction in welfare state doctrine (Saunders, 1990).

Equality before the law is a foundational principle of any free society, and a *sine qua non* for genuine democracy. Equality of opportunity, in the strictly limited sense of minimization by legal measures of irrelevant and inequitable barriers to employment, housing, education and so on, while less fundamental than equality before the law (which it presupposes) is also a proper, and continuing, obective in any democratic society.

Pursuit of equality beyond these basic parameters is not feasible in the real world, and is powerfully counter-productive, producing much higher costs – in freedom and in economic efficiency – than any imagined benefits. Even among supporters of state welfare, the *inegalitarian* effects of current arrangements, which redistribute resources further in favour of privileged groups, are now widely recognized (Goodin and Le Grand, 1987). Moreover, egalitarianism is typically a sectarian, minority dream to which large majorities of most populations are positively antagonistic. They recognize that it is not only an impractical illusion, but also incompatible with equity, since effort and success merit higher rewards than idleness and failure.

Despite this, the most avid supporters of the Welfare State have regularly and from the beginning sought to elide the proper equitable objectives of welfare provision with politically unpopular and philosophically unjustifiable egalitarian goals. It is essential to insist on this distinction, and to enquire, in relation to any existing or proposed element of state welfare, whether it serves the traditional, legitimate, and politically popular objective of improving equity as between persons or groups, or whether on the contrary its justification is pursuit of the alien, unpopular, and utopian purposes of some unelectable minority.

Efforts by the state to improve the situation of citizens are of course entirely legitimate, and in some respects and to some degree such efforts may be desirable, particularly in relation to those who are most disadvantaged. However, it can be no proper objective of the state, through its welfare arrangements or by any other means, to equalize as such any aspect of the conditions of the population. In a free society it must always be presumed that individuals will be allowed and encouraged to improve their own and their families' circumstances by their own legitimate efforts. This presumption discounts egalitarian objectives altogether, since some individuals and groups are likely to be continuously pressing standards – in income, wealth, consumption, education, health care, and so on – ahead of the general level, however high, which has been reached at any particular time. Confusion in welfare theory between equity and equality, which would subvert and contravert this fundamental principle, should at all costs be avoided.

Needs and Rights

Needs and rights are two of the most basic concepts in the philosophy of the Welfare State. Neither of these ideas, taken separately, is altogether free – to put it rather modestly – of incoherence. Neither is philosophically unproblematical (Rawls, 1972; Miller, 1976; Gewirth, 1982). Combined in a single policy discourse, they produce ideological Babel and institutional chaos (Barry in Plant and Barry, 1990; Harris, 1987; Goodin, 1988).

On the one hand, the Welfare State seeks to identify and answer objectively definable 'basic needs'. On the other, it urges people to demand more and more of everything from the state 'as of right'. Thus, while yesterday's need becomes tomorrow's right all round, at the same time your rights can be arbitrarily denied by the state because they supposedly conflict with my needs, and spuriously legitimate neglect of my established needs can be justified in terms of your newly authenticated rights. It is a recipe for beggar-my-neighbour in personal relations, and for financial and moral bankruptcy in the nation as a whole.

Glibly contradictory use of this ill-assorted pair of concepts has enabled champions of the Welfare State to ratchet up demands on the state's resources continuously throughout this century. Thus, acknowledgement of the supposed need of a small number of people for help with their housing has been elaborated into the right, even of immigrant aliens lacking any established or likely status as genuine political refugees, to free, state-provided shelter. On a broader front, this same philosophical illogicality has provided the justification for escalating housing benefit payments now costing £9 billion annually, having doubled since 1988.

Or again, the supposed need for the state to provide basic general education has been transmuted magically into the right of suitably – which is to say rather modestly – qualified young people to state-financed higher education. Even more absurdly, this same 'need' has somehow translated itself into the apparently inalienable right of the prosperous middle classes to free or highly subsidized adult education designed to enliven their leisure.

Or again, where the founders of the National Health Service once absurdly supposed that free health care would clear up health problems once and for all within a decade or so, public expenditure is nowadays escalating towards infinity as every medico-technological breakthrough reveals a new, exorbitantly costly treatment to which every last member of the whole population has a 'right' which somehow trumps and transcends any notion of real need. Public expenditure on the NHS in 1993 was almost £30 billion.

The height of this self-indulgent folly of confusing rights with needs has ironically been scaled only during these very recent, supposedly welfare-resistant, years. This consists of extravagantly costly, government-financed campaigns – in the press, on television, and through special publications – designed to draw the attention of an unconcerned populace to 'needs' they were never aware they had by informing them of 'rights' they never sought! (Anderson, 1988.) State-financed institutions, such as universities, the NHS, and the BBC join in enthusiastically. Consider a 1989 poster for the BBC's Advice Shop programme, shown weekly on BBC2 and repeated on BBC1: 'For advice and information on benefits, housing, pensions, the Poll Tax (*sic*), the NHS, and much more...', it urges with all the sanctimonious incoherence which is typical of welfare-speak, 'watch Advice Shop'. 'Watch the costs to taxpayers', one might add, and more pertinently in relation to contradictions in welfare theory, 'Watch out for your responsibilities as well as your rights, and don't ask anyone for anything unless you really need it.'

The concept of rights, one should not need to emphasize, is as complex and contested as any (Nozick, 1981 and 1984; Flew, 1981 and 1992; Sen, 1987; Campbell, 1988). It is notably liable to ambitious over-expansion, incorporating absolutely anything that the user of the term happens personally to define as desirable. One can readily imagine, for example, a purported 'right to beauty' justifying claims for free NHS cosmetic surgery. Or consider the imaginary right 'to the highest level of education' being used as an argument for winning access to PhD programmes at Cambridge or MIT – for the mentally handicapped.

It seems to me that it is probably foolish to use the term rights in relation to welfare provision *at all*, since nothing of what is promised can be guaranteed except at the cost of lowering all round the quality of what is offered (Quest, 1992). The state pension provides a good example.

We have in all the welfare state societies a serious problem with pensions. This is not primarily because life expectancy has improved beyond anyone's predictions, although it has, nor merely because state pension schemes have invariably been, in financial terms, extraordinarily badly organized, although they do indeed for the most part rely on unbelievably, even recklessly, foolish arrangements. The difficulty is altogether more fundamental. The state simply lacks – because of its multiple and conflicting responsibilities, and because it is inherently and unavoidably a political organization – the capacity to deliver on long-term financial promises. (See Norman Barry's analysis in Jordan and Ashford, 1993.)

Only specialist and independent organizations, such as pension funds and insurance companies, can reliably deliver on the promises entailed in a pension contract. Pension rights outside the context of a legal contract enforceable on genuinely free agents are entirely spurious, or – perhaps one should more accurately say – fictional. An editorial response to an important analysis by Georges Lane (1994) of what he calls 'A-Securité Sociale' makes this point neatly and definitively:

> En socialisant les assurances, on évacue le contrat et la responsabilité qui l'accompagne. On rend certaines personnes irresponsables, et d'autres arbitrairement responsables (comme l'employeur pour les accidents du travail). Quand la faillité des assurances sociales sera consommée, il faudra accepter les contrats d'assurance, qui constituent la securité sociale véritable.

Even on the left of British politics, the destructive incoherence of the concept of welfare rights is beginning to be recognized. In an article boldly entitled 'The wrongs of standing up for rights' (1994), Melanie Phillips suggests that 'To challenge the rights-based culture is seen as forfeiting one's claim to moral virtue'. She argues, none the less, that 'What is needed is a society of reciprocal rights and duties, with primary responsibilities for ourselves and for each other, and with the role of the State redefined mainly as educator and enabler.' 'In welfare', she continues, 'the original community ideals of the Left have been subverted by the rights agenda. Making benefits conditional upon behaviour is a taboo because benefits are seen as rights and claimants have no responsibilities. But that was not at all how the architects of the Welfare State saw it.' 'The rights-based culture', she concludes, 'is immensely strong... The politician who challenges *that* will need a sense of history, intellectual toughness, and moral courage.'

Need is also a difficult concept (Bradshaw, 1972; Wilkin *et al.*, 1992; Smith, 1980; Flew, 1992; Sen and Williams, 1982; Sen, 1987). The bare minima of human survival are more modest by far than modern man dares to admit. Beyond survival, the process of defining needs is always contentious and inherently conventional (Doyal, 1989). At least, however, by contrast with the concept of rights, needs are open, even if with difficulty, to definition, measurement and monitoring. A needs concept provides, therefore, in sharp contrast with the altogether opaque concept of rights, a reasonable – if not unproblematical – philosophical and theoretical basis for welfare arrangements. It can be used effectively in this role provided that – *and only provided that* – we forswear entirely any of the incoherent confusion between needs and rights which utopian welfare theorists have always been so eager to promote (Wilson, 1994).

Extravagance and Austerity

Its champions make great claims about the Welfare State being the appropriate modern instrument of economic progress compared with the chaos of 'unfettered capitalism'. It is supposedly – through control of employment and unemployment, by means of income redistribution, and with the assistance of generous state benefits – the only reliable guarantor of prosperity for the population as a whole. Yet at the same time they are riddled with the rankest prejudices against affluence, and never happier than when economic mismanagement or misfortune can be used as a justification for punitive austerity. It is no accident that a key study of the period 1945 to 1951, when the foundations of the modern Welfare State were being laid down, is called *The Age of Austerity* (Sissons and French, 1963).

Even recent apologists for the Welfare State, writing at a time when standards of living are incomparably higher than forty years ago, and when even the poorest people take entirely for granted what even in the 1950s were luxuries, talk nostalgically about the siege economy of the war years and the era of rationing fronted by socialist Chancellor Stafford Cripps (Hennessy, 1992). 'Materialism', it seems, belongs in the uncontrolled, competitive world of the market, and as such is to be regarded *de haut en bas* by the high priests of the Welfare State's more spiritual, transcendent values.

This contradiction between the promise of affluence and the preference for austerity is characteristic of welfare state thinking. It is associated with policy confusion between planning and investment on the one hand, and extravagant short-term state expenditure on the other. For example, despite its absolute commitment in principle to the NHS, it was the Labour Party which found itself obliged to introduce charges for prescriptions, and it has been left largely to Conservative governments to build new hospitals. Labour has preferred to fritter away resources on wage increases and on uncontrolled expansion in the scale of ineffectually used ancillary manpower (Gammon, 1987). Despite the current spate of unjustified complaints about under-investment and cost-cutting in the sphere of welfare, it was a Labour Government and Labour Ministers who were committed supporters of state welfare who in 1976 had to cut health-care investment with a savagery which was unparalleled either before or since.

Again, it was the Welfare State's most avid supporters who sought most fervently to prevent ordinary people from gaining access to the modest but crucial stake in prosperity provided by home-ownership. The same abstemious puritanism prevents supporters of the Welfare State from acknowledging the right of the mass of the population to pay from their own hard-earned income for the best education for their children, and commits the Labour Party to repeal of the Assisted Places Scheme regardless of its meritocratic impact. It underwrites the left's ferocious resistance to health-care reform, and legitimates their antagonism to personal health insurance, even where it is provided by trade unions. One suspects that, given stronger political support, the levelling tendency in welfare state thinking would have outlawed foreign holidays and limited the availability of cars to the 'essential use' of 'key workers'!

In populations subject to these oscillating signals – affluence as of right and the ethical duty of saintly poverty – the confusion generates nervousness about prudent saving combined with bouts of guilty spending on leisure and personal consumption. It encourages excessive wage demands, fuels inflation, creates prejudice against successful entrepreneurs, stifles enterprise, and rewards the idle and incompetent. It habituates the whole population to squalid conditions and execrable levels of service in health care, education, and the public sector generally. It reinforces antiquated envy of the 'idle rich', and schools us all to dreams of effortless prosperity (Gilder, 1981).

Over the decades since 1945, the symbolism of hair-shirted welfare state austerity has served to aggravate anti-Americanism (over-rich but fortunately over there!), and to accentuate a wider xenophobia against 'mere foreigners' in general on account of their economic progress and increasing affluence. It has tricked us, almost as effectively as did socialism in the Soviet Union, into servile acceptance of standards of living and a quality of life such as even Puerto Ricans and illegal Mexican immigrants in the United States aspire beyond. Like a battered wife, we return and cling in sentimental disregard of the evidence of our own senses to the familiar, destructive setting which is at least, for all its gross inadequacies, our own.

Through these same declining years, this self-satisfied lack of ambition generated by Welfare State austerity has jostled incongruously with greedy envy – fed by welfare Micawberism – of the greener grass of other people's prosperity. Gulled by the Welfare State's glib promises of effort-less ease and its empty guarantees of our right to a living, a place in the sun, and protection from cradle to grave against the unavoidable risks of life, the British people had become by the 1970's a nation of greedy wastrels. Despite the IMF's 1976 visit, despite Margaret Thatcher's best efforts, and precisely *because of* the Welfare State's spurious commitment to free lunches all round, imperious beggars we remain.

Thus we have in the oscillating polarity of austerity and extravagance a third fundamental contradiction built into the concept of the Welfare State. State welfare stamps on the people's aspirations, and punishes the careful, self-disciplined planning by individuals and families which the realization of ambitions entails (Himmelfarb, 1987). At the same time it breeds avaricious envy of more successful and more fortunate fellow-citizens, occasioning poisonous social divisions, and encouraging a spirit of grab-what-you-can by whatever means throughout the nation (Minogue, 1989).

Freedom and Control

The tempting attractions of austerity to welfare ideologues reflects in part the constant tendency in Welfare States to subject the population to centralized control. Thus post-war rationing was not simply a device for preventing inequities in a period of shortages, but at least as much an instrument of control over the behaviour and life-styles of ordinary people. And just as the Welfare State's inclination to austerity is contradicted by its persistent spendthrift extravagance, so its authoritarian inclinations are combined incoherently with a tendency to pseudo-liberal permissivism which seeks to undermine every form of natural and normal social control by the family, the neighbourhood, and the established forces of law and order.

Normal, healthy societies seek to achieve a sensible balance between maintaining adequate social control to prevent disorder and inhibit negative behaviours, and guaranteeing the maximum feasible extent of freedom and personal responsibility (Marsland, 1991 [2]). The Welfare

State, by contrast, appears to go to extremes in both directions, thus losing the essential balance between freedom and control which civilized living requires. It increasingly consigns the population to a chaotic combination of uninhibited licence and bureaucratic subjection.

The Welfare State's reponsibility for undermining the influence of essential social controls in Britain is patent. The attack on the family has been largely led by people whose dogmatic, ideological preference is for state control of education, income support, health care, children's discipline, and all the other crucial duties of the family (Anderson and Dawson, 1986). The same collectivist critics persistently challenge the efforts of the police and the courts at social control of delinquency and crime, castigating them as prejudiced, reactionary interferences with the rights of the individual to pursue his own freely chosen inclinations. The churches have been thoroughly subverted by sanctimonious relativists intent on substituting welfare rights for moral responsibilities. The schools have had all their vital responsibilities for disciplining young people and for civilizing the rising generation progressively stripped away by play-way theorists whose concept of education is limited to maximizing self-expression (Marsland, 1992 [3]). Above all, the Welfare State and its army of tenured servants is the prime source of the parroted emphasis on rights without commensurate responsibilities which has increasingly made of the British people an ungovernable, unemployable mob, bereft of values and scornful of rules (Dennis, 1993).

These contradictory effects are not accidental. They arise directly, inevitably and incorrigibly from philosophical incoherence in the theory of welfare. Either persons are to be conceived of as autonomous agents, responsible alike for their own welfare, for disciplined self-control, and for supporting co-operative agencies of social control of minority deviance; or they are incompetent subjects of the state, incapable of agency without state facilitation and regulation, and liable to arbitrary authoritarian interventions at any moment in any sphere of their lives. The Welfare State makes both sets of presumptions simultaneously, with predictably incoherent effects.

The Purposes of State Welfare

One last contradiction in the principles of the Welfare State must be addressed, which underlies and compounds each of the four others I have examined. Like the contradictions between equity and equality, between needs and rights, between austerity and extravagance, and between licence and over-regulation, this last contradiction reveals itself both in the writing of welfare theorists and in the history of the Welfare State's institutional practice. This is the conflict between practical and utopian goals.

Taxed by critics with the Welfare State's inefficiency and extravagance, its apologists characteristically argue that, whatever its shortcomings in these regards, it is none the less essential to the point of indispensability as a means of helping the poor and the deprived with the real practical problems they face in their daily lives (Fraser, 1993). Without the practical assistance provided by the Welfare State, they argue, this disadvantaged minority would be excluded from participation in the normal life of the community. Unshielded by welfare provision from the effects of un-fettered market forces, they would languish as ineffective citizens, their lives spoiled, their talents wasted, and ripe for disaffection.

From this perspective, the Welfare State is an essentially practical insti-tution designed to provide concrete help with the genuine problems of small minorities of people with special and largely temporary needs – needs which cannot be answered at the relevant time, it is presumed, by other means. No assumption is made that such needs are permanent, or that there is anything positively attractive or especially desirable about any human needs being answered by special welfare arrangements organized by the state. The underlying justification of the Welfare State from this perspective is the supposedly unavoidable necessity of providing practical assistance which would not otherwise be available (Goodin, 1985).

Such was the modest, practical perspective of most of the early welfare pioneers, including the Victorian and Edwardian philanthropists who pressed for the extension of education, health care and housing beyond what the market and charities seemed to them at the time able to provide for the poorest people. Such was the perspective also of the reformers who urged the development of unemployment protection at the beginning of this century. Octavia Hill, with her consistent, unapologetic insistence in all her valuable work in the housing sphere on the distinction between the deser-ving and the undeserving poor, was a characteristic example (Boyd, 1982).

The perspective of Lord Beveridge, as the founder of the modern Welfare State, was broadly similar (however, see pp. 32ff. below). He would probably have dismissed the idea of the Welfare State serving as some sort of paradisical, semi-socialist alternative to the competitive, effortful real world of capitalism and the market as altogether laughable, if not actually positively mischievous (Harris, 1977).

This limited, practical view of the Welfare State's goals was also largely shared by the Ministers in the Labour governments of 1945–51. Like Beveridge, and with even less justice, they are too often blamed for subsequent distortions of their modest, if flawed, ideals. Certainly the objectives of leading Ministers in the successive post-war Conservative governments which happily and positively supported the Welfare State never went beyond these limited practical aspirations (Hennessy and Seldon, 1987). Even Harold Macmillan, with his between-wars concept of 'the third way', viewed state welfare as a remedial and secondary component of an essentially free-enterprise society. Probably, indeed, no more than this was intended by the leading figures of the Wilson-Callaghan governments of the 1960s and 1970s. Hence, of course, the vitriolic antagonism towards the policies of these governments from the left wing of the Labour Party, and from ideological proponents of welfare concepts of an entirely different, altogether more ambitious, sort.

For the modest, practical concept of the Welfare State described in preceding paragraphs comprises precisely what its critics dismissively characterize as 'the residual model' (Page, 1993; Lee and Raban, 1988; Sutherland, 1994). This has long been rejected and resisted by influential welfare theorists, by leading socialist politicians, by public sector union leaders, and by the swelling band of professional welfare lobbyists. Their alternative, which they deliberately seek to confuse in the public mind with provision of practical welfare for the most needy, is a vision of the Welfare State as a radically new type of society (Abel-Smith and Titmuss, 1987; Myrdal, 1960). This is either (in some versions) a socialist heaven on earth to which we are moving gradually by means of continually expanding state welfare, or (in other versions) a New Jerusalem which transcends capitalism and mere democracy once and for all by creating the basis for a fraternal, egalitarian community in which competition and the market are superseded, and the needs of the whole population are answered through elaborated welfare state institutions. Poverty, defined speciously to mean a lower income – however high – than that of some other people, is to be abolished by instituting equality. Opting out of state welfare provision is to be disallowed, since this would create a 'two tier system' incompatible with an egalitarian community.

This more extreme version of the Welfare State's objectives has been urged, by communists, by socialists, and by idealistic liberals alike, throughout the century (Fraser, 1981; Pope *et al.*, 1986). However, it has been particularly in the period since 1950, and increasingly throughout the 1960s and 1970s that it has proved influential in practice. In Richard Titmuss (1958, 1968 and 1970) and Peter Townsend (1979) it found two sophisticated and eloquent spokesmen who dominated academic social policy analysis for decades. They won unchallenged influence in the liberal media, and thoroughly subverted the Labour Party's capacity for rational thought about welfare issues.

From this second socialist or otherwise collectivist perspective, the Welfare State is not to be limited to the modest, useful business of ensuring that practical help is provided for needy people. Its objectives are far more ambitious than this, enshrining in the last resort the dream – or rather nightmare – of incorporating the whole of society within an all-encompassing framework of state welfare institutions, with the totality of social life, including politics and the economy, subordinated to re-distributive, egalitarian controls.

Even the more modest and practical model of the Welfare State produces effects which are economically damaging and morally harmful. The consequences of the utopian model are even more savagely destructive, as the complete economic and moral bankruptcy of the socialist world more than sufficiently demonstrates. Moreover, the principles governing the two models of state welfare – residual and universalist, practical and utopian – and the social policies which arise from them are mutually exclusive and entirely contradictory. The resulting institutional incoherence and ideological confusion have characterized the British Welfare State for decades. Little wonder if it has proved beyond measure incomprehensible, unmanageable and inefficient.

The Role of Lord Beveridge in Facilitating Confusion in Welfare State Thinking

I suggested earlier that Lord Beveridge was often unfairly blamed for recent excesses in the operation of the Welfare State. There can be no doubt that he was not a socialist or an egalitarian, and that he was personally strongly committed to the work ethic, to the value of self-reliance, and to the crucial role of voluntary action, by contrast with state control, in a free society (*Voluntary Action*, 1948). On the other hand, he does, in my judgement, bear some serious responsibility for subsequent misinterpretation and misuse of his ideas. His writing and his life are a primary source of the confusions and contradictions in welfare theory and welfare policy which it is the business of this chapter to examine. We need, therefore, to examine the meaning of his work.

Marx explicitly denied that he was a Marxist. Christ himself, and even St Paul, would have been more than a little surprised by what their followers have made of Christianity. Freud could certainly not be satisfied that all of the mutually contradictory Freudian theories of the decades since his death are compatible with what he intended in his writing.

This third example exposes, however, the difficulty of this sort of analysis, the insurmountable difficulty of any attempt to identify and define any one singular meaning in the work of any substantial thinker. For there is not only one book: there are many. There are not only writings: there are also people and groups influenced directly and indirectly. There are not only writings and influences: there are also social and cultural contexts, which serve to shape and complicate interpretations. Of course we cannot be infinitely elastic in our interpretations of Marx, or of Christ, or of Freud, or indeed – to come to the case at issue here – of Beveridge. We certainly cannot afford to follow the deconstructionists into contentedly reading into either texts or lives the opposite of what all the relevant evidence, judged by reasonable, objective criteria, apparently indicates (Gellner, 1992; Harris, 1977).

But this still leaves a good deal of scope for variation and even contradiction in interpretations of the intentions and influence of Lord Beveridge. I am aware that he was a Liberal rather than a Socialist. But on the other hand he was equally a Liberal rather than a Conservative, and a Liberal of the London rather than the Manchester variety, with ideological attachments to Lloyd George, the originator of the modern British Welfare State, rather than to Gladstone with his ultra-Thatcherite commitment to sound money and careful national housekeeping.

I know perfectly well that Lord Beveridge understood – as many who have taken his name in vain have certainly not understood – the significance of economic incentives in motivating effort and enterprise. On the other hand, his own celebrated report (Beveridge, 1942) initiated social policies which inevitably reduced the effectiveness of economic incentives by establishing a more ambitious and more generous welfare system than any market economy can psychologically afford (Gilder, 1981).

Again, I admit readily that Beveridge warned British socialists and radicals not once but often about the dangers to freedom and prosperity posed in principle by centralized control and state bureaucracy under socialism. On the other hand, in the Report itself and elsewhere, he continually emphasized the need for 'comprehensive' provision and for 'adequate' – and therefore, at least up to some generalized minimum, universal – standards. He explicitly urged the necessity of welfare provision by the state in realms extending far beyond the narrow confines of mere social security – covering at least health care, education, and all of the rest of the social space over which his five 'Giant Evils' supposedly stalked. This was large in any case, by his own account, and almost infinitely extensible without much rhetorical difficulty by politicians and civil servants less chary about the dangers of socialism than he was himself.

Moreover, there is little evidence that either between 1945 and 1951, when Labour governments were installing a hugely expanded Welfare

State in his name, nor later when bureaucratic socialism was gradually ratcheted forward under Butskellite Conservative governments, he used any of his considerable influence to warn the British people in explicit practical terms of the dangerous risks they were taking with their freedom and with their prospects of economic progress. Courageous opponents of collectivism and paternalism were pretty thin on the ground in those consensual days, and Beveridge does not seem to have been among them.

I will mention one other area of Beveridgean ambivalence where apparent theoretical concern is contradicted by actual and practical nonchalance about paternalist and collectivist dangers. He was a great supporter of voluntary associations of all sorts, and an eloquent advocate of their crucial role in a free society (Williams and Williams, 1987). On the other hand he was, in terms of character as much as experience, the prototypical civil servant. His concept of public service was ultra-Reithian, his image of society a vast corporate BBC. His impatience with mere politics and with the imprecision and irrationality of democracy was eminently suited to wartime consensus and centralized wartime state planning.

His analysis of the inadequacies in welfare provision occasioned, as he saw it, by variations and contradictions between voluntary and charitable schemes, by overlaps between them, and above all by apparent gaps between them down which some of the population might accidentally fall, provides a carte blanche justification for every stage of the subsequent comprehensivization and universalization of the Welfare State. His sweeping confidence in the capacity of the state to act in the public's behalf dispassionately and efficiently is as magisterial as that of even the most fervent Jacobin or Leninist.

Thus, whatever his own explicit criticisms from time to time of paternalism and collectivism, and despite the undeniable fact that some Conservatives and some Liberals who claim to be neither paternalist nor collectivist proclaim themselves as his heirs, none the less, his report, his other writings, his influence and the main line of his intellectual inheritance are, in my contention, both paternalist and collectivist.

Indeed, until 1976 or 1979, or until the election of 1983, or whenever precisely the cultural and political hegemony of paternalist collectivism was first seriously challenged in Britain, there would have been little argument about this question. Since we were nearly all to a more or less degree, in various styles, contentedly paternalist and collectivist, the general inclination was for positive acclaim for Beveridge alongside Keynes as glorious heroes of the taming and civilizing of capitalism precisely by paternalism and collectivism.

At first the resistance to this general view came only from eccentrics and dissidents such as Ralph Harris and Arthur Seldon at the Institute of Economic Affairs. Then came the débâcle of 1976, with a Labour Government running in panic to the International Monetary Fund to bail it out, and axing public expenditure. Then came the 'Winter of Discontents', Margaret Thatcher and the 1979 election, and the gradually dawning realization that the Butskellite consensus – together with its intellectual underpinnings established by Beveridge in wartime reconstructionism – really was being challenged root and branch. From that point on – I suspect the watershed was 1983 – it has been essential to determine what the role of Lord Beveridge has been in Britain's postwar history. I have given my verdict in the preceding paragraphs. We were all of us quite right about him before 1976, and we should stick to the same judgement now. He was the author of an immensely influential report on welfare which exudes throughout a thoroughly paternalistic and collectivist spirit, and this is the spirit of his influence overall on British social policy. The Report and the way it was read and interpreted had a powerful and particular influence. It encouraged widespread reliance on the central state, ever-expanding state intervention, bureaucratic control of people's lives and massively increased public expenditure. It had the effect, whatever its author's intentions, of discouraging individualism, self-reliance, voluntary organizations and private initiatives. It tipped the balance in the development of British social policy decisively against competition and in favour of planning (Marsland, 1991).

Despite being himself a Liberal rather than a Socialist, Beveridge lent immense credibility, by his championing of the utopian thinking of the reconstructionist movement, to socialism, and undermined confidence in the potential of democratic capitalism to provide successfully for the needs and wishes of the population as a whole (Barnett, 1986). This paternalist-collectivist influence has continued and expanded from the 1940s through to the present. Even during the 1980s, it continued to shape social policy thinking despite attempts to find more effective alternatives. It has distorted and deformed the development of the Welfare State as a whole. It has impinged powerfully on every sphere of social policy. Across the board, this collectivist influence has served producers rather than consumers, reduced efficiency and flexibility, squandered public resources, favoured the privileged and powerful over the weak and genuinely needy, and created morally destructive welfare dependency.

Despite the manifest harm which the collectivist concept of welfare has done and is doing, it is not easy to challenge it definitively. Norman Barry (1990, p. 129) has indicated the source of this difficulty:

> Despite the resurgence of a more individualistic approach to public affairs, and an acceptance by many writers that well-being is a subjective phenomenon, there is no consensus on this. To many theorists, individuals do have needs that are independent of their desires, and indeed it is claimed *pari passu* that a society does have ends which are not reducible to individual choices. It is this claim which justifies the assimilation of welfare to the welfare state, and hence the inevitable paternalism that accompanies that form of social organization. This dichotomy, between individualism and collectivism, this apparently unbridgeable gulf between the potential ethical nihilism of subjectivism and the prospective authoritarianism of objectivism, in theorizing about welfare is but a special case of the larger division within social and poitical theory as a whole.

However, the rootedness of the conceptual intractability of welfare in larger and more antique conflicts in general social theory between individualism and collectivism (which Barry establishes) does not necessarily exclude the possibility of a degree of progress in clarification of the issue within the more limited sphere of welfare itself. We must surely at least try.

Distortions in Welfare Policy Arising from Theoretical Confusion

It is the purpose of this book to persuade proponents of the Welfare State that:

1. A market system would provide for the welfare needs of the prosperous majority more effectively than our established arrangements;
2. The special needs of the disadvantaged minority temporarily incapable of self-reliance would be at least as adequately answered as under the current dispensation by a new system which offered the additional benefit of avoiding waste, fraud, and dependency.

However, even supposing the main lines of my case for welfare reform were thus vindicated, there would remain – over and above the impregnable ideological resistance of egalitarian socialists and welfare fundamentalists – two distinct types of instrumental arguments in support of the welfare status quo which arise specifically out of confusions and contradictions in welfare theory.

The first emphasizes the function of state welfare provision as a necessary form of *social investment*. The second finds in the Welfare State an indispensable mechanism for securing *social solidarity*.

The defence of state welfare provision as a rational system of social investment is not implausible. It finds sophisticated support on the right of the Labour Party, among Liberal Democrats, on the 'Butskellite' left of the Conservative Party, and among the senior Civil Service technocracy. Its spokesmen argue that it is an essential interest of the state to provide at least for education – in order to secure an adequately trained workforce – and for health care – to maintain the strength and efficiency of the population – and possibly also for regional funding, unemployment schemes, environmental projects and transport – in order to maintain the economic infrastructure of society. It tends to be assumed that without state involvement, these crucial investments would not be made (Gray, 1993).

Plausible as it may seem, the argument for 'welfare as social investment' is readily refuted. Firstly, its underlying assumption that, without the state's involvement, essential investments would be neglected is contradicted by the experience of nineteenth-century Britain and contemporary America, Germany and Japan (Green, 1984; West, 1970; Hanson, 1974). To various degrees and in various ways, these examples demonstrate the scope for private and independent investment in the whole range of essential social infrastructure, given appropriate legal and economic conditions, and provided that entrepreneurs and companies are not crowded out by the state.

Secondly, the presumption, which is essential to the argument, that state investment – in education, in health care, or in anything much else besides – is likely to be wise and effective is contradicted by all the available evidence. The whole history of state intervention in any specifically economic role is a farce if it is not a tragedy. Can we be seriously expected to believe that, if education and health care had been handled since the War by the market, their condition could conceivably be any less satisfactory than they are today as a result of consistent state monopoly control and unmitigated state investment decisions?

Thirdly and finally, it does not in any case follow logically from the proposition that a state should ensure certain outcomes that the state should itself deliver them or even control their delivery. A legal requirement for parents to educate their children or for adults to insure themselves and their dependents against illness would of itself call into existence and mobilize into effective operation the required institutions and organizations – schools, colleges, hospitals, clinics and the rest. Similarly, intelligent economic policies, particularly in relation to monetary discipline and labour market flexibility, would do more to protect and upgrade the economic infrastructure than any amount of state investment or governmental regulation.

In short, while this first argument pretends to be rational and instrumental, it is actually as emotional and ideological as any other apologia for state welfare. It provides no persuasive grounds for resisting radical welfare reform.

The second argument, concerning the role of state welfare in securing and maintaining social solidarity, is similarly plausible, and similarly fallacious. In its essentials, it emphasizes the role of a shared commitment to collective welfare in symbolizing, and in sustaining in practice, the population's unity in the face of its diversities (Wicks, 1987; Halsey & Dennis, 1988; Ignatieff, 1984). The Welfare State, it is claimed, is what binds together – is all that binds together – the rich and the poor, the old and the young, black and white, region with region, the fashionable and the outmoded, insiders and outsiders, the establishment and the masses, the powerful and the powerless. Scrap the Welfare State, and society will split apart along its multitudinous seams into confrontational, or at best mutually indifferent, clans and factions (Galbraith, 1993).

This argument is not merely fallacious. It is, despite its current fashionability, a downright contradiction of the truth. It is difficult to think of any institution which has done more in practice to sustain and exacerbate social divisions than the Welfare State. For example: it falsely represents normal and necessary differences in income as unjust inequalities; it encourages demands for privileges as of right which are properly achieved only by merit and effort; it invalidates people's belief in the work ethic and in the feasibility of improving their economic conditions and social status by their own efforts and regardless of background; it provides the disadvantaged with excuses for inertia and alibis for lost opportunities, and deprives them of the essential stimulus of challenge; it underpins with spurious rights and stigmatizing institutional arrangements such divisive partial identities as 'poor', 'unemployed', 'immigrant', 'unskilled', or 'council tenant', and sectarian categories such as 'inner city', 'working class', or 'deprivation'.

Conversely, this argument neglects and discredits the genuine and essential bases of social solidarity, which the Welfare State consistently subverts and undermines. National identity is dismissed as an outmoded mystification (Shils, 1982). Local voluntary organizations and initiatives are seen as laughably amateur efforts due for replacement by comprehensive, state-organized systems. The family's crucial role in the socialization of children into a shared national and civilizational culture is sabotaged by

Welfare State ideology and practices. The market – which provides the ultimate arena of unity in all free societies – is ironically and scandalously maligned for its allegedly divisive effects, and prevented by over-regulation and state interference from carrying through the natural and normal process in capitalist societies of incorporating the whole population, regardless of irrelevant differences, into the market economy (Williams, 1982 and 1994; Sowell, 1981).

Thus, right across the board of all those intermediate institutions which comprise the intimate bonds of civil society, which stand protectively between the atomized individual and the all-powerful bureaucratic state, which define and sustain the grounds of our belief in ourselves as belonging together as one people – across all this precious cultural territory, the impact of the Welfare State is entirely negative (Green, 1993; Gellner, 1994). Far from providing a source of social solidarity, the Welfare State corrupts and destroys like a corrosive acid all those long-established institutions which comprise the whole basis of our genuine unity as a people with a common history and a shared destiny.

Conclusion

The concept of the Welfare State is thus riddled with incoherence and contradiction. I have argued here that the main lines of confusion in the theory and practice of state welfare can be defined in terms of five questions:

- Is it intended to deliver equity or, more ambitiously, equality?
- Are its distributive decisions to be based on needs or on rights?
- Is it promising a cornucopia of affluence or a hair-shirt of mere adequacy?
- Is its priority freedom or regulation?
- Is its fundamental concern with solving practical problems or with instituting a new social order?

I have also pursued aspects of each of these questions by examining two key expressions of the incoherence of state welfare theory: the ideas of Lord Beveridge, and the ambitiously instrumentalist arguments of exponents of the Welfare State's role as a channel of social investment and as a mechanism of social solidarity.

The Beveridge blueprint has failed. The idea of the Welfare State as society's primary economic governor has failed laughably. The proposition that state welfare can protect and enhance the communal integrity of society has been dramatically refuted. Moreover, these failures are not merely – which would be quite bad enough – falsifications of fundamental elements of welfare state theory. They are also inevitable outcomes of basic contradictions within that theory as a whole.

The Welfare State will continue to generate failure after failure because it is an inherently flawed concept. The concept is temptingly plausible precisely because of its challenge-proof incoherence, popular because it means all things to all men, and as difficult to contravert decisively as the Hydra was to kill, because its internal contradictions serve to square the circle of all the key social policy choices we need urgently to make.

3 Who Needs the Welfare State? Relative Poverty as Absolute Prosperity

One common answer to the question in the title of this chapter is that we *all* need the Welfare State. From the perspective of utopian welfare theorists such as Titmuss and Townsend, the Welfare State is not essentially, or even primarily, concerned with answering the special needs of the disadvantaged as such, however defined. The Welfare State is there to serve us all. Universal welfare provision is simply a defining characteristic of a civilized society.

From this egalitarian point of view, a genuine welfare state is defined by the communitarian nature of social relationships between citizens, with fundamental needs answered by universal welfare institutions, rather than through the market and other voluntary mechanisms. Citizenship means rights, and a regime of genuine rights requires, they suppose, universal provision of welfare. Hence, however high the standard of living may reach, however widely prosperity may be spread, the Welfare State remains essential. However few the poor may become, on whatever generous definition of poverty, utopian welfare theorists insist none the less that the institutions of the Welfare State remain absolutely indispensable. They argue indeed that, regardless of economic progress, the scope and power of these institutions should be continually extended.

This influential argument seems to me as incoherent as it is erroneous. Its incoherence arises from the systematic confusion of equity with equality and of welfare with socialism which has been examined in the preceding chapter. It fails in any case because it cannot be shown that the institutions of the Welfare State do in fact produce or encourage genuinely fraternal relations between people, as its exponents claim (Titmuss, 1968 and 1970). Such evidence as there is suggests that, on the contrary, nothing kills hospitality, real charity, neighbourliness, and genuine fellow-feeling quite as completely as state monopoly control of welfare (Seldon, 1990; O'Keeffe, 1994).

Despite the incoherence and fallibility of the utopian argument that the Welfare State is permanently essential as an instrument for answering population-wide needs in all conceivable economic circumstances, there is no sign of its being abandoned. Indeed, ironically, increasing prosperity appears to have driven apologists for the Welfare State towards deploying it more vigorously and brazenly than ever (Loney, 1986; Wicks, 1987; Commission on Social Justice, 1994).

None the less, it is nowadays commonly – if illogically – accompanied and supported by arguments appropriate to more modest and more pragmatic welfare theories. These seek to identify groups of poor, deprived and disadvantaged people to whose special needs Welfare State institutions are presumed to provide an indispensable answer. This concept leaves no escape from the necessity of finding an honest answer to the question of who really does need the Welfare State. It constrains those who seek to maintain the existence of the Welfare State indefinitely to show that there really are people with special needs in numbers large enough to justify large-scale state welfare. It requires of the Welfare State's champions that they should demonstrate how their arguments take account of recent economic progress and contemporary levels of prosperity. Typically, they do not (Abel Smith and Townsend, 1965).

Poverty-speak

Much nonsense is talked about poverty in the affluent societies of the free world, particularly at Christmas. This is commonly a 'season of ill-will' against the Government and a carnival of philanthropic hypocrisy. The tendency is especially strong in Britain, where the theologically implausible alliance between religious leaders guiltily parading their delicate consciences and left-wing pressure groups looking to extend their malign control of social policy is uniquely powerful.

For example, just in time for Christmas of 1989 – and it is the same every Christmas – Church Action for Poverty initiated yet another jihad against government policies with public meetings and the publication of a fifth gospel, entitled, with disarming sentimentality, *Hearing the Cry of the Poor*. 'We are outraged', one of their spokesmen was reported in the *Guardian* (4 December 1989) as saying, 'by the divisive effects of present policies.' According to the same report, Church Action's leaders were due to meet at Westminster Abbey 'to criticize the privatization of essential services, hospital ward closures, tax cuts, teacher shortages, and trade union and media restrictions'. Remarkably, there was apparently no mention on this occasion of the impact of defence spending on orphans, or of the shining exemplars of Christian charity and humanitarian welfare provided by the People's Democracies, at that time still, within socialist limits, thriving!

We have to reject with contempt, I suggest, the Poverty Lobby's scandalous misinterpretations of the facts about living standards if we are to have any chance at all of straight thinking about welfare. For the sake of the truth, for the sake of democracy, and for the sake above all of those who genuinely do need special help and protection, sensible people should dismiss all this mendacious poverty-speak nonsense out of hand.

John (now Lord) Moore was impolitic perhaps in his celebrated speech of 11 May 1989 about the concept and reality of poverty. He was, however, essentially correct. If we are to continue the improvement of the people's welfare in Britain, we have to think straight and clear, and stand firm against the emotional blandishments of sentimental sloganizing, from whatever distinguished academic sources (Atkinson, 1989).

We should, for example, refuse to be overawed by the spurious imagery of 'Cardboard City' gloatingly brandished in our faces by well-heeled journalists and comfortably-housed academic experts in homelessness. Its temporary denizens include the usual high proportions of alcoholics, recent Irish immigrants, and the casualties of personal and domestic tragedy. There are in addition significant numbers of mentally ill and handicapped people pitched out of protective asylum as a result of ill-considered radical campaigning against the supposed horrors of 'institutions'. There are also young people escaping inadequate families or worse, and prevented by decades of anti-landlord legislation from finding the lodgings which would enable them to take the jobs still amply available in London and the other big cities.

There are serious problems in the housing sphere, of course, but none that could not be ameliorated substantially if the intellectual atmosphere allowed rational policy-making. None, certainly, that can be brought one whit nearer to a real solution by pseudo-Christian sermonizing, expanded welfare expenditure, or welfare policies which ignore the moral dimensions of social problems. For example, when David Donnison (1994), a leading expert on housing policy, describes the commitment to owner occupation as an 'obsession' and dismisses it as 'a political virility symbol', we can be certain that he is in the business of equality-mongering rather than problem-solving.

Nor, I suggest, should people who are genuinely concerned to find ways of helping those who truly need help allow themselves to to be gulled or bullied into support for ill-considered welfare policies by flashy media extravaganzas. For example, during 1989 – in the same week, as it ironically happens, as the announcement of a new and stricter Press Code of Practice – the *Independent* (2 December) published a characteristically misleading account of contemporary life in Bradford. Under a glaringly sensational headline – 'The Hungry Poor Fail to Bounce Back' – readers are informed that 'Peter Dunn reports'. Now, admittedly 'reporting' is a complex concept, but one might have thought that it necessarily entails balance, and that it unarguably implies the presentation of evidenced facts. Yet, out of twenty-nine and a quarter column inches (pictures excluded), only six inches are allowed to counter-argument and counter-evidence. All the rest – four-fifths of the 'reporting' – supplies partisan support for the one-sided headline. So much for balance.

As to facts, the evidence is largely uncorroborated hearsay. Readers are not even told how many people live on the ill-starred Brierly Estate which is the main focus of the article. Neither date nor source is given for the 20 per cent unemployment rate alleged. A section reporting recent distribution of EC surplus food – which is the sole source for the imagery of 'starvation' in the headline – is woefully inadequate. Readers are not told whether any of the claimants were themselves from Brierly: it is entirely unclear whether any of them actually needed it, or simply fancied it because it was free; in relation to none of the so-called 'community organizations' which the article zealously defends is any evidence at all provided about how many Brierly people, if any, they have ever actually managed to help.

Then there are the pictures. They take up *three-quarters* of the whole page devoted to these revelations. Not one of them shows the new developments which the City has entered on to boost Bradford's image and to stimulate progress. All five depict a gloomy, pessimistic image. At least three of them seem clearly propagandistic in conception and in effect. The lead photograph – of an unfortunate gentleman on crutches walking, very conveniently from a photographer's point of view, past a run-down medical centre – seems to be a product of either considerable patience, subtle contrivance, or remarkable luck.

The last word in this whole feature (apparently part of an *Independent* tradition of photo-socialism, to judge from a recent full-page item in the issue for 25 November 1994, showing a child caught in a poverty trap) is allowed, unsurprisingly, to Ruth Lister, a member of the Commission on Social Justice and a tirelessly consistent spokesman for the professional poverty lobby. 'Unfortunately', she is reported as saying, 'poverty just doesn't go away.' Nor *will* the complex of problems she calls 'poverty' go away until we have more honesty about the manifest failings of the Welfare State, and instead of apologetics some open-minded consideration of new policies better calculated to produce real welfare.

However, this is not easily achieved while bias in public debate about poverty is so blatant. For example, the course outline for an entirely typical BSc Sociology and Applied Social Studies degree (1990) advises students as follows: 'For recent up-to-date statistical data, consult *Poverty*, the journal of the Child Poverty Action Group.' One might almost as well recommend an enquirer interested in learning about the geography of the Middle East to consult Saddam Hussein. Yet data provided by partisan campaigning bodies are regularly treated as reliable sources by teachers in schools and colleges and by the media.

Again, on a rather more influential front, the Parliamentary Social Services Select Committee, no less, supported its Ninth Report, on the social security reforms of 1986, with evidence presented by the following: Disability Alliance; Child Poverty Action Group; Family Service Units; Camden Tribunal & Rights Unit; Campaign for the Homeless and Rootless; Maternity Alliance; National Association of Citizens' Advice Bureaux; Social Security Consortium; British Association of Social Workers; British Refugee Council; Department of Sociological Studies, Sheffield University; Wandsworth Rights Group; Hounslow Benefits Action Group; and the West Midlands Welfare Rights Agency. The predictable views and special pleading of these proselytizing, not to say partisan, bodies, appears not to have been balanced by any alternative approaches at all.

Again, in Parliament recently, the Labour Party's chief spokesman on social security went so far (according to a report in *The Times* of 31 January 1990) as to accuse the Government of 'deliberately creating poverty' and the Prime Minister of being 'indifferent to those in need'. Serious analysis of welfare policies is impossible unless the issue of poverty is examined more dispassionately than has become usual.

No doubt even more progress along the road towards continuing prosperity might have been achieved in recent years. But what has prevented it is the persisting power of the reactionary forces which destroyed the 1970s: trade union chauvinism, institutionalized envy, antiquated anxieties about social change, the belief that the world owes us a living – and, above all, the destructive myths of the Poverty Lobby.

Prime examples of this myth-making are Harrison's *Inside the Inner City* of 1983, which has become an unjustifiably authoritative standard text on urban inequality; the hysterical 1985 report of the Archbishop of Canterbury's Commission on Urban Priority Areas, *Faith in the City*; and a more recent but logically identical instance provided by the Rowntree Foundation's one-sided and misleading 1995 report, *Income and Wealth*. They exaggerate the extent of poverty absurdly. They deliberately confuse poverty with inequality. They demand the same old, failed remedies: more government spending, more taxes, more state control. They feverishly defend the Welfare State as if it were the Holy Grail. We need instead to hear the truth about living standards, and about the sorts of policies which are likely to inhibit rather than exacerbate economic failure and poverty.

The same spurious claims about widespread poverty are made in the United States as in Britain, yet according to a recent report (Macrae, 1995) consumer surveys suggest that 'many of the 10 per cent poorest Americans spend three times as much as they say they earn'! According to the same report:

> When the last census reported that 39.3 million Americans lived in absolute poverty, we wailed that so many of these were children. The US health authorities now report that these 'starving' kids eat twice as much protein (the most expensive nutrient) as is medically desirable, so their chief food-related problem is obesity. By age 19 the sons of welfare mothers average one inch taller and 10 pounds heavier than the GIs who stormed the beaches of Normandy.

In Britain, as in America, in every situation which allows free expression of opinion without providing an adequate forum for systematic evaluation of supposed social facts, the legend of poverty is elaborated by mischief-makers and professional sentimentalists as an antidote to their own failed neurotic dreams (Horowitz, 1994; Marsland, 1988, 1992 [6], and 1993 [5]). The persistence of poverty guarantees a meaning for the lives of all those for whom the humdrum satisfactions of successful domesticity and useful practical work are either unavailable or never enough. If neurotic identification with the outcast (what one might call 'the Pilger Syndrome' or 'the Robin Hood Complex') also provides a mantle of sanctity, even of martyrdom, so much the better, it seems, for them, and so much the worse for the mainstream majority and especially for the minority of people who really do need and deserve special help.

The Truth about Poverty

It goes without saying that some people and some families have much lower incomes and much lower living standards than others. However, income differences and inequalities have nothing whatsoever to do with 'poverty'. Mistaken judgements about this issue continue to be made even by otherwise sensible, and therefore unfortunately influential, analysts such as the authors published by the Institute for Fiscal Studies (Giles and Webb, 1993), and even by the least arrogant and unattractive of our bishops (Shepherd, 1983).

The differential between two millionaires, one of them living on the income from one million pounds, the other possessed of one thousand million pounds, is bigger by far than the sort of differences in income which the Poverty Lobby glibly labels as a 'gulf' or an 'intolerable social division', and interprets routinely as evidence of 'polarization'. Yet patently the poorer of the two millionaires is in no genuine sense of the term 'poor'. There is no way he could plausibly be characterized – except no doubt by a radical Association of Low Income Millionaires – as enduring 'poverty'.

The same argument holds at any point up and down the whole range of the income scale. *There is simply no logical connection at all between income differences as such and 'poverty'*. The so-called relative concept of poverty is a pure nonsense designed to keep alive the guttering flame of Marxist and socialist critique of capitalism (Moynihan ed., 1969). Its implication, which is self-evidently ludicrous, is that there is worse poverty in Britain than in Uganda, more poor people in Los Angeles than Cairo, and less deprivation in Mexico City than in London. It underpins ludicrous headlines such as 'Third of Britons Live in Poverty' (*Times Higher Educational Supplement*, 11 March 1994), which sub-editors with any professional pride left should resign over.

Peter Saunders makes this crucial point nicely with a mythical simile (1994, p. 88):

No matter how much capitalism improves the lot of all the people, relativist critics will forever complain that nothing is 'really' changing because some people still enjoy greater opportunities than others. Once upon a time a giant and a dwarf clambered into a hot air balloon. The balloon's efficiency exceeded all expectations and most observers were delighted to see its continuing ascent toward the clouds. One group of disaffected sociologists remained resolutely unimpressed, however. When asked why, they triumphantly replied that the giant was still closer to the clouds than the dwarf. Far better, they assured their bemused audience, to have dug a hole in the ground for the giant to stand in and never to have got involved with balloons in the first place.

This infinitely elastic relativism has to be avoided. If we are to use the term 'poverty' at all, it has to refer to some objectively given level of deprivation of necessities. As John Moore put it, in commenting on Poverty Lobby manipulations of income data, 'It is utterly absurd to speak as if one in three people in Britain today is in dire need. These claims are false and they are dangerous.'

Yet just such absurd claims are the staple message of the Poverty Lobby, most social scientists, and the social affairs correspondents of the media. They are the main basis of arguments used by champions of the Welfare State to justify continuance of large-scale state welfare provision. A particularly influential example was provided by Mack and Lansley's book *Poor Britain* (1985), which was based on the even more influential television series, *Breadline Britain*, and on a MORI poll associated with it. The book epitomizes the characteristic vices and weaknesses of British sociology: contamination of scholarly analysis by ideological commitment; prejudice against capitalism; illiterate allegiance to economic egalitarianism; chronic incapacity to see the wood for the trees; and studied lack of common sense. Worst of all, it typifies the confusion between inequality and poverty, and the resolute, not to say pig-headed, refusal to acknowledge the level and extent of prosperity and economic progress in Britain which seem to be the fundamental articles of faith of *soi-disant* experts on social affairs.

Fortunately, John Moore's analysis of these errors has been followed up in depth in a recent study by David Green (1990). He demonstrates that the so-called 'rediscovery of poverty' in the 1960s by Marxist and left-socialist academics was actually a manipulative redefinition of poverty rather than the discovery of anything at all in the real world: 'Instead of defining poverty in terms of hardship, the poverty line was calculated in relation to average earnings.' Even if one were to grant that conceptions of hardship change as prosperity increases, which seems to be implausibly generous anyway, Green shows that this provides no justification whatsoever for linking the poverty line to average earnings rather than prices. The effect of this absurd equation is to ensure that a large proportion of the population can always be characterized as poor, entirely regardless of their actual standards of living.

Thus, in a report of 14 May 1989 of Moore's speech, the *Sunday Times* (not the *Morning Star*, nor even the *Guardian*, one should note, but the *Sunday Times*) was able to claim, apparently seriously, that 'Most commentators' estimate that 'around 15 million, just under a third of the population' are in poverty. This was too much even for the Child Poverty Action Group, who – no doubt fearful for their already slender credibility – insisted that the right figure for what they called 'people in or at the margins of poverty' was only 9.5 million! Quite why people at the upper margin of an already arbitrary and implausible boundary should be allocated downwards into poverty rather than upwards into the 'margins of prosperity' is not clear.

It seems to provide further confirmation, if any were needed, that the whole exercise of defining poverty in relative terms, as if it were an aspect of inequality rather than a feature of objective living conditions, is a specious political sleight-of-hand rather than a scholarly or scientific endeavour. Green's study provides strong evidence for this interpretation. In a careful analysis of *The Growing Divide* (Walker and Walker, 1987), which purports to assess the first eight years of Thatcherism, he shows that:

a) Having themselves reported that recipients of supplementary benefit enjoyed increased income in real terms of about 5 per cent, the authors, by introducing a comparison with average earnings, manage to claim that supplementary benefit levels have 'fallen considerably'. In other words, they say the living standards of poorer people have fallen although they know they have actually risen. The Grand Old Duke of York just isn't in it.

b) The authors systematically and surreptitiously slip between reference to those 'on the SB level' and those 'at or 40 per cent above SB'. This manoeuvre facilitates gross exaggeration of the number of 'the poor', even if one were to grant that the SB level itself represented poverty other than in purely political and distributional terms.

c) One of the authors, Martin Loney of the Open University, claims that the Government has 'reduced the incomes of the poorest', when in fact, as is admitted elsewhere in the book, their real incomes have gone up significantly.

d) Another author, Alan Walker, who asserts quite contrary to the evidence that the 'fissure between rich and poor has widened into a chasm since 1979', manages simultaneously to falsify the nature and extent of so-called poverty, and to foist on his (mostly youthful and unsuspecting) readers the tendentious presumption that inequalities in income are morally indefensible, economically counter-productive, and incompatible with improved living standards for the least well-off. None of these propositions is true.

The undeniable conclusion of any clear-headed analysis of the recent literature on poverty is that the arguments it offers – which serve, we should recall, as the main justification for continuing with the provision of large-scale social welfare – are entirely false where they are not wholly meaningless.

There are, of course, substantial income differences in modern Britain. Such differences are entirely natural and normal. Moreover, any dynamic society positively needs such differences in order to provide economic and

social incentives, as most of the population acknowleges. Egalitarian societies invariably have high levels of real poverty. Eventually, as in the
socialist world of Eastern Europe and the former USSR, they collapse in
chaos and bankruptcy. Their collapse is in large part due to their systematic commitment over many decades to levelling incomes downwards
and squeezing out economic inequality.

There are, of course, small but significant numbers of people and families in real economic difficulty. However, these cases are not – with some
very few exceptions, and these only on a temporarary basis – properly
classified as poor. Even among the very least well-off, as John Moore has
shown, *half have a telephone and central heating, and significant numbers
own a car, and even their own home. Even the poorest fifth of families
with children spend close to a tenth of their modest incomes on alcohol
and tobacco.*

Moreover, in many of these cases the causes of their economic difficulty
are not themselves economic at all, and their problems are not such as can be
solved by economic assistance as such. This applies, for example, to large
numbers of the chronically ill, criminals and young runaways, who together
comprise a substantial proportion of the least well-off. Another substantial
segment of the least well-off comprise lone parents, whose 'poverty', such as
it is, is for the fathers of their children rather than tax payers to remedy.

The fact is that prosperity in Britain is at a high level by international
and historical standards. The way in which British society and the British
economy have successfully incorporated since the Second World War
several millions of immigrants from Ireland and the Commonwealth,
almost all of them penniless and unqualified at the time of their arrival, is
proof enough in itself that the myth of poverty is precisely that.

The number of people who cannot fend for themselves in economic
terms, who cannot achieve individual and family self-reliance, is
immensely smaller than the Poverty Lobby pretends. These cases need and
deserve help of course, but their number is so small compared with the
specious claims made by collectivist campaigners that it provides no
justification at all for large-scale state welfare. Indeed, as I suggest in a
later chapter, the Welfare State is actually harmful to the real interests of
the genuinely disadvantaged minority, and serves to multiply their
numbers. The poorest people in Britain need the Welfare State least of all.

Economic Progress and Prosperity

A significant element in the slender plausibility of the Poverty Lobby's
implausible case is contributed by our recent experience of high levels of

unemployment. A large proportion of those currently living on state benefits – few of them, in consequence, suffering serious hardship – are unemployed.

While this is deeply regrettable, it does not of itself confirm the pessimistic diagnosis of current economic conditions which supporters of state welfare call on to justify its continuance and expansion. In a free society unemployment is unavoidable, and in un-free societies its apparent absence is purely fictitious. A 10 per cent unemployment rate – much lower in any case than in many other advanced countries – is a 90 per cent employment rate. A significant proportion of official unemployment is a spurious product of the black economy (Wood, 1975). Moreover, recent British unemployment has largely been caused by overpriced wages, state interference in the market, high taxes, and extravagant welfare benefits – the same causes as have held back economic progress and prosperity by comparison with our foreign competitors.

Even so, support for the unemployed and their families has been held at a high and improving level. If state unemployment benefits were replaced by personally-insured employment protection (which would offer a much better deal), this last shred of plausibility in the Poverty Lobby's implausible case for massive state welfare would vanish. The true facts about Britain's economic progress and prosperity would be undeniably apparent.

The bottom-line criterion of prosperity is life-expectancy. As economic progress in Britain has gone from strength to strength over the past hundred years, people have been living longer and longer. With typical casuistry, socialists like the authors of the Black Report on health inequalities (DHSS, 1980; Townsend and Davidson 1982; Townsend *et al.*, 1988) prefer to focus on persisting differentials, even though these have been narrowing rapidly in recent years (Le Fanu, 1993). Instead, an objective analysis requires consideration of long-term trends (OPCS, 1989).

Since 1841/5 crude death rates have declined from 21.4 per thousand to 11.8 in 1985. The Standard Mortality Ratio, a more valid measure than crude death rates, has plummeted from 344 to 75 in the same period. Improvements in infant mortality have been even more massive, reducing from 148 deaths of children under one year per thousand live births in 1841/5 to as few as 9 per thousand in 1985. The details of trends in infant mortality – which largely control mortality rates as a whole and provide incontrovertible evidence of continuous comprehensive economic progress – are set out below (Marsland and Leoussi, 1995).

Life expectancy at birth has improved from 45.5 for men and 49.0 for women in 1901 to 73.2 for men and 78.6 for women in 1991 (*Social Trends*, 1993, Table 7.4). The Queen sent eight times as many 100th

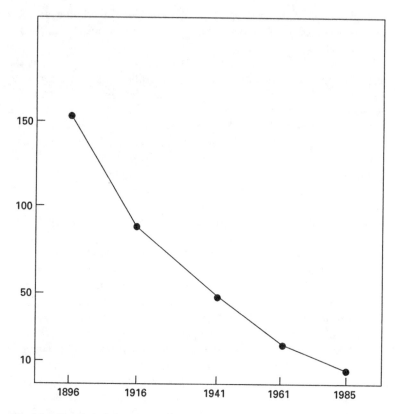

Fig. 3.1   Trends in infant mortality
Deaths of infants under one year per thousand live births.

birthday messages in 1993 as she did as recently as 1963, and there are now two million Britons over 80 and a quarter of a million over 90! Life expectancy is currently increasing by 2 years every decade. While advances in health care have certainly made a significant contribution to these astonishing improvements, the consensus of opinion among epidemiologists and other experts is that they are very largely due to economic progress and the general increase in standards of living (Farmer and Miller, 1991), not least the continuing, if irregular, improvements in the quality of diet (Burnett, 1979).

Their effects are also evident in the physiological characteristics of the population. Reliable evidence about these basic aspects of the outcomes of living standards is sadly as inadequate, on Burnett's expert account (ibid.), as it is in relation to diet. Scholars have generally been more intent on finding confirmation for their prejudiced views about persisting inequalities than on systematic collation of comprehensive, descriptive data. Fortunately, recent work by Roderick Floud (1990) has begun to produce the evidence we need. Average height has increased consistently and substantially ever since the process of social modernization began. Other relevant indicators point to a similar conclusion. Over the past century and from decade to decade since industrial capitalism established itself in Britain, standards of living have consistently improved for the whole population (Gash, 1974). Thus real disposable income has risen by 80 per cent since 1971. Reliable long-run details are more difficult to establish than they might be if the discipline of economic history had not been subject to so complete a take-over by socialism, but they are available.

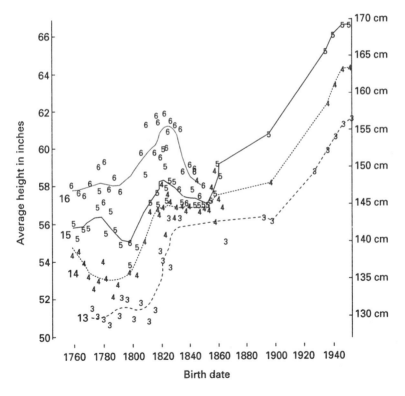

Fig. 3.2   Trends in height
Mean height of working-class children at age 13, 14, 15, and 16 since 1758 (Floud, 1990, p. 166).

Welfare or Welfare State?

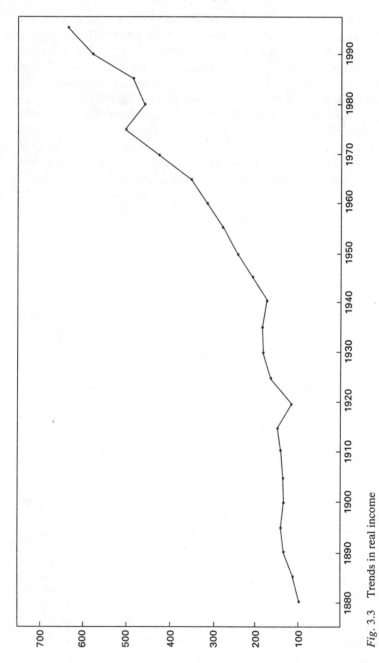

Fig. 3.3   Trends in real income
Average personal wages, adjusted for inflation with 1881 = 100 (Based on Rigby, 1995).

A further basic indicator of quality of life is provided by home ownership. Of the 24 million dwellings in the UK in 1992, more than twice as many were owner-occupied compared with the position in 1961 (*Social Trends* 1994, p. 110). Seventy per cent of households (as of June 1993) now live in their own homes, a higher proportion than almost anywhere else in the world, and likely, despite current glum muttering about the housing market by policy experts, to increase still further before the turn of the century. This should include a further increase in the large number of 1.5 million public sector tenants who have bought their homes as a result of the 'Right to Buy' policy. Between 1981 and 1990 owner-occupation increased in every socio-economic group, including the semi-skilled manual, the unskilled manual, and the economically inactive (*Social Trends*, 1993, Chart 8.25). We are indeed, as the title of Peter Saunders' important study of the topic suggests, *A Nation of Home Owners* (1990 [2]). A temporary increase in negative equity affecting a small minority of home owners may be a source of encouragement to

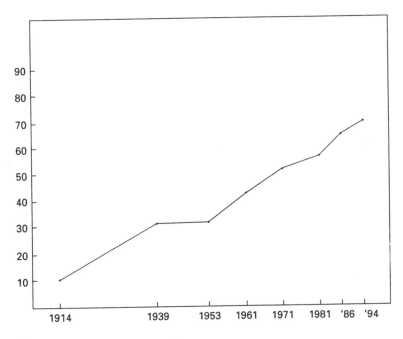

Fig. 3.4   Trends in home ownership

Percentage of households in owner-occupied homes (Holman, 1987; Saunders, 1990 [2]).

enemies of free markets, but it cannot provide any real challenge to the genuine increase in wealth which expanding home ownership comprises.

Nor are these the only indicators of improving generalized prosperity. Cars are owned by almost 70 per cent of families, a large proportion of those without being pensioners and others less capable of driving. Central heating is available in 81 per cent of households, a washing machine in more than 87 per cent, and a telephone in more than 88 per cent – having risen from 75 per cent during the 'Hard Times' of the 1980s (all figures 1992; source: *Annual Abstract of Statistics*, 1994). By 1992 the number of holidays taken abroad had more than quadrupled compared with twenty-five years ago to 22 million, the highest figure ever, and predicted to continue rising (*Social Trends* 1994, p. 138). Personal savings are massively high.

Thus, even allowing for the inclusion in all these figures of pensioners and recent immigrants, who have been prevented by time and absence respectively from participating to the same extent as others in recent economic progress, the economic condition of the British population is objectively very good and continually improving. In the face of biased reporting by the media, where most social affairs correspondents define one beggar as worth ten times as much coverage as a hundred prosperous families, and where the alcoholic homeless and the bankrupt are regarded as incomparably more photogenic and newsworthy than successful graduates and first-time home-buyers, we need to remind ourselves of the scale and persistence, over the long term and in recent years alike, of our economic progress.

Celebrating Progress

In relation to the years since 1979, a recent article by Stephen Glover, reflecting on the new edition of *Social Trends*, 'We've never had it so good – honestly' (*Evening Standard*, 9 February 1995), addressed this bias:

> The truth is that nearly all of us have grown fantastically richer since 1979 and that expenditure on infrastructure has soared in nearly every area of government. [The statistics] show a country which is very difficult indeed to categorize as poor, though such is the image unthinkingly peddled in countless newspaper columns and articles. Take, for example, real gross weekly earnings. Since the Tories came to power these have risen in almost every walk of life you care to mention. Adjusted to April 1994 prices, i.e. stripping out inflation, the average weekly wage of a nurse has risen from £188 in 1981 to £316 in 1994 –

an increase of 68%. For a doctor the equivalent rise has been from £550 to £745; for a secondary school teacher from £314 to £427; for a waitress from £138 to £157; for a receptionist from £135 to £182...it is impossible to read Social Trends without concluding that for most people the quality of life has improved very greatly over the last 16 years. Britain has become a much wealthier country.

Proponents of capitalism have always argued, in the teeth of dogmatic scepticism on the part of socialists, that levelling success upwards works, and that the fruits of economic growth automatically 'trickle down' to poorer segments of the population, provided that the process is not sabotaged by socialist levelling-down through excessive taxation and extravagant public expenditure. This hypothesis is amply confirmed by British historical data.

Indeed 'trickle down' is altogether too modest a characterization of recent improvements in standards of living. Liberal capitalism has produced in Britain a veritable cascade of wealth, which has transformed the standard of living and the quality of life of the whole population to levels scarcely imagined as recently as the 1960s, let alone the 1930s (Pollard, 1983; Court, 1965; Breach and Hartwell, 1972). This is admitted by default even by critics of capitalism such as Stuart Lansley (1994). For in urging restraint and increased social controls, he reveals that:

> Last year United States citizens spent more on potted plants than the regular budget of the United Nations. North Americans now spend more on private security than in taxation on public policing. In Britain consumer spending has soared as a proportion of national wealth.

The Guardians of the People's Morals may object to the choices people are making about what they spend their money on, but they can hardly claim at the same time that they have no money to spend.

Even in a characteristically hysterical critique of inequality (*Independent on Sunday*, 4 July 1993), Christopher Huhne has to confess that between 1979 and 1990/91 average household income in real terms rose by 36 per cent. To make his negative case, he is obliged to focus on the bottom 10 per cent, whose 'income fell between 1 per cent and 14 per cent'. Moreover, he supports his implausible anti-government argument by torturing his source – an official government document (Department of Social Security, 1993) – unmercifully.

Thus he focuses his attention on the *possible* 14 per cent ceiling of reduction among the poorest rather than the *more probable* 1 per cent within the range of uncertainty identified by the study. He distracts his readers' attention by means of studied rhetoric from the fact that even in his worst case scenario the income of 86 per cent of the population – hardly a narrow élite of privileged rich – has, even during a period of radical economic re-structuring on the global and domestic fronts alike, increased significantly in real terms. He makes no allowance at all for the fact that the lower income group of 1990/91 does not comprise the same people at all as in 1979 – with many more lone parents and large numbers of new immigrants. Citizens of the Irish Republic continued to flow into the UK throughout the 1980s, despite the gross poverty and intolerable inequality alleged by this latterday Engels! Worst of all, Huhne simply assumes that inequality is 'a bad thing', and evidently finds it inconceivable that more egalitarian policies would have produced worse results. If Huhne's preferred tax and benefits policies had been deployed, the chances of achieving a 36 per cent increase in real incomes would have been negligible.

In this sphere of living standards, even more than in most, a dispassionate attention to the facts in all their complexity is to be preferred to philanthropic emotionalism, however strongly this may seem to be justified. Even the Hammonds, those influential purveyors of the Satanic Mills myth, whose work is still cited by socialists as evidence of the oppressive poverty of capitalism, confess that their own influential account of conditions in nineteenth-century Britain was exaggerated and inaccurate (1947, p. 15):

> Statisticians tell us that when they have put in order such data as they can find, they are satisfied that earnings increased and that most men and women were less poor when this discontent was loud and active than they were when the eighteenth century was beginning to grow old in a silence like that of autumn. The evidence, of course, is scanty, but this general view is probably more or less correct.

Thus in relation to the whole period of capitalism, as much as if not more than in relation to the early period studied by the Hammonds, progress towards increasing prosperity has been substantial and continuing. Protest movements, romantic intellectuals and political campaigning notwithstanding, the myth of poverty in modern Britain is just that.

In relation to more contemporary British circumstances, I have seen little note taken by our media specialists in poverty of a remarkable study by the Economist Intelligence Group (1991). Headlined accurately in *The Times* (Jones, 1991), 'British Workers Among World's Wealthiest', a report of the study indicates that 'Only the Swiss and Americans have more purchasing power than the British'. The average Swedish production worker with two children has (or had in 1989) £7156 take-home pay, while the British equivalent was almost £3000 per annum better off at £10 061. German, French, Italian, and Danish workers, all from European countries supposedly ahead of Britain, are also behind their British equivalents in real purchasing power terms. So much for stereotypes.

In the light of the figures reported here, even Gustave Doré, the gloomy painter of desolate scenes from supposedly starving Victorian London, would have to add a little brightness to his palette. Even Engels, that most famous and influential of professional pessimists, would have to cheer up just a little.

Exceptions to Prosperity?

The concepts and measures of poverty, so-called, adopted by socialists, the Poverty Lobby, and most academic social policy analysts are irrelevant and misleading as indicators of deprivation or need. Since they are wholly relative in character, they provide no useful guidance at all about real standards of living, or about the capacity of the population to provide for itself autonomously without state welfare support.

Nor does the rising volume of state benefits – which the media commonly use as evidence of impoverishment – provide a more valid indicator of poverty or need. More people receive state benefits today than in earlier decades simply because more state benefits are available. A proper and objective understanding of the economic conditions of the population can only be derived from analysis of trends and patterns in real incomes. All the evidence, by whatever criteria, shows that the standard of living of the whole population has improved, is improving, and will continue to improve further. Indeed, our standard of living is at very high levels by historical and comparative standards alike. The vast majority of the British population in 1994 is thoroughly well-off in economic terms. Everyone is better-off by several times than when the Welfare State was first established. The poverty which state welfare was designed to alleviate has to all intents and purposes vanished, and this without any significant contribution on the positive side by state welfare.

The exceptions to majority prosperity comprise a very small minority. Even during the worst period of the early 1980s' recession, the unemployed comprised no more than 12 per cent (without discounting for fraud, which is widespread) of the potentially employed population, and an even smaller proportion of all households. Unemployment is not, in any case, a permanent condition except for a very special minority of unemployables and near-unemployables within the minority of the unemployed. In normal circumstances, about a third of those who are unemployed will find a job within three months, another third within six, and half the remainder within a year. Long-term unemployment, even by the generous definition usually adopted of more than twelve months out of work, is higher than it should be, higher than it needs to be, but still very exceptional indeed. Moreover, all the unemployed have continuing access to adequate and improving benefits to protect them against the worst effects of their situation.

In short, this first category among the economically disadvantaged minority – the unemployed – is modest in number (less than in France, Italy, Belgium, Holland and Denmark, and a third of the Spanish level), adequately protected, and capable for the most part of having this same or better protection made available by means of personal insurance instead of state guarantee. There is no justification for the apocalyptic vision of large-scale permanent unemployment with which the media is preoccupied (Marsland, 1994). Nor, in any case, would a genuine threat of increasing unemployment provide any justification for maintaining the massive state welfare system – since the Welfare State itself, because of its impact on wage costs and on incentives, is among the primary causes of unemployment.

A second relatively large block of the population on lower incomes is comprised of pensioners. Here, too, state benefits provide substantial assistance. A large and increasing proportion provide more adequately for themselves by means of occupational or personal pension schemes. Provided that an increasing number of people can be persuaded, by rational argument and by changes in the tax structure, to discount the state pension as anything more than a basic minimum, and to provide for themselves on their own account by saving for their retirement, there need be no great pensions crisis such as some experts predict. Even given increasing life expectancy, there is no reason why more than a very small proportion of pensioners should be in financial difficulties or impose in consequence any significant demand on a state welfare system.

Over and above the unemployed and pensioners, the vast majority of the 'needy' in contemporary Britain are people in special and unpredictable personal circumstances: one-parent families, the chronically sick, the seriously handicapped and the homeless. *In toto* these comprise a very small minority of the population. Their problems are not caused for the most part by economic factors, and financial assistance cannot provide an adequate answer to most of their problems. Nor do their problems and needs provide any justification at all for the Welfare State and its comprehensive, universalist provision. On the contrary, their situations cry out for special provision targeted sharply on their varied and special needs, with the vast majority of the whole prosperous population allowed and encouraged to look after themselves without state interference.

Thus, if we really want to find out who needs the Welfare State, we ought – first discounting altogether the wholly spurious answer provided in terms of relativist and redistributionist criteria by socialists and the Poverty Lobby – to identify carefully the relatively small number of categories and cases of genuine hardship and real need. This might reduce Welfare State coverage from the current 100 per cent – with state education, health care, pensions, child benefit, leisure provision and all the rest available even to the wealthiest – to some 15 per cent. The whole of the large, prosperous majority of 85 per cent of the population could easily fend for themselves without state welfare help, given tax reductions and tax incentives (Goodin and Le Grand, 1987).

Even a realistic analysis along these lines exaggerates the extent of need for the Welfare State substantially. For many, even among this 15 per cent minority, could manage to provide for themselves adequately out of their own resources by means of savings and personal insurance, given encouraging tax incentives and personal planning. Welfare reform should be directed both to providing the necessary tax cuts and to guiding people in temporary need towards a more prudent and planned approach to their own and their families' lives. The independent, non-state assistance available is examined in Appendix 1 and in a recent article by Reece (1994) on the alternatives to failing and inadequate state care available through the market.

This might leave a hard core of 5–8 per cent who unavoidably need welfare assistance. The whole of the costly, complex, bureaucratic machinery of the Welfare State is thus needed at most by about two million families. Even this could probably be reduced by sensible social policies such as I discuss in Chapter 9, and the remainder could certainly be more effectively helped if the delivery of welfare were radically reformed.

Conclusion: Bringing the Minority on Board

One of the oldest Welfare States in the world is New Zealand. Under the pressures of economic crisis largely caused by extravagant public expenditure, the Government of New Zealand is currently cutting back state welfare savagely. Similar moves are in train in Australia, in Sweden and in the United States. Why should we in Britain wait for economic crisis? The Welfare State is a redundant trace-effect of antique ideological errors and historical accidents. Who needs it? Not all of us. Not most of us. Just a very few at most, and even they would be much better off without it in its present form.

As the evidence presented in this chapter demonstrates, prosperity, living standards and quality of life have all been improving consistently throughout this century and before. The data presented in the several graphs above show incontrovertibly that, despite wars and recessions, huge progress has been achieved in *reducing infant mortality* (and therefore increasing life expectancy), in *improving the physical condition of the population* evidenced by average height (an indicator of dietary quality), in *raising the real income of the people*, taking full account of costs and inflation, and in *extending the scale of home ownership*, a measure of prosperity which represents a crucial stake in the ongoing progress of society as a whole.

This same pattern of continuing economic progress and sustained popular prosperity is evident throughout the free world. It is plainly a function of that combination of market capitalism and liberal democracy which defines the culture and civilization of freedom. Collapsed communist societies which have pursued the alternative path of planned socialist development are unlikely to provide similar standards of living unless and until their leaders prove capable of initiating a genuine democratic politics and real markets unencumbered by political interference. Third World societies will remain squalidly poor until they find the means – in terms of values, leadership, and the key institutions of property, law and competitive markets – to create, like Chile in the South American context, Taiwan and Hong Kong in Asia, and perhaps South Africa, those essential conditions of progress which socialists have always opposed.

The several indicators of progress which I have examined leave room, of course, for wide variation – from the richest to the poorest, from the longest to the shortest lived, from families with two homes of their own to the genuinely homeless, and so on. However, the trend of all the figures, and any others that might have been included, is so consistent and so steeply upwards that denial of general improvement involving everyone except small minorities is implausible in the extreme. Nor can the persistence of inequalities be legitimately used to contradict or even to qualify this positive interpretation of the condition of the population. They are much less severe than the routinely negative sociological accounts pretend, and they are in any case unavoidable, morally justified and necessary if the competitive dynamism which produces economic progress and prosperity is to be assured.

Moreover, Britain and other free societies have achieved and are sustaining economic progress and popular prosperity despite increasing numbers of social passengers who are able to contribute little on their own account to the conditions from which they benefit. These include young people spending more and more time in full-time education (three times more tertiary-level students today than in 1979), the refugees and immigrants who have flooded into all the free societies throughout the modern era, and the elderly who in huge numbers are living on – and living well – much beyond three score years and ten, and to an age which even recently was exceptional in the extreme.

There are, of course, many – far too many – who are left behind as the prosperous majority moves forward, or who are driven out of prosperity they themselves once enjoyed. In the context of the overall analysis presented in this book, two comments on this situation are necessary. First, the number of such people is much smaller than is commonly claimed, and they do not, as yet, constitute a permanent caste of the excluded. People move in and out, up and down, much more than orthodox sociological analysis acknowledges, and with little of the simple, inescapable structuring of disadvantage by class which forms the fundamental item of faith in the vision of society propagated by socialists and sociologists.

Second, we have to consider the reasons why general progress has not been shared even more widely, and the causes which have to-date excluded a significant minority from full participation in the prosperity which has become increasingly available. The contention which is argued throughout this book, and in detail in Chapters 6, 7 and 9, is that no blame at all can be attributed in this regard, as supporters of state welfare claim, to the competitive character of capitalism or to the effects of market processes. On the contrary, it is these essential features of a genuinely free society which have produced all the economic progress so far achieved, and which will guarantee, if they are allowed, continuing improvements in prosperity.

The minority of our populations who comprise the disadvantaged and deprived are driven into deprivation and disadvantage – and held prisoner in these intolerable conditions – by state welfare. They will not be permanently liberated from this lesser Gulag of petty socialism until the ideas and arguments of witting and unwitting agents of influence who serve from time to time the socialism of Russia, the socialism of China, and the dispossessed international socialism which pre-dated and outlasted 1917, are answered, contained and defeated once and for all.

4 Bankrupting Britain: The Costs of the Welfare State

Wherever Welfare States have been established, grave damage to the economy is evident. Jacques (1994) comments as follows, for example, on the situation in OECD countries:

> Reform of national welfare systems is now under consideration throughout the OECD as government expenditure rises inexorably. Total government spending in these countries has grown from 28.1% of GDP in 1960 to 43.8% in 1990. The biggest single element in this increase has been the cost of pensions, health, unemployment benefits and family support. Social security payments more than doubled during this period, from 7% of GDP to 15.4%. Health expenditure also doubled, from 3.9% to 7.8%.

Again, to take a more exotic and less well-known example, Uruguay is known as 'South America's first Welfare State' (Biddulph, 1990). By the beginning of the 1990s, the country faced economic crisis, and the government of Louis Lacalle was desperately struggling to privatize the bloated public sector in the face of popular resistance. According to local reports, Uruguayans had 'grown quite comfortable with a government that provides salaries of some sort for sixty percent of the population'. However: 'the cost of maintaining these benefits is out of control. With a $7 billion foreign debt, Uruguay has one of the highest per capita debts in the world.' Meanwhile, in New Zealand, commonly referred to as the world's oldest Welfare State, there are similar problems. For the past few years the government has been forced to cut the extravagant welfare budget to the bone in response to a serious economic crisis occasioned primarily by excessive public expenditure (Morgan, 1994).

Even socialist governments, faced by similar economic problems, have been adopting similar strategies of reducing welfare provision to minimum essential levels in order to balance the national books. For example, in August 1990 the Australian government completely abolished unemployment benefits, and cut back severely on medical and other welfare support. Indefinite unemployment benefit, long available to Australians, was abandoned altogether, and replaced by a short-term job-search allowance and a form of work-fare. Those unwilling to work – the legendary 'dole-bludgers', or cheats – will get no help from the state. Moreover, it seems the majority of Australians recognize that unemployment benefit has been largely squandered in preceding decades, and acknowledge that it has proven counter-productive and a gross waste of public financial resources. Support for the proposed reforms is widespread.

In Sweden, too, that latterday paradise for visiting welfare fellow-travellers from Britain, these past several years have seen a radical restructuring of welfare. For many years, the Swedes – like the Dutch and the French, but unlike the British, even under Margaret Thatcher's administrations – have operated 'workfare' as a means of preventing abuses of unemployment benefit and of inhibiting its dependency-creating effects. Now the whole intricate panoply of cradle-to-grave state support is being cut back, as the impact of excessive public expenditure on public debt, economic growth and standards of living is at last being recognized (Stein, 1990; Sillen, 1990; Hilton, 1991). The tax burden of 57 per cent of GNP and expenditure in the public sector amounting, incredibly, to 65 per cent of GNP, are both being reduced substantially to deal with the problems characterized graphically by Stein in the following terms: 'We have one of the lowest growth rates and one of the highest inflation rates in Europe. Radicalisation of public policy and an ever-increasing government intervention have eroded wealth creation.'

Thus, far from providing, as British apologists for the Welfare State tirelessly claim, definitive evidence of the feasibility of combining large-scale state welfare with economic efficiency, the Swedish case offers in fact (as does the Austrian) an exemplary case-study of the inevitably destructive impact on economic progress of extravagant public expenditure and grandiloquent, cradle-to-grave welfare provision. This even in societies which have managed to avoid state intervention in industry such as we have had in Britain for fifty years.

These economic problems of the Welfare State are general. In a recent study, *The Crisis of Redistribution in European Welfare States*, J. P. Jallade (1987) claims that 'European Welfare States are in crisis. Governments everywhere are trying to restore the financial balance of social budgets either by cutting benefits or by increasing taxes and contributions, or both.' He admits, if somewhat coyly, that European societies are becoming 'more aware of the price to be paid for more protection and social equality', and that they are asking 'how egalitarian a society do we want or can we afford?' This important study – the more telling because its initial assumptions are strongly supportive of state welfare – suggests on the basis of detailed investigation of social security in the UK, Sweden,

Hungary, the Netherlands and France, that the redistributive goals of state welfare are unattainable, and that the vast sums of money spent in pursuing them are largely wasted.

Indeed, so general has concern become in recent years with the wasteful inefficiency of state expenditure that, even in the pre-lapsarian Soviet Union, Mr Shevardnaze (reported in the *Guardian*, 27 June 1990) was able to claim (in relation to defence expenditure) without apology or qualification that 'Soviet taxpayers have a right to know what security they are getting for their money'. In a speech by a top leader of a society officially committed throughout the whole of its existence to the sacred propriety of state expenditure, and ideologically hostile to private spending, these are telling words. The interests of taxpayers as such are to be treated seriously; their right to know about the scale and efficacy of public expenditure is explicitly acknowledged; and the significance of value for money in state spending is admitted openly and embraced as warmly as in Reagan's USA!

We ought, surely, to expect these perfectly obvious ideas to be applied at least as rigorously to public expenditure in Britain as in the Soviet Union! The USSR at least had the tragically magnificent excuse of socialism to justify extravagant state spending, whereas here in Britain we still claim to believe that government money is not 'the people's money' but your money and mine. As a recent French analysis concludes (Mackaay, 1993): 'tous les systèmes de protection sociale occidentaux sont en crise ouverte, parfois en explosion'.

We must attend urgently to the causes of this manifest crisis of the Welfare State and to the roots of its potentially explosive collapse. This is essential, if for no other reason, because of the destructive effects of excessive public expenditure on the economy (Flew, 1994). The nature and extent of these effects are described as follows by Michael Bell (1994, p. 30):

> It is no coincidence that successful economies have low levels of public spending. State spending is itself seldom economically well allocated, and is often spent wastefully even where the objects of spending are legitimate. And there is a double whammy: high state spending means high levels of taxation, reducing the incentive to work for citizens. If the state is taking even 40% of GNP, taxation on the margin for wealth-creating entrepreneurs and managers is at least 55% (50% direct taxation and at least 10% on the balance consumed). Incentive is severely reduced at these levels of taxation; no one can pretend otherwise. While the middle classes are being held back at one end of the income scale, universal benefits are sapping the will to work of all those in or near the poverty trap.

Patterns of Public Expenditure

Jacques (1994) points to the difficulty of finding solutions to the economic problems associated with state welfare:

> There are no easy answers to this rising fiscal pressure. One possibility is raising taxes, and in the short run this may well happen, as in the UK, US, Italy, and Germany, for example, where taxes have been increased to deal with the public debt and reduce government borrowing. But there is little evidence that the public has the appetite for long-term tax increases to meet the rising burden of welfare expenditure. Indeed, the origins of the present fiscal crisis of the welfare state lie partly in the tax revolts of the 1970s.

Jacques considers sceptically the possibility of finding a solution by means of hypothecated taxes, before dismissing outright and with some vehemence the suggestion made by some that the problem can be dealt with by increased government borrowing. 'Financing increased welfare expenditure', he says, 'by borrowing alone would increase borrowing to totally unacceptable levels.' The likely outcome, he concludes – and we should note that Jacques, as a former distinguished editor of *Marxism Today*, is hardly a man of the right – is that:

> the emphasis tends to be on finding ways of capping the rise in welfare expenditure. In this context we may well see an increasing resort to user charges, to an extension of targeting and the means test, to greater use of the quasi-market in the public sector, and to the replacement of state by private provision.

Two of the most profound investigations of the topic, Correlli Barnett's *The Audit of War* (1986) and Bacon and Eltis' *Britain's Economic Problem: Too Few Producers* (1976) both conclude that public expenditure in modern Britain has been excessive, wasteful and economically damaging. Yet public expenditure, particularly on welfare, has continued to increase inexorably, even during the past decade and a half of governments explicitly committed to keeping it under control. Despite brave reductions in income tax, overall taxation required to pay for swelling public expenditure has increased similarly.

Throughout the 1980s, the Government was continually and viciously criticized by the Opposition parties, the media and academics for supposedly savage and mean-minded cuts in public expenditure. In fact, public expenditure on most fronts and overall continued throughout these years and since, as throughout the whole postwar period, to expand in money terms, in real terms, as a proportion of GDP, and in terms of every other conceivable indicator. Following the replacement of Margaret Thatcher as Prime Minister by John Major, the rate of expansion of public expenditure has escalated further.

From his revealing insider's perspective as a former senior civil servant responsible for public expenditure, Sir Leo Pliatzky (1982) usefully reminds us that 'What we now call public expenditure consisted, for the greater part of history, very largely of the costs of wars and armies – in present day parlance, defence expenditure.' Until as late as the middle of the last century, defence spending comprised the bulk of public expenditure. Moreover, the whole of public expenditure, after a sharp rise during the Napoleonic Wars, fell back to the pre-war level of scarcely 10 per cent of gross national product. It only began to rise substantially above this sensible figure in the later part of the century, as state intervention started out on its headlong expansion beyond modest local government spending on poor relief.

From then onwards, with predictable spurts during both World Wars, and including a substantial proportional increase even during the depression years of the 1930s, public expenditure has increased regularly and substantially 'not merely in line with national wealth, but as a percentage of it'. From some 10 per cent at the beginning of the nineteenth century, through 25 per cent in the early 1930s, it had by the 1970s reached 40 per cent. By 1979–80 public expenditure was £83.5 billion, GDP was £201.8 billion, and the ratio of PE to GDP was 41.4 per cent (Pliatzky, p. 213). Especially large annual increases in public spending occurred in the inauspicious years of 1967–68 (12.6 per cent) and 1974–75 (12.4 per cent), both increases in real terms, at 1978–80 prices.

Writing in 1982, Pliatzky urged – rather modestly, one might have thought – the importance of avoiding 'long-term expenditure measures which would build into the economy a ratio of public expenditure to GDP of 45–50% on a continuing basis'. This, he says, in the inimitably understated manner of the senior civil servant, 'would be likely to involve rather burdensome tax rates at all levels of income'.

While public expenditure is not composed entirely of welfare spending, it does comprise the bulk of it (Peacock and Wiseman, 1967). By the 1990s public expenditure as a whole and welfare spending specifically had increased still further. Consider the figures presented in the most recent 'Red Book' – the Financial Statement and Budget Report for 1994–95 (HMG, 1993).

Estimated total government expenditure is £269.2 billion, at some 44 per cent of GDP well within Pliatzky's range of danger, and continuing to increase despite the Government's efforts. Of this total, almost 70 per cent is welfare spending: 30 per cent on social security, 15 per cent on health, 12 per cent on education, and 6 per cent on housing. To this should be added a signficant proportion of employment expenditure and a large proportion of the funding allocated to local authorities. Still further increases in spending are envisaged in the Government's future planning (ibid., p. 97) on employment, education in particular, health, social security (up from £62 billion to £76 billion by 1997, even with a cyclical element excluded from the figures), and on Scotland, Wales and Northern Ireland, each of them heavy consumers of welfare. By 1997 a hugely increased public expenditure total is anticipated. Little wonder if so much painful effort is having to be put into reducing the public borrowing requirement, including increased taxes even for those on lower incomes.

The trend of public expenditure in real terms over recent years – the vast majority of it devoted to welfare – is set out in Table 4.1 below. It should be noted that the figures indicating a slight improvement in public expenditure as a proportion of GDP for 1994 onwards are plans rather than facts. Whether this can be achieved remains to be seen. Moreover, even

Table 4.1   Trends in public expenditure

Year	Real terms £ billion	% of GDP	Year	Real terms £ billion	% of GDP
1963–64	120.1	36.75	1980–81	219.0	46.5
1964–65	124.2	36.5	1981–82	222.0	47.25
1965–66	131.6	37.75	1982–83	228.0	47.5
1966–67	139.8	39.5	1983–84	231.7	46.5
1967–68	157.5	43.25	1984–85	238.2	46.75
1968–69	156.6	41.5	1985–86	238.0	45
1969–70	157.7	41	1986–87	242.8	44
1970–71	162.9	41.25	1987–88	242.9	41.75
1971–72	168.3	41.75	1988–89	238.5	39.25
1972–73	176.5	41.5	1989–90	244.7	39.75
1973–74	191.1	43.5	1990–91	246.7	40.25
1974–75	214.2	48.75	1991–92	253.5	42.25
1975–76	214.4	49.25	1992–93	269.2	44.75
1976–77	209.1	46.75	1993–94	277.0	45
1977–78	198.9	43.25	1994–95	276.9	43.75
1978–79	208.4	44	1995–96	281.0	43.25
1979–80	215.1	44	1996–97	284.7	42.5

Source: HMG (1994), p. 115

the hypothetical proportional decrease cloaks a substantial increase in real and absolute terms to £284.7 billion annually – an increase since 1963 of approaching 150 per cent.

In only six out of thirty-three years has there been a decrease in public spending, and the average decrease is a mere £3.5 billion compared with an average increase in the twenty-seven 'fat' years nearly twice as high at £6.8 billion. Since the mid-1960s the proportion of GDP devoted to public expenditure has been held below 40 per cent only twice. The norm appears to have moved up a step from 40 per cent to 45 per cent and rising, with recessionary high points of public expenditure corrected and compensated less and less adequately by proportional reductions during periods of economic growth.

Some apologists for state extravagance seek to explain away this trend by reference to 'inadequate growth' and the assumption that somehow growth can be accelerated to cover whatever increases in public expenditure may seem from time to time desirable. Such arguments can be faulted on two counts. First, we cannot be confident that increased economic growth can be assured. Secondly, there are strong grounds for believing that excessive public expenditure is itself a primary barrier to the achievement of our real economic growth potential (Bacon and Eltis, 1976).

The root of the problem is clear: year on year increases in real terms of government expenditure, most of it on welfare. Figure 4.1 displays the phenomenon graphically. Admittedly the growth rate in expenditure of £7.3 billion per annum for the years 1963 to 1976 had been reduced to an average of £4.1 billion per annum in the years 1979 to 1994. However, even without account being taken of predictable (and in the absence of radical policy change, unavoidable) increases in need and demand – for example the demographic effect on the pensions bill, and the impact of technological development on the costs of health care – the implication of these figures is patent: continuing and escalating costs to the Exchequer of public expenditure, particularly welfare costs; an inexorable rise in the level of taxation; worsening pressures on the public debt; reduced capacity for unpredictable necessary expenditure on emergencies such as defence; and increasing dependence on the whims of the global market and the goodwill of allies and partners.

In the mid-term, let alone the long term, continuation of these trends in public expenditure – a large and increasing proportion of it devoted to state welfare – will bankrupt Britain and subvert our national sovereignty. In Michael Bell's words (1994, p. 31): 'If there is to be a significant reduction in the state's share of GDP, there is eventually no alternative but to reduce state involvement in the main headings of health, pensions, and education.' Unless continued pressure is kept resolutely on public spending, which is to say primarily on welfare spending, current trends will rapidly worsen to the immediate and irreparable detriment of the real welfare of the whole population.

Shopping for What?

Besides levels and trends in expenditure, we need also to consider the breakdown of expenditure into different heads of spending. What exactly

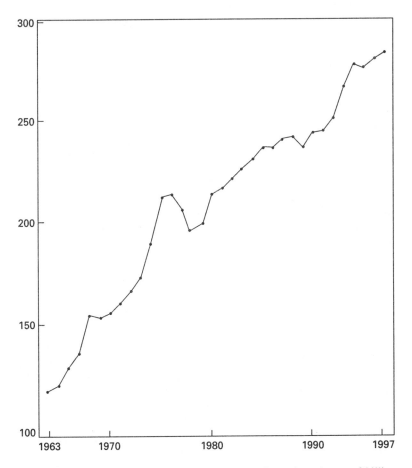

Fig. 4.1   Recent and planned trends in public expenditure, in real terms, £ billion (HMG, 1994)

are we getting for our huge welfare budget? All the figures in this section are taken from the *Annual Abstract of Statistics 1994*, reporting actual expenditures for 1990, 1991 or 1992, according to information availability. The figures for any recent year reflect a similar pattern and logic. Total government expenditure in 1990/1 on 'social services and housing' – a category which represents a large proportion of welfare expenditure – was £118.6 billion, up from £71 billion in 1982/3. It was divided as follows (main heads of spending only):

Table 4.2   Government expenditure on social services and housing, 1990/1, £ billion

Education	26.7
National Health Service	27.8
Personal Social Services	5.4
Social Security Benefits	54.7
Housing	3.9
Total	118.6

These are vast sums of money, continually expanding and altogether too vast to be entrusted to the singular, monopolistic decision-making apparatus of *any* government, however intelligent, however efficient. The scope for transferring large tranches of expenditure on education, health and social security into differentiated, private hands is manifestly substantial. Consider social security spending, the largest block of public expenditure by far, in more detail.

Only a very few of the twenty heads of expenditure listed in Table 4.3 are absolutely essential at the level indicated: widows' benefits, the redundancy fund, and war pensions on my reckoning. These items cost less than 5 per cent of the total budget. All seventeen of the remaining heads of expenditure could be either reduced, in some cases substantially, or eliminated altogether.

There is massive scope for privatization, reducing public expenditure by a substantial proportion under the following six heads: retirement pensions, unemployment benefit, sickness benefit, sick pay, maternity pay, income support, family credit and the social fund. Under each of these heads – costing together some £45 billion, or about 60 per cent of the total social security budget – effective protection could be provided at least as adequately as the state manages, and probably to a much better standard, by personal insurance in the private sector combined with deals between employees and employers requiring no public expenditure input. These

Table 4.3   Government expenditure on social security benefits, 1992, £ million, main heads only

1.	Retirement pensions	27 019
2.	Widows' benefits etc.	1 045
3.	Unemployment benefit	1 811
4.	Sickness benefit	318
5.	Invalidity benefit	6 380
6.	Statutory sick pay	716
7.	Statutory maternity pay	384
8.	Redundancy fund	321
9.	War pensions	1 002
10.	Child benefit	5 974
11.	One parent benefit	275
12.	Family credit	930
13.	Income support	15 396
14.	Social fund	151
15.	Attendance allowance	1 825
16.	Invalid care allowance	354
17.	Mobility allowance	2 116
18.	Invalidity pension/severe disablement allowance	654
19.	Housing benefit	3 603
20.	Administration	3 531
	Total	74 006

savings could be introduced only gradually, of course, and no doubt there would be a small minority of people who could manage private self-protection only with considerable difficulty. At least the scope for movement in this direction, in the light of the enormous scale of public expenditure involved, ought to be under close scrutiny by the Government and in the Department of Social Security.

This leaves nine more problematical heads of expenditure. Among these, administration of the whole system costs three and a half billion pounds per year – enough to pay nearly a quarter of the vast bill for income support. Litle wonder when the system is, in crucial parts, so heavily and so mischievously unionized. Privatization would reduce the scale of the system substantially and save administrative costs falling on the public purse *pro rata*. Moreover, at any level of operations it *must* be possible to reduce this huge bill for administration substantially. In the private sector, it would be halved on principle.

Child benefit is, of course, among the most contentious issues in the whole budget. At a cost of almost £6 billion per annum, with most of it going to families with little real need of it, there has to be a case for substantial reduction, or even for its elimination and replacement with a benefit targeted specifically on children in real need. The one-parent family benefit costs relatively little at present, but current trends in marital lifestyles will increase public expenditure under this head rapidly and substantially. I can see no rational justification for it. The Child Support Agency must be made to work so that the costs involved can be recouped from fathers.

Housing benefit, at £3.6 billion annually and rising, is an absurd burden on the tax-payer. Substantial savings could be made under this head, as under several others, by much tougher policing to eliminate fraud. Beyond this, however, we need to review and amend our whole housing policy drastically. The budget could be held and then eventually halved by tighter prescription of the size and type of housing to be allowed to those accepting benefit, and by the return of the prefab, brought up-to-date by modern technology.

This leaves invalidity benefit and the four other benefits (items 15, 16, 17 and 18) associated with it. Together they cost about £11 billion pounds every year, with further substantial costs incurred outside the Social Security budget by Personal Social Services. Legislation currently being prepared is likely to add still further to this massive bill for invalidity broadly defined, more than £200 a year for every single member of the population. And who knows where it will end, when an article in *Disability Now* can complain that terrorists in Northern Ireland receive no compensation for injuries received while on 'active service'! Resistance to reductions is likely to be fierce, but there has to be scope in a population which is getting healthier and healthier, fitter and fitter, year by year for some substantial containment of this budget. There is a substantial degree of fraud involved. Some of the bill could be covered by private insurance. Other savings could be made by privatizing all delivery. Certainly a bill for what will shortly be as much as half of the whole education budget has to be substantially reduced somehow.

It is not my purpose here to propose systematic plans for cost saving, or even to suggest the lines of reform which would be required to reduce public expenditure on welfare. I turn to these matters later in Chapters 7, 8 and 9. What I hope I may have accomplished in this section is simply to display the scale and nature of the expenditure entailed by our current welfare regime. The sums involved, in welfare broadly and in social security specifically, are astronomical. Like the wife of a long-term gambler and boozer, we have become habituated to seeing half the family budget squandered on indulgencies and inessentials while the long-term needs of the family are ignored.

Moreover, much could be done to remedy the situation, once it is fully and honestly acknowledged. A large proportion of this huge budget could be eliminated by reducing fraud, privatizing delivery, outright privatization of whole services, and radical efficiency savings such as the private sector has taken on courageously during the past decade. I turn now to consider supporters of state welfare who apparently believe that budgets such as those above are easily affordable and provide scope for further expansion.

The Planner's Micawber

In 1993 the Joseph Rowntree Foundation published John Hills's *The Future of Welfare: a Guide to the Debate*. The study was pressed into immediate use – in which it has continued regularly ever since – as a primary source of justification for the belief that there is no real problem at all about the financial future of the Welfare State.

Among my other teaching duties, I am an instructor in statistics. I am not usually much inclined, therefore, to look with any enthusiastic favour on Disraeli's cynical view of the discipline – 'lies, damned lies, and statistics'. Hills's analysis, however, is almost enough to change one's mind. It is an exemplary demonstration of the fact that if you throw a set of figures around enough, you can make them mean almost anything you like. Provided you are distracted by the conjuror's cunning, he really does succeed in making rabbits appear out of thin air. He gave a similarly prestidigitatious performance in his more recent evidence to the House of Commons Social Security Committee (1993), strongly supported by Andrew Dilnot of the Institute for Fiscal Studies who calmly claims at one point (p. 2) that: 'I do not have a great deal to add to what John [Hills] has said. The problem in a nutshell is that there is really no problem with financing social security if we go on as we are now.'

In respect of one key aspect of welfare spending, this sanguine, not to say casually irresponsible, analysis is entirely refuted by an important recent study of pensions (Taverne, 1994). The report warns that a demographic 'pensions time-bomb' is about to explode, with effects right across Europe, unless there are fundamental changes to the current state pensions system. 'Without radical changes', Taverne writes, 'maintaining levels of benefits provided by pay-as-you-go schemes in line with present expectations will impose a burden on future generations of taxpayers which is likely to prove unacceptable, will worsen the competitiveness of industry, and will harm the prospects for employment and for the economy as a whole.' The study argues that an increasing share of the cost of retirement must be taken up by privately-funded pension schemes.

Proposing a new European Commission directive guaranteeing freedom of management and investment for pension funds, the report argues that 'a move to a greater role for private schemes with maximum freedom to invest should increase the savings available for investment, will make capital markets in Europe more efficient, and will increase the availability of capital generally.' In comments reported in the press (*Evening Standard*, 6 January 1994), the Chairman of the study group responsible for the report said: 'The generation now approaching retirement is wealthier than its predecessors and correspondingly better able to to make provision for its own retirement needs.' Thus in relation to the most expensive component of state welfare, Taverne's study demonstrates that unless the effects of demographic changes are addressed urgently by a large-scale switch to private funding, pensions will simply not be affordable except at an intolerable cost to the economy. In overall terms also there are serious problems with Hills's analysis. Madsen Pirie has characterized them graphically (1994, p. 24):

> The survey commissioned by the Rowntree Trust blithely reported that Britain could happily continue to fund its welfare programmes well into the new millennium, despite the adverse demographic changes which are taking place. Alas, their definition of affording something is not one which everyone agrees with. Their report spoke of only a 5% increase in the proportion of GNP needed in taxation. This translates as doubling VAT from 17.5% to 35%, or putting 20p onto income tax. *This is not affordable at all....*The swingeing increases [in taxation] postulated in the Rowntree study would cripple our economy and wipe out its ability to create wealth and jobs in the future.

That Hills does believe that there is no serious financial problem in continuing with the welfare status quo – a misconception in which he is not alone, to judge from several contributions to Page and Deakin's recent collection (1993) on the costs of welfare – is clear from a shorter account of his research, published (in 1994) after he had had time to reflect on criticisms of his analysis. The sub-title to this article provides in itself a clear indication of his views, thus: 'A major LSE report demonstrates the continued resilience of the British welfare state'. In the body of the text he says of his report that 'in contrast to much of the current debate which starts from the assumption that policy is boxed in by fiscal constraints, it highlights the wide range of inter-related options which face welfare policy'. Of attention to the impact on welfare costs of likely demographic changes, he says that 'Such concerns have been considerably exaggerated' – though he does not say by whom.

The Future of Welfare: a Guide to the Debate (1993) is a glossy, expensively produced document of 91 pages. Its empirical basis is provided by selected data drawn from a variety of sources, rather than from any research conducted by the authors of the report themselves. The overall logic of its argument is from beginning to end carefully attuned to defending the status quo in state welfare. No serious consideration is given at any point to radical reform. It is notably over-confident and un-self-critical in tone.

Consider a series of propositions from the summary of the report – each of them presumably included after careful reflection because the authors believe they represent the crux of their case. The numbering is mine, but they are presented in the order in which they appear in the summary (pp. 4–6).

1. *'Over the past twenty years or so, Britain's welfare spending has been stable as a share of GDP.'*

'Twenty years or so' is both a remarkably vague and a wholly arbitrary period of analysis to choose. Why not thirty years? Why not post-war? Why not since 1900? Perhaps because their pre-ordained case is better suited by the period chosen? The truth of the proposition depends in any case on what one defines as welfare spending: they define it narrowly and widely by turns as suits the argument. Its relevance depends on whether or not one is satisfied, as I am not, that proportional spending is the best criterion of affordability. Why not spending in real, absolute terms – which has sky-rocketed over any period one might choose (see Table 4.1 above).

2. *'That share – about a quarter of GDP – is below that in most other European countries.'*

So what, one should ask. One could equally accurately say that it is 'higher than in the USA, Japan, and many European countries'. Certainly it is much lower than in the former USSR, and look where that led to!

3. *'even if benefit levels kept up with overall living standards, the total net effects on public finances over the next fifty years would add up to an addition of about 5 per cent of GDP.'*

I have already indicated above the extravagant tax implications of this proposition, even supposing it were accurate (not to say better written). In fact, the information and technique underlying the estimate are highly suspect, involving little more than simple extrapolation. It takes no account of predictable pressures for additional benefits, nor of the knock-on effects of likely expansion in existing benefits, such as those provided for one-parent families and for invalidity. So implausible, indeed, is this major conclusion of the report – which has been flaunted without qualification all over the media – that I would liken it to the fairy-tale prediction of the founders of the NHS that health costs would be reduced in the future as a result of their new scheme. This was not just mistaken: it was completely and laughably wrong.

4. *'The welfare state has much wider aims than just the relief of poverty.'*
Only people have aims. This statement is a rhetorical attempt to cozen readers into accepting unargued the authors' view of what we should be seeking to achieve through state welfare. The re-distributive aim which they attribute to the Welfare State is not a necessary or widely agreed part of its objectives, nor is income-smoothing over the life-cycle. As for 'stepping in where the family fails' and 'evening out income between men and women', these are highly contentious issues which should be the subject of debate rather than unarguable assumptions.

5. *'Side-effects of welfare provision may deter people from working... or from accumulating savings'*, etcetera.
It is good to see *any* negative effects of state welfare acknowledged by key spokesmen for the welfare lobby. However, they mainly use the opportunity to criticize means-testing – to which they appear to be opposed in principle – while largely ignoring the massive negative effects of universal welfare provision as a whole on initiative and enterprise.

6. *'Things have changed since Beveridge.'*
This too is a remarkable and potentially valuable acknowledgement of a truth long denied by those opposed to welfare reform. Here too, however, they abuse a genuine discovery in order to urge expansion of state welfare. 'The scale of the problems faced by the welfare state', they say, 'has increased whatever kind of measuring rod is used.' This is plain nonsense. Standards of living have increased enormously since the 1940s (see Chapter 3). If the scale of problems *has* increased since Beveridge, despite hugely expanded state welfare provision, they are by no means necessarily problems which the Welfare State has to face, or can face, and they may quite conceivably be problems which the Welfare State has actually itself caused.

7. *'Part 2 of the report examines proposals for reform of different parts of the welfare state.'*
This is true, but the mode of examination adopted is superficial and subjective in the extreme. The long section of the report devoted to the authors' analysis of reform proposals (pp. 39–77) reads more like a newspaper article than an academic research study. None of their conclusions challenge their own collectivist assumptions in the slightest

degree, and their whole mode of argument – particularly in relation to private sector alternatives and expanded means-testing – is calculated to strengthen their case for universal contributory state insurance. Their treatment of private sector alternatives at pp. 40–1 is a travesty of objective analysis. Only wholesale privatization of pensions will address the problems in this sphere adequately.

8. *'Much current debate starts from the assumption that welfare policy is boxed in by fiscal constraints. This report suggests there is actually a wide range of options...'.*

This proposition seems to me wholly disingenuous, as does the argument it arises from in the conclusion to the report. The fact that there may be several policy options available is in no way incompatible with there being a serious problem about the future of welfare. No doubt Hitler had several options besides suicide available as the Allied armies closed in on Berlin. This hardly lessened the gravity of the problem he faced, and nor did it alter the eventual outcome. By the same token, supporters of state welfare should not be allowed to get away with suggesting that any of a wide range of remedial measures they might propose can necessarily save the Welfare State from collapse occasioned by financial extravagance.

9. *'There is no demographic time-bomb.'*

If they believe this, they will believe anything. See the analysis at p. 75 of this chapter, and Chapter 8 (Taverne, 1994; Seldon, 1994).

10. *'Whichever form of targeting is used, incentives are affected.'*

This is a disingenuous truism, deployed, it would seem, to distract attention from the major disincentives of state welfare as a whole, to the minor – and less than fully demonstrated – disincentives of means-testing.

11. *'Further choices come in the balance between different ways of paying for public welfare.'*

'Balance' is a curious word to use in the context of an argument which from beginning to end proscribes absolutely any possibility of shifting away from public funding to personal and insurance-based payment. It is rather as if an ecological imbalance between sheep and wolves were adjusted not by shooting some wolves, but by adding in some foxes!

12. *'Some efficiency gains are being realized, but there are costs to running internal markets, difficulties in ensuring equity in treatment and funding arrangements, and in "empowering" users rather than providers (or professional purchasers).'*

This part of their argument is the nearest the authors manage to get in the whole report to acknowledging any gains at all arising from welfare reform since 1979. To classify it as a case of 'damning with faint praise' would be a considerable understatement. Their anti-market prejudices are manifest here and throughout. They evince not the slightest aware-ness of the considerable advantages of internal markets, let alone real markets, as an antidote to deficiencies in state welfare provision which even they recognize. Nor do they even report on evidence and arguments to this effect presented by others. This seems more than somewhat one-sided in a document purporting to offer 'a guide to the debate'. More broadly, their extensive lists of further reading are remarkably one-sided too. They contain not a single publication by the Institute of Economic Affairs, none of Charles Murray's work, and indeed nothing at all that I can discover which is not strongly supportive in principle of the Welfare State in its current form. This trumps the Open University, whose publications usually include at least token alternatives.

13. *'Massive changes to labour markets and family structures are leading to increased inequality, greatly raising the demands made on the welfare state.'*

With this flourish, the authors of *The Future of Welfare* blow the gaff on the claims of the report to provide a balanced account of the relevant debate. Their position is pre-emptive and extreme. It lays a basis for a Labour Government – rather to the left of any Tony Blair might lead, I suspect – to maintain the existing state welfare provisions, to expand them by shifting from a selective to a universal approach and by orient-ing the Welfare State to a wider range of new 'problems', and to make equality the watchword of social policy as a whole. Little wonder, then, that they are so keen to demonstrate, however inadequately and implausibly, the affordability now and into the future of state welfare as currently organized. For given the opportunity, they would clearly increase public expenditure on state welfare substantially.

The Government's Perspective

In 1993 the Secretary of State for Social Security delivered the MAIS Lecture, speaking to the title 'Benefits and Costs: Securing the Future of Social Security'. Speaking in the balanced and closely argued terms one would expect, Mr Lilley reminds us from the start that the impact of the social security system on the economy is a secondary matter by compari-son with its primary purpose – to provide positive support for those in need, which he suggests, it has done and is doing successfully. He also, however, reminds us that the system is not and should not be a state monopoly, and that it has to be affordable. By way of evidence of the potentially negative impact of welfare on economic performance he cites the cases of Eastern Europe and Sweden. His analysis of the first of these stands as a telling warning to those who would glibly expand welfare in Britain:

> In the People's Republics, the State generally monopolised the provision of social security to provide a generous level of support relative to national income, and to protect people from the impact of economic change. People who were in effect redundant and unemployed usually remained on their firm's payroll until they voluntarily moved elsewhere or retired. The net effect was a massive level of unemployment (albeit concealed), a labour force lacking motivation, mobility, or self reliance, and a low level of voluntary saving and provision for retirement or temporary loss of income. The economies stagnated, stalled, and eventually collapsed.

Turning next to countries more like Britain than the extreme cases of actually existing Bolshevik or Scandinavian socialism, he shows how excessively generous benefits price people out of work and magnify unemployment. 'Generous, unconditional help for the unemployed sounds', he says, 'humane. But if it discourages job search and prolongs unemployment, it damages the chances of the very people it is intended to help.' On this basis he examines the size, growth and likely growth prospects of social security in Britain, indicating that the budget 'is huge, has grown rapidly, and is set to continue outstripping national income in the future'. He also identifies a substantial increase in dependency on benefits, and observes as follows on this crucial matter:

> It is true that as a country gets richer it ought to be able to afford better provision for those in need. But other things being equal, one would expect that as a country gets more prosperous, *fewer* of its people would need to depend on state benefits and *more* people would make an increasing share of provision for future needs out of their own resources.
>
> If we are to understand why this has not happened, let alone address the daunting welfare problems of the next century, we need to analyse what has caused the growth in Britain's social security budget. Where has the money gone, and why?'

After a passage examining carefully the diverse patterns and sources of the huge continuing increase in the Social Security budget, he asks what can be done about it, and proposes 'a constructive public debate on the reform of our social security system', a debate in which he sees both the Government's own Long-Term Review and the Labour-Party-initiated Social Justice Commission playing a part.

He frames the debate he wants to see in terms of nine plausibly defended propositions:

1. There are no easy solutions.
2. Any effective structural reform must involve either better targeting, or more self-provision or both.
3. Disincentives are inherent in statutory benefits.
4. Means testing is not the only way of targeting benefits more closely on need.
5. The existing array of benefits – contributory, universal and income related – are rather more targeted than some comment suggests.
6. No one has the right to opt out of contributing to help those who cannot provide for their own needs.
7. Contracting out inevitably involves a switch from pay as you go to fully funded provision.
8. The more the provision for needs and risks is monopolized by the state the less the incentive to work and save to provide them.
9. Reform of something as vast as the social security system is best carried out sector by sector rather than by the 'big bang' approach.

In conclusion, Mr Lilley argues that failure to reform the system effectively would damage above all those in most need, and claims that by contrast 'successful reform will guarantee the position of the most needy. It will reduce dependency, encourage self-reliance, harness popular energies, give people greater control of their own resources, boost savings, and strengthen the economy on which the material well being of all of us depends.'

By comparison with most statements by senior politicians – of whatever party, anywhere in the world, and particularly on the complex and contentious topic of welfare – Mr Lilley's lecture seems to me magisterially authoritative, comprehensive and coherent, carefully grounded in genuine understanding of the relevant facts, and unusually bold. It is not altogether free, however, of the influence of orthodox mandarin-think and of that overcautious nervousness about imaginative innovation which besets, understandably enough, most senior politicians in democratic societies. His analysis of the extent and nature of the problem caused by the damaging impact of expanding welfare expenditure on economic progress is correct and persuasively put. We should trust no one who resists it. His initiation of a wide-ranging, open debate about the future of social security is both sensible and courageous. His acknowledgement of the problem of dependency is an important breakthrough. His unapologetic incorporation of independent sector self-provisioning into official analysis of welfare is long overdue and much to be welcomed, as is the tone of scepticism he adopts throughout in relation to the usual hand-wringing, bleeding-hearts terms of reference of orthodox welfare discourse.

None the less, and notwithstanding these and other advances in the analysis of welfare reflected in the lecture, it seems to me to fall short to some significant degree of providing an adequate basis for the scale and urgency of reform which is necessary if the economically destructive impact of the Welfare State is to be staved off effectively.

First, we ought perhaps to be a little suspicious about the idea of a nation-wide welfare debate, attractive though it sounds. Mr Callaghan's ringing 1976 plea for a 'Great Debate' on education availed nothing. Actual and practical radical reform required a new government, the appointment of effective Ministers genuinely committed to complete overhaul of the antique education system, and wholehearted backing for change from the Cabinet and the Prime Minister (Marsland, 1989 [2]). While we chatter endlessly about welfare reform, the social security budget will continue to escalate through the roof, bringing economic collapse ever closer.

Secondly, there is perhaps an excess of careful balance to the lecture. Particularly in the long section setting out the propositions which comprise his framework for debate, Mr Lilley is worryingly successful in finding problems in every direction. Senior civil servants, less radical Cabinet colleagues, and welfare-addicts in the media are likely to find more than sufficient ammunition here for justifying inaction across the board. It can be read as a recipe for maintaining the welfare status quo as the devil we know.

There is, third, a remarkable lack of attention to fraud in the social security system or to its gross inefficiency. Together they impose huge costs on the public purse. Serious reduction in fraud and inefficiency could produce enormous savings. The media should not be allowed to get away with their snivelling protestations that only marginal improvements could be achieved. A big business leader, faced with evidence of waste from these sources of what I estimate as between 10 per cent and 20 per cent of the total budget, would sack and replace senior managers in large numbers, and install new systems and procedures right across the enterprise.

Fourthly, there is no challenge in the lecture, even in *sub rosa* form, even as an idea attributed to others, to the concept of the Welfare State as such or to the ideology of universal state provision. It provides in consequence a less than adequate intellectual or moral basis for political argument such as radical reform requires, and such as underlay the reforms of the 1980s (Cockett, 1995). Similarly, and fifth, there is no explicit acknowledgement of the powerful vested ideological interests involved in resisting reform. The lecture is too instrumental and technical to serve as the basis for radical reform, which requires, in addition to careful analysis of the facts, a commitment to values and the development of a rhetorically persuasive mission statement.

Finally, there is no explicit recognition anywhere in the lecture that private provision is inherently better – more efficient, more reliable, more appropriate as the normal mechanism of securing genuine welfare in a free society – than the established state system. Nor, therefore, is there any indication of the enormous cost savings which would be produced by opting out of state provision in large numbers.

One might hope that at least some of Mr Lilley's boffins are busily occupied in making systematic, comprehensive estimates of the reduction in his budget which radical liberalization of the whole system would allow. It would also have been reassuring to hear from him that others of his senior civil servants are working now on detailed plans of incentive schemes to encourage early opt-out from state social security by as many people as possible, and thus to bring forward substantial cost savings to the earliest possible date. One fears, however, if one may judge from the weight of emphasis in the lecture on problems and complexities, that they are more likely devoting their expensive, tax-payer-financed time to formulating elegant arguments designed to inhibit rather than expedite radical reform. There is an awful lot of scope for the 'Yes, Minister' phenomenon at the Department of Social Security!

An Extravagant Luxury

From time to time the media get themselves worked up into fits of concern about waste in public expenditure. Defence, the monarchy, MPs' foreign travel, the salaries of privatized industry bosses, and more recently the EC are favourite targets. It is very rare, by contrast, for these zealous, if for the most part hypocritical, cost-saving campaigns to identify any targets in the sphere of welfare.

Why, for example, should pensioners, pregnant women and children be entitled simply as a result of being pensioners, pregnant women and children, and entirely regardless of the level of income to which they have access, to free prescriptions? Can there be any rational justification for as many as five out of six prescriptions being free – at a cost to the Exchequer and the taxpayer of more than £2 billion every year? Should we not fall into line with almost every other country in Europe by introducing a modest cash barrier to unnnecessary GP consultations? Why are the children of the elderly sick not expected to make any contribution at all to the costs of caring for their own parents? Why should the author of a draft Cabinet paper (leaked to the *Guardian*, 9 November 1993) dismiss a proposal for requiring from parents a modest degree of accountability for their children's behaviour on the grounds that 'savings would be less than £10 million'? So one might go on through every single line of welfare expenditure, finding potential savings of a substantial order at every turn.

This is precisely what every big company does regularly and continually, with the sack or at least an unpleasant demotion for managers who fail to identify wastage, savings and improved alternative expenditure patterns. But far from suggesting or supporting even such modest measures of cost saving, the social affairs correspondents and leader writers of the quality press and the news and current affairs programmes on our television screens devote their energies instead to bemoaning alleged cuts in welfare, to portraying the allegedly poor and oppressed in implausibly attractive colours, and to demanding more and yet more public expenditure on education, on health care, on pensions, on housing and on the whole Byzantine range of more than three dozen different benefits.

Yet the Welfare State represents by far the biggest segment of public expenditure. The social security budget specifically and welfare spending as a whole have swollen consistently ever since the Second World War. They now comprise a hugely extravagant luxury which is impeding economic progress, crippling our capacity for effective competition with our global rivals, and gradually driving Britain into bankruptcy. In this respect Peter Lilley's analysis is entirely correct, and John Hills's view wholly mistaken. This despite continuing support for a sanguine – not to say Micawberist – opinion about the costs and benefits of state welfare in Barr's bible of welfare orthodoxy, *The Economics of the Welfare State* (1993). The positive contributions to social efficiency and social justice which Hills, Barr, Glennerster (1992) and others attribute to the Welfare State are largely fictional. Its negative impacts, not least those arising from its extravagant costs, which they disingenuously deny, are real and profound.

We cannot afford it now. Still less shall we able to afford it, organized as it is, in the future. We can't afford it period. It is a gross waste of money that would be much better used if it were spent on almost anything else. Separately from all of the other deficiencies of the Welfare State, its costs are extravagantly excessive, with unacceptably destructive effects on the prospects of the economy as a whole. Reviewing welfare systems across Europe from an American perspective, Tyler Marshall concludes that:

the difficulties lie in the worrisome structure of the welfare state and intractable problems such as rapidly aging populations, a large and growing army of long-term, hard-core unemployed, and spiraling health care costs. All have increasingly sucked up resources, driving the welfare bill to untenable levels. Traditional sources of funding such as pay-roll taxes can no longer bear the load. Wage costs in the region have gone so high that they are beginning to price Western Europeans out of competitive world markets.

It is no accident, and no mere passing fad, that regimes of every political hue and right across the world are preoccupied with cutting back the costs of welfare. We shall have to be much tougher on state welfare than any politicians, including even Margaret Thatcher and Newt Gingrich, have so far envisaged if the destructive bill for the Welfare State is to be brought under firm control. Warwick Lightfoot has pressed the argument in a recent article (1994) as far as demanding that government expenditure 'should be reduced to one-third of national income'.

Even in the course of a systematic treatise, *Paying for Welfare*, which is devoted entirely to demonstrating the efficacy and affordability of state welfare, Howard Glennerster (1992) lets the inadmissible cat of welfare costs out of his voluminous bag of collectivist apologetics. Thus (p. 271): 'The cost of producing social services has risen for all these reasons *and has an inherent tendency to do so*' (my emphasis). 'The tax price people must pay to buy the same quantity of care or service', he infers accurately from the evidence, 'has risen' – and he implies, quite correctly, that this increase in costs is likely to continue.

Curiously, however, he is unfazed by the prospect of infinitely increasing welfare costs, finding in some warmed-over opinion polling data, purporting to show the British people's commitment to tax-financed welfare, support for the view that state welfare can go on expanding indefinitely entirely regardless of the cost. In actual fact, the data on which he relies (Jowell *et al.*, 1989 and Taylor-Gooby, 1991) show merely what people might ideally wish for, and provide no evidence at all about what they would be realistically prepared to pay.

Indeed, even in the highly unlikely circumstance of willing acceptance by the electorate of the large tax increases likely to be necessary to fund expanding state welfare, the damagingly negative effects of welfare costs would be expressed in economic instead of political terms, through their impacts on savings, investment and incentives. One way or another, increasing welfare costs must reduce demand. Either this, or the whole system will collapse in chaos. Irwin Stelzer's report (1994) on reactions to the Bipartisan Commission on Entitlement and Tax Reform speaks both with its title – 'Runaway Welfare Costs Stoke Fears of Inflation' – and in its analysis as much for Britain as for the United States. Welfare expenditure must be controlled and reduced. 'If the centre cannot hold', he concludes, 'there is a 1970s Britain in America's 21st century future.' The implication for Britain of failing to reverse the swelling tide of welfare spending is *pro rata* worse: economic crisis such as would threaten the whole basis of political stability.

In a recent article entitled 'Cruel Tide of History Drags Sweden from its Dreams of Utopia', Mark Frankland (1994) describes the agonized realization of the Swedish people that they really cannot afford any longer the absurd costs of their extravagant Welfare State. With two out of three of the population receiving state monies, all indexed against inflation, something had to give. The situation, he says, is beautifully summarized in the title of the left-wing journalist Anders Isaksson's latest book – *Always More, Never Enough*. Isaksson's words make an appropriate ending to this chapter, in which I have sought to controvert the still utopian belief of British supporters of state welfare that we can keep on paying the ever-expanding bills of the Welfare State without, as it were, turning an economic hair: 'There is no limit to what a welfare state can do with other people's money. But however much it does, there are always more demands to satisfy.'

5 Monopoly, Bureaucracy and Inhumanity: The Inefficiency of the Welfare State

One might imagine, to judge from the hysterical reactions of the Opposition, the media, and academic social policy analysts, that the Government's current reforms of education and health care threatened the immediate and irreversible extinction of the Welfare State in its totality. In fact, while these reforms are certainly radical and long overdue, they leave the fundamental status quo in both spheres largely intact. No privatization has been introduced, not even in the attenuated form of vouchers, let alone genuine opportunities for real people to purchase services of their choice with real money. The state retains its monopoly. The emphasis given, not before time one might think, by the Acts of Parliament underlying these reforms to competition, to costs and to consumer choice does not diminish by so much as an inch the extensive, bureaucratically impervious boundaries of state monopoly control.

In the welfare sphere – in stark contrast with the industrial sector, where privatization has been driven through triumphantly – state monopoly and its heavy freight of bureaucratic and other inefficiencies is apparently to remain unchallenged except at the margins. The thousands of millions of pounds extracted each year from taxpayers to finance state welfare are still to be pumped uselessly round the clumsy circuits of state bureaucracy, and delivered haphazardly to more or less the same people in the shape of services worth a fraction of the original cost.

In general, supporters of the Welfare State are sceptical in the extreme about economics as a discipline. Arguments presented by bona fide liberal and libertarian social scientists in terms of economic reality, market forces and the laws of supply and demand are commonly treated by the champions of state welfare with outright derision. There is, however, one element of economic analysis they typically welcome with unconsidered acclaim. This is the demonstration of the harm done by monopolies. Even socialists are against monopoly.

Yet curiously, in relation to welfare services – which are controlled by that supreme monopoly of monopolies, the state – the grave damage done routinely by monopoly is consistently ignored or explicitly denied by socialists and welfarists, and played down even by conservative supporters of the Welfare State. This is, to say the least, disturbing, given the demonstrated benefits of pluralist competition and the mounting evidence of the inefficiencies and destructive effects of monopoly in general and state monopoly in particular (Friedman and Friedman, 1980; Seldon, 1990).

Monopoly Health Care

Take, as an example of some topical significance, the case of health care. In Britain, as everywhere else where market mechanisms and consumer choice are systematically excluded or held in tight check, the amount spent on health care is substantially less than where the public are allowed and encouraged to spend for themselves. Supporters of the NHS actually boast about its efficiency as a mechanism of rationing. Again, in the monopoly conditions promoted by the NHS, the professional associations and trade unions of health workers have for years been able to slow down innovation, to seize for themselves disproportionate amounts of available resources, and to treat patients with gross insensitivity. In such circumstances, effectiveness, efficiency, standards and patient satisfaction are inevitably gradually reduced (Gammon, 1987; Whitney, 1988).

In Britain this process of decay had by the mid-1980s reached such a point that it had become evident even to the most zealous defenders of the status quo that no amount of extra resources could make any significant difference in the long term. In any case, as research by Grosse (1987) shows, revealing patterns confirmed also by other studies, there is little popular support for increased public expenditure on health care. Less than a third of people want more spent specifically on health, and fewer than one in five are willing to pay more tax for health spending. Only 10 per cent of people would be prepared to pay even 3p more on the standard rate of tax, which is scarcely enough to produce more than a marginal increase in health care spending.

Furthermore, the NHS is already in many particular aspects over-resourced: OHE figures showed that as long ago as 1987 there were in Britain more than twice as many nurses proportionately as in West Germany, and at least 50 per cent more than in the USA or France – and still this is allegedly not enough. Quite new approaches to the organization of health care – relying on genuine insurance principles, ensuring competition, and allowing real consumer choice – were by 1985 manifestly essential (Scrivens, 1991 and 1993; Caines, 1994).

Green's analysis, *Challenge to the NHS* (1986), provided a cogent early demonstration of the damage done to British health care by monopoly control, and indicated the potential advantages of shifting towards a more competitive system such as the current NHS reforms have at long last initiated. By way of illustration of the gravity of the harm which can be done in this sphere by state monopoly control, consider an extreme case which graphically demonstrates where denial of consumer preferences leads to if it is applied consistently and systematically. This is from a report (Gedye, 1987) of the situation in Poland after forty years of socialist planning in health care:

> The corridors of Orlowskiego hospital are clogged with beds. Some of the sick lie in sheets covered in blood and streaked with excrement because the laundry cannot cope and the nursing staff is so small that bedding could not be changed regularly even if the laundry worked.
>
> Visitors not only bring food to supplement inadequate diets, but bring clean sheets and clothes, as well as any medication they can get their hands on which is requested by doctors.
>
> Thirty-five per cent of Poland's patients come out of hospital with at least one more illness than they entered with because of the almost total lack of disinfectant and inadequate sterilization methods.

And again:

> A free medical service is claimed, but nothing could be further from the truth. Patients cannot even hope to see a general practitioner without the occasional box of chocolates or bottle of vodka.
>
> Anything more elaborate and you are talking serious money. The average bribe for an operation is 10,000 zloty (£18), two weeks' salary, paid to the surgeon or head sister.
>
> People are so used to employing bribes and gifts as a means of easing wheels in Eastern Europe that no one thinks the behaviour of medical personnel to be particularly abhorrent.

Monopoly Housing

As a second example of the destructive effects of monopoly welfare, consider next the case of housing. In this sphere protagonists of state welfare have fortunately been less successful than in health, education or social services. Even in the worst phase of the quasi-Maoist campaign for state control in the 1960s and 1970s, family home ownership remained fairly high. Indeed it increased somewhat, and private rental housing was not entirely squeezed out of existence. This is not to claim much, however.

Labour governments and Labour-controlled councils persisted throughout this period in building council housing in huge quantities, despite readily available evidence of its excessive costs and its damaging psychosocial effects. After 1979 Labour politicians continued to resist the Conservative Government's policy of selling off council housing to tenants, right up to the point where even they could no longer ignore the fact that it was an immensely popular policy. Even after the purchase of hundreds of thousands of homes by their tenants, the proportion of council 'housing units' (as they are, in a significant phrase, commonly described in planning documentation) remains enormously high compared with any other free society. In Scotland, local authority monopoly in housing remains substantially higher than it ever was in Eastern Europe in the condition of 'actually existing socialism'.

In many of the inner-city areas of the conurbations there is hardly any privately owned or rented housing at all, even if housing association and charitable housing is included on the liberal side of the equation. Furthermore, the Rent Acts introduced by the Labour Party as part of its long-term, systematic campaign for complete state expropriation of housing remain even today, owing to Conservative timidity, largely in force. They continue to have their entirely predictable effect of reducing the amount of available low-priced housing, and thus swelling the number of homeless people on the streets and in emergency hostels.

Consider more broadly the effects of monopoly housing. First, Alice Coleman (1985) has demonstrated that careless, paternalistic local authority housing policies must accept a large share of responsibility for rampant crime in inner city areas. Defensible family territory has been deliberately destroyed, and replaced by huge high-rise towers and massive blocks set in urban wastelands which are indefensible even by the police, let alone by normal local community action. All over Britain these abortions of state control and socialist planning are being demolished. Professor Coleman is currently involved in literally deconstructing the worst design features of the estates we cannot afford to demolish entirely in order to reduce their crime-generating capacity.

Secondly, Ian Robinson (1983) has shown through careful empirical research how council housing creates – as a result of the inferior status associated with it, and the poor quality of its design and management – a destructive stigma and an even more destructive dependency which combine together to prevent social involvement and enterprise. Where capitalism failed to produce a proletariat according to Marxist prescriptions, monopoly council housing has succeeded triumphantly in generating a lumpenproletariat of exploited tenants. Their liberation is essential if democracy is not to be put in danger (Power, 1993).

Another aspect of the damage done by monopoly control in this sphere is illuminated by a little noticed but important report by the Audit Commission (1987) on councils' management of the huge tracts of land and swathes of property they bought up to advance their monopoly welfarist concepts of housing and employment. The Commission, whose job is to monitor local government efficiency, accuses councils of the following deficiencies:

- Failing to adopt a commercial approach in the management of their vast property portfolios, often in prime town-centre sites, and in some cases not even knowing what they consist of. If they did, the Report says, they might conclude they would achieve a better return by selling up and investing the money;
- Holding up to 100 000 acres of surplus land instead of releasing it to developers;
- Failing to estimate how much they need to spend on repairing buildings, especially schools.

One of the councils in question, Sheffield City Council, owns *75 per cent* of all the property in the town centre, a level of monopoly – with its usual destructive effects – which would cause an indignant outcry from the Opposition benches in Parliament, from the media and from social researchers if it were private rather than public.

The Monopoloy of Monopolies

One could extend this analysis of the harm done by monopoly into all the areas of social life where welfare provision has been allowed to fall under unilateral state control. This has been fully documented by Savas in *Privatising the Public Sector* (1982 and also 1987). His analysis is all the more compelling because it relates to the United States, where welfarist beliefs have never taken the intractable hold on the imagination of intellectuals, politicians and other influential people which they have had in Britain for many decades. His conclusions apply *a fortiori*, therefore, in the British context (on which specifically, see Forsythe, 1986). Monopoly domination of welfare, as of other sectors of the economy, is enormously damaging. It can be and should be radically reduced in the interests of free citizens in their roles as consumers.

A primary rationale for state control of welfare, still heard from some on the left and used when it suits them by those of a different political complexion, is that it provides an effective antidote to private monopoly and oligopoly. This has always been a nonsense, and in many of its expressions it serves as a disingenuous undercover argument against capitalism. The State is *the monopoly of monopolies.*

All the deficiencies of private monopoly are multiplied a thousand-fold by state monopoly, which is a pre-condition and precursor of socialism and a contradiction both of capitalism and democracy. In the the welfare sphere, state monopoly control threatens an open road to serfdom, as Hayek (1944) recognized and demonstrated half a century ago. By escalating public expenditure, it inflicts on societies inflation and eventual bankruptcy. By destroying incentives and motivation, it strangles enterprise. By pulling all the diverse threads of control over the population into a single power centre, it threatens democracy at its roots and promises totalitarian rule.

If monopoly as such is dangerous and damaging, a singular state monopoly in welfare such as prevails still in Britain holds out far worse dangers and threatens even more destructive damage. Its gross inefficiency compared with provision through the market and through market-related voluntary and co-operative mechanisms is patent, querulous arguments to the contrary notwithstanding (Barr, 1989). The harm it does to the poor in particular by reducing them to abject dependency is transparent. The danger that it will snuff out altogether the role of the independent consumer, and with it all the benefits of consumer sovereignty, producer efficiency, and a dynamic, open, free society, is apparent to all except those who are in principle opposed to the continuance of liberal democratic capitalism – that form of society which uniquely produces and guarantees these benefits.

Mechanisms of Inefficiency in State Welfare

I have so far considered in broad and general terms the negative impacts of state monopoly. I turn next to examine separately the several distinct correlates and consequences of state monopoly. They are all inter-related in practice, but each makes its own distinctive contribution to the overall inefficiency of state welfare, in social security, in education, in health care, and across the board. I deal in turn with: monopoly; bureaucracy; excessive scale; planning mania; and inhumanity.

A Competition-Free Zone

The power of a state monopoly – the arbitrary power challenged by Adam Smith and his eighteenth century intellectual confrères in their argument on behalf of the market and civil society – is almost limitless, even in a democracy. In the last resort it can even, from time to time, controvert the law with impunity. For example, gross abuses for year after year in the state's old people's and children's homes could not conceivably have been tolerated in the independent sector, where investigative journalism and the law would have played their usual regulatory role effectively. Indeed, so long as the alternative party regimes – Conservative and Labour, Republican and Democrat – are equally content to leave a monopoly intact, it is immune to democratic challenge. Provided that it retains a base of support, however corrupt, among the placemen of the intelligentsia, even media campaigns against abuses by a state monopoly are likely to be futile. The only significant opponent of a state monopoly is – another state monopoly, and then only occasionally and by chance, if there is competition for crucial resources (as between the Departments of Employment and Education) or a turf-war over some intermediate terrain of control (for example between Social Security and Health).

Even without the commanding power of the state behind it, however, monopoly is extremely damaging to the interests of individuals and of society. Free from the natural and proper challenge of competition, a monopoly can artificially speed up (as with the dissemination of progressivist educational ideas), or in the more usual case drastically slow down (for example new genetic technologies in health care) the process of innovation in goods and services. It can drive prices or their equivalent as high as it likes, or artificially reduce them on a temporary basis to kill off potential competition. Within broad limits it can exploit its workforce and abuse the environment without let or hindrance. More commonly and more dangerously, a monopoly reaches a corporatist accommodation with symmetrically monopolistic trade unions and professional associations to share the spoils at the expense of customers and clients and long-term social interests.

The surprise is that state schooling is not even *more* ineffective than it is, given the protected monopoly position allowed to it since the late nineteenth century. By the same token, we should perhaps be less sympathetic to the growing chorus of complaint about the NHS: for a monopoly supplier, deprived of the incomparable advantage of challenge from competitors other than New Age mumbo jumbo and the latest health food fads, it does remarkably well. The social security system has been similarly encouraged for decades in its worst habits – administrative incompetence, excessive costs and casual impersonality – by the dubious privilege of decades of monopoly. Until very recently, when, in pensions particularly, legislative changes and improving standards of living have enabled ordinary people to experience the altogether higher quality of service in the independent sector, clients had no basis for comparison and no freedom of choice.

Monopoly is a major source of inefficiency in the Welfare State. So long as it is allowed to persist, with agencies of state power protected more securely than high-risk prisoners against the challenge of competition, the routinized incompetence which we have come to take for granted in education, in health care and throughout the welfare services will continue.

Bureaucracy

Bureaucracy, in that pejorative sense which is all that the short-sightedly misdirected behaviour of generations of bureaucrats has allowed the concept to retain, is not of course restricted to the public sector. Consider the banks, or IBM, or ICI before it was shaken up by serious challenge from real entrepreneurs (Heller, 1993). There cannot be much doubt, however, whatever the protestations of the bureaucrats' influential and gentlemanly spokesmen, that the state sector is altogether more prone, and this not for accidental reasons, to bureaucratic deformation than even the big business sector of private enterprise. It is the sphere of modern society most completely protected against competition which exemplifies most perfectly the primary characteristics of bureaucracy identified by Max Weber: formalistic impersonality, rigidity of response, proliferation of hierarchical positions, demand for ritually defined qualifications, comprehensive regulation and suppression of individual initiative (Gammon 1992).

Christopher Huhne (1993 [2]) is surely absolutely right, even if one is not obliged to follow him as far as believing that *anything* can justify what he apparently fondly calls 'high taxes', in claiming that:

> There will only ever be a consensus behind public spending programmes to relieve poverty, sickness, and ignorance if they can be shown to be effective. One weevil undermining backing for the Welfare State is an arrogant bureaucracy that treats tenants or claimants like serfs. Another is public suspicion of waste, corruption, and bloated payrolls. Every T. Dan Smith and London Borough of Lambeth is another hammer blow against the legitimacy of high taxes.

If Huhne is more than somewhat over-sanguine about the feasibility of fundamental improvement in the quality of administration in the public sector, at least he is accurate about the nature and extent of the damage which its bureaucratic rules have produced. They have, he says:

> stifled initiative and encouraged paper-pushing. Implicitly they say: 'You're stupid. We don't trust you.' Rules made it more important to

avoid mistakes than to achieve successes. That may not have mattered much in a relatively simple world delivering simple services, but it looks much less appropriate now. The inflexibility that those procedures introduced into the system has outlived its usefulness. Long live a public sector that sets clear goals, takes risks, experiments – and even makes mistakes.

On my analysis there has for decades been no shortage of mistakes in the public sector, but little sign of initiative or flexibility. Typical of modern state bureaucracy is the Department of Transport. The Chief Executive of the new Highways Agency, recruited recently from British Aerospace, has the daunting task of streamlining a basically decrepit organization. He has to effect a drastic re-organization of its regional offices, which currently take such little notice of each other that conflicting maintenance plans on contiguous sections of the motorways produce high levels of avoidable congestion. Lawrie Haynes also has to downsize its swollen staff by some 20 per cent. As one manager told *The Times* (30 December 1994): 'The private sector has always been able to get rid of dead wood. But the public sector has accumulated decades of time-servers. If managers are going to manage, they have to be able to get rid of people who just aren't up to the job.'

The routine goal displacement demonstrated in this example, with primary objectives entirely forgotten in the pursuit of ritual obligations and job security, is apparent throughout the ramifying state welfare structure. In the Byzantine central, regional and local offices of state social security, health care and education, civil servants and local government officers join in their hundreds of thousands in a stately dance to the infinitely tedious music of innumerable contradictory, inconsequential memoranda. Elaborate procedures have been perfected over decades for avoiding necessary initiatives and postponing essential decisions. Mystificatory rituals, as arcane as any from the South Seas, have been painstakingly developed to serve as impediments to the legitimate demands of the public, and as distractions from the proper concerns of clients and citizens.

The Government has tried hard to improve matters, with an energetic programme of diverse initiatives described and explained fully and persuasively by William Waldegrave in a speech in 1993 to the Institute of Directors. Referring to the 'excessive growth of government' as 'a parasite which thrives on free institutions', he suggests that it can 'swamp the fragile balance necessary to the maintenance of a vigorous free society'. The lesson, he argues, is clear:

Only if we get competition into the provision of public services will we get the efficiency gains we want. That is the central perception. From it flows a whole doctrine of devolved, entrepreneurial, competitive public service of which we in Britain are the pioneers.

And again, in a passage which combines to an unusual degree elegance of expression with factual and logical cogency:

When Government is looked at in this way, certain other policies fall into place. As you work to establish internal competitive markets, it becomes obvious that where there is a real, external market, one that can be used for public benefit, then it should be used: privatise, or franchise, or contract out if the private sector can meet the needs better. Bring the Government itself back towards its true role, steering, not rowing the boat. If there has to be monopoly (though this is the case much less often than might be assumed) then regulate it, set it targets, test it against common satisfaction measures – but if possible disentangle Government, as champion of the users, from the dangerous embrace of itself becoming a provider. It was not democracy, in the end, which gained in power from bringing the 'commanding heights' of the economy into Whitehall. As a dozen stories, from Advanced Gas-Cooled Reactors via Concorde to coal mining showed, it was Whitehall which too often was itself captured.

There is first, within the programme of reform which Waldegrave commends, the Citizen's Charter initiative, which seeks to discipline public sector derelictions by empowering consumers. There is secondly the translation of civil service departments into quasi-enterprises. The Prison Service, and crucially the Benefits system have been hived off, like transport, into semi-autonomous agencies operating under business-like private sector norms. Scores of such agencies have been established already, and more are in the pipe-line. Thirdly, market-testing is being pushed through toughly and quickly in the face of bitter union resistance right across the public sector, with a view to privatizing whatever functions can be operated at a profit. Large-scale bureaucracies, in the education system and the health service particularly, are being scaled down and split up, with autonomy delegated as far down-stream as possible to local operating units such as Grant Maintained Schools and NHS Trusts. Throughout the public sector, systematic attention is being given to the evaluation of effectiveness and efficiency (Jackson and Palmer, 1993).

All these initiatives, anticipating and re-inforcing the persuasive guidelines for transforming dead bureaucracies spelled out graphically in

Osborne and Gaebler's *Reinventing Government: How the Entrepreneurial Spirit is Transforming the Public Sector* (1993), are having a considerable positive effect. Bureaucrats are at least a little apologetic in consequence about their bureaucracy. The Kafkaesque gloom of state machinery has been successfully, if fitfully, penetrated by the occasional shaft of illuminating light shed by commonsense and business-like straight dealing.

As Professor Eric Caines has shown ('How Competition is Creating Winners', 1994), while those in charge of the bureaucracies may 'try to hold tenaciously onto their power and influence, and by so doing make the changes more painful than they ought to be... there is accumulating evidence that where it has had time to take root, the new approach is working.' Moreover, even the worst excesses of state bureaucracy have not, for the most part, produced in Britain the corruption and downright criminality which it routinely generates elsewhere. Gross inefficiency in the delivery of vital services does not represent, however, all *that* much of an improvement compared with straight-forward brigandage. Crime can be policed, but bureaucracy is for the most part merely regretted.

Bureaucracy *can* be brought under control, of course, but apparently not by any measure short of genuine privatization. There is evidently no reliable antidote to bureaucracy except the discipline of self-management and real competition in a genuine market. The public utilities, gas and electricity in particular, and the telephone system scarcely less, were havens of rampant bureaucracy for years. Privatization – resisted frenziedly by the unions, by the Labour Party, and by socialist intellectuals – has transformed them for the good in no time.

Alas, the fund of prejudice against the market, competition, and profit built up during the long, dead years of socialist and quasi-socialist planning is so considerable that privatization even of the mines and the railways has been endlessly postponed, and liberation of the Post Office from the enervating clutches of the state has, at the first attempt at least, been successfully blocked. In the Welfare sphere, of course, matters are even worse. We have somehow managed, with some exceptions such as Glennerster (1993), to define social security, education and health care as not a part of the economy at all, and thus in principle unamenable to privatization, and not susceptible to competition.

We do at least now have an internal market in health care, with bureaucratic state purchasers acting to the best of their abilities on behalf of consumers vis-à-vis semi-autonomous suppliers. We do now have the beginnings of real choice in state education, with self-managing schools competing on quality, if not on price, for the custom of parents in localized areas. As Osborne and Gaebler (1993) have shown in relation to the

East Harlem ghetto, reform along these lines can improve even the worst school system considerably. Similar changes have provided the faintest signs of quasi-market institutions even in the heart of the welfare system, with companies and voluntary agencies competing to supply the state, local authorities and the health service with provision of housing, residential homes, community care and other services.

These are all advances towards a rational and efficient welfare system. Hence the frenzied resistance to every sign of a quasi-market on the part of welfare state ideologues, such as those represented in the recently published book, *The Politics of the Welfare State* (Oakley and Williams, 1994), which I examine in detail in Chapter 10 below. On the right road, however, a step or two is insufficient. The bureaucracy of state welfare will not – cannot – be finally defeated and displaced, as Savas (1982) and Forsythe (1986) have demonstrated, until genuine privatization into real markets is accomplished. Indeed, unless it is controlled and suppressed, bureaucracy tends towards its pure form, where 'that which is not commanded is forbidden' (Gammon, 1992; and for an unusual plea for privatization in higher education as a means of defence against state control, see Salter and Tapper, 1994).

Nor should it be forgotten that bureaucracy is not a merely abstract matter of inappropriate systems, structures and rules. Its destructive impacts arise concretely out of the incompetent behaviour of real individuals in powerful positions. There are the clerks in Health Authorities who send out notifications of screening appointments for five successive years after they have been informed, and reminded, and reminded again, that the person in question has moved away. There are hospital administrators who take a perverse pride in arranging for patients to be kept waiting. There are the heads of university departments who compensate for their incompetence in teaching, research and management, and their guilt at having published nothing, by bullying young members of staff unmercifully. There are senior teachers who specialize in successful avoidance of meetings with their pupils' parents. There are social workers who shuffle papers endlessly while wives are battered and children abused. There are welfare workers whose capacity for requiring clients to come back again next week to fill in yet another form is apparently infinite. There are highly paid civil servants whose inability over a period of years to organize matters so that key decisions about the siting of an office or the purchase of an IT system can be taken swiftly and sensibly would get them the sack in a matter of weeks if they worked in the private sector. Across the vast terrain of the Welfare State there is a cast of thousands upon thousands of such bureaucratic parasites. We should get rid of the system which produces and permits them, without allowing them even the absolution granted ironically to 'mediocrities everywhere' by Salieri in Peter Shaffer's *Amadeus*.

Excessive Scale

Throughout much of this century organizational theorists, industrial economists and senior managers have urged on the world the presumptive benefits of what they laughably call 'economies of scale'. Large size was supposed in and of itself to provide advantages denied absolutely to smaller organizations. The lesson was learned only too well in the state sector. The size of operating organizations such as schools and hospitals was expanded in the face of popular and commonsensical resistance. On the same dubious grounds, the massive scale of national welfare services, such as the NHS and Social Security, was tolerated, and even acclaimed for the cost-savings and scope for planning it was supposed to facilitate, despite the resulting bureaucratic complexity and patent inefficiency.

Examples of what I have called 'social mass production' (Marsland, 1980) increasingly constitute the unavoidable context and texture of everyday life, a Kafkaesque forest of irresponsible organizations, unchallengeable assumptions, ill-considered policies, compulsory payments and ignorant experts, where the light of common sense percolates at best fitfully and dimly. Mass production is enshrined in nationalized industry, the civil service, the health service, social security, social services and local government more generally (Marsland, 1981).

Yet the myth of so-called 'economies of scale' has been decisively challenged. For example, in a recent paper called 'The Dubious Economics of Scale' (1994), which addresses the question 'Is largeness a liability?', Robert Heller argues that 'The fashionable tide turned against large companies long ago. Yet fashion doesn't always reflect reality.' He instances IBM, which he says was 'bogged down in bureaucracy. To fill a typical corporate order, 13 managers had to sign off on various decisions.' He specifies four endemic flaws in large-scale organization: 'self-perpetuating bureaucracy; lagging behind smaller rivals on basic efficiencies; fast-breeding of products and facilities; and imposition of constricting strategies from on high'. All these problems arising from excessive scale – which are rampant throughout the colossal bureaucracy of the Welfare State – can in principle be solved effectively, according to Heller, by systematic de-merger and de-scaling. However, resistance by the bureaucrats is typically fierce, as research by Bennett Harrison, reported in *Lean and Mean* (1994), demonstrates: 'Power, finance, distribution, and control remain concentrated among the big firms. That power can still corrupt.'

The issue of scale is analytically distinct from state control, monopoly, expropriation of local initiatives by central planning, and bureaucracy. The state sector – and the welfare sphere in particular – has produced the most Gargantuan organizations in the world and in world history, alike in terms of the density of employees, turnover, costs and plant (Marsland, 1980). A large-scale map of Britain with all the state welfare agencies marked in red would look not unlike the map of the world before the Empire was disbanded.

The rivalry which the NHS – the largest employing organization in the free world – offered in terms of scale even to the massive Red Army at full complement is well known. The vast size of the education system is disguised only by its – largely fictitious – internal local authority boundaries. The escalating plethora of social workers, counter clerks and paper-pushing office staff in Social Security and its client agencies is immense, and to judge from the classified section of the *Guardian* any Wednesday, still expanding steadily. Despite recent initiatives to downsize and privatize their functions, local authorities are the largest employers by a long way in many communities up and down the country. Right across the state welfare sector, man-power costs comprise a large and increasing proportion of all costs.

In a context of high, if declining, unemployment, there are even those who defend this state of affairs, resist streamlining and cost-cutting, and call for an expansion of central and local state employment, in welfare and across the board. Nothing could be better calculated to reduce efficiency in the public sector (and in the economy as a whole) still further. Its excessive scale and impervious bureaucracy has arisen precisely as a result of years of timorous feather-bedding and futile empire-building. For every incompetent protected and preserved in the aspic of trade-union rule-books, there is a charlatan busily inventing and expanding a new section or department devoted expensively to some entirely unnecessary and usually impractical objective. The soft-hearted retention of poor-quality manpower and the uncontrolled growth of uselessly novel new functions conspire together to realize Gammon's Law of Bureaucratic Displacement, with increased resource input matched by lowered production. In bureaucratic systems 'the more you put in, the less you get out' (Gammon 1992), and, conversely, 'the less efficiently state organizations perform, the bigger they grow'.

Planning Mania

Planning by individuals and by families of their own life-projects is of course an entirely feasible and wholly desirable aspect of liberty. Planning by autonomous organizations, and even – within strict limits – by governments is also possible and proper. But central planning of the economy by states is neither necessary nor feasible (Marsland, 1991). This has been powerfully demonstrated in Hayek's refutation of Oskar Lange's thesis of the possibility of socialist calculation – and graphically illustrated, quite contrary to the author's apparent intention, in Gordon Cherry's revealing study, *Pioneers in British Planning* (1981).

Lange claims that all the information available to capitalist entrepreneurs necessary for them to make optimal decisions about resource allocation is available in practice to socialist planners. Given this data, they can then plan the socialist economy rationally. Or, as Heilbronner, following Lange, puts it: 'A central planning board would receive exactly the same information from a socialist economic system as did the entrepreneurs under the market system.' This assumption – strengthened in some quarters recently by over-imaginative interpretations of new developments in information science and technology, which speed up the flow of any sort of information and make it potentially much more comprehensive – is required by even the most modest concepts of planning. It is absolutely essential to systematic detailed planning such as would be required to replace the market. Hayek's response (1982) is as follows:

> I am afraid this is a blatant untruth, an assertion so absurd that it is difficult to understand how an intelligent person could ever honestly make it. It asserts a sheer impossibility which only a miracle could realize.
>
> In the first instance: most of the information which the capitalist entrepreneurs have consists of prices determined on a competitive market. This knowledge would not be available to anyone in a socialist economy where prices are not provided by the market.
>
> So far as the particular case of the production function is concerned, the relevant production functions which guide the competitive market are, of course, not (as the theoretical models simplifyingly assume) relations between general, generic categories of commodities, but very specific relations showing how, in a particular plant under the specific local conditions, changes in the combinations of the particular goods and services employed will affect the size of the output.

Moreover, even if the information were available – which by definition cannot occur in a socialist society – there is still no way it could be collated and analysed by a planning unit or by a single person or by any other means than the infinite complexity of the market itself. *Dispersed market knowledge simply cannot be mobilized centrally.*

Even on more modest assumptions about the range and specificity of the knowledge required, such that a kind of 'accountancy planning' could be possible, it couldn't work in practice. As Hayek says:

The mere idea that the planning authority could ever possess a complete inventory of the amounts and qualities of all the different materials and instruments of production of which the the manager of a particular plant will know or be able to find out makes the whole proposal a somewhat comic fiction. Once this is recognized it becomes obvious that what prices ought to be can never be determined without relying on competitive markets.

The suggestion that the planning authority could enable the managers of particular plants to make use of their specific knowledge by fixing uniform prices for certain classes of goods that will then have to remain in force until the planning authority learns whether at these prices inventories generally increase or decrease is just the crowning folly of the whole farce (ibid).

This is why all planning systems – but only some markets – fail. A competitive market system capitalizes naturally on a complex interaction of individual decisions which cannot be adequately recorded, let alone reproduced in the abstract, by any artificial means. That is why Central Europe, and eventually Russia and the Ukraine too, closely followed by China, will simply have to marketize fully if they intend to progress at all beyond central planning.

Without a market, economic decisions are bound to be guesswork, and usually mistaken. This is also why rational planning within the Welfare State is so difficult, why state functions which cannot be privatized such as defence are so expensive and inefficient, and why it is at those boundaries between national economies which are not made transparent by free trade that major dislocations of economic efficiency and dynamism routinely occur. In the absence of a market, there is simply no rational basis available for resource allocation decisions. If a plan, of whatever sort, is used instead, systematic resource misallocation is inevitable. Moreover, corrective reactions to the consequences of these errors will multiply them still further, resulting sooner or later in complete economic collapse – in an economic crisis such as socialists have long expected in capitalist societies but actually occurs only in socialist societies.

I have in front of me a graph showing steel production in the USSR and the USA between 1965 and 1975. It is from a book, written as late as 1978 by Erwin Marquit, devoted to extolling the Soviet socialist system. The graph, which is headed 'Planning versus Chaos', shows US production moving along gradually in zig-zags up and down ('Chaos'), while Soviet production leaps upward in a perfect straight line ('Planning'). Planners love straight lines. The fact that US development took realistic and precise account of need and demand, while planned Soviet development ensured the ready availability in the wrong place and at the wrong time of vast amounts of steel which no one who wanted it could afford, and no one who could afford it wanted, is apparently a matter of complete indifference to victims of planning mania.

Even the much more modest and commonsensical notions of planning typically recommended by socialists in Britain – for example, organizing the health service either nationally or regionally in terms of prescriptions derived other than from a market, or distorting the natural flow of regional investment in order supposedly to protect economically weaker regions – are subject to the same fundamental errors. Socialist planning, however desirable it might seem in principle, is, as Hayek has surely demonstrated more than adequately, simply not feasible in practice. The planning arm of the state's monopoly control of welfare is inherently flawed, destructive and futile. Commitment to planning the delivery of welfare is a major source of the Welfare State's ineffectiveness.

Inhumanity

The Welfare State is supposed to express and realize the disposition of people to care for one another, and in particular to care for the unfortunate and for those in need. Its spokesmen trade brazenly on carefully selected images of the neglected poor from Dickens and from 1930s films to persuade us all that only the Welfare State has vouchsafed to the poor salvation, and to us all a state of civilized grace. This is arrant nonsense. The Welfare State is an oppressive instrument of inhuman control. Eventually, like some monstrous Dantesque Ugolino, it voraciously devours its own children.

Its supporters are proud of the universalistic impersonality of its claim to treat everyone alike. By the same token, however, its 'clients' are all mere cyphers, each interchangeable *ad infinitum* for any other, and none of them valuable, or even meaningful, in the slightest to the blind machinery of state. Without a value allowed to concrete individuals, with the private actions which constitute the meaning of our chosen life-worlds systematically ignored, with praise and blame and all responsibility denied, any scope for genuine care – which is to say for *caritas*, for charity – is fundamentally undermined (O'Keeffe, 1994).

Little wonder if the so-called caring undertaken by the Welfare State does little good and much actual harm. Instead of real care for individual people in need of help, it provides at best a species of service maintenance for the universal class of worker-citizens. The Good Samaritan would make a poor social worker. Consider an example from the NHS (Clark, 1994):

> In the Accident and Emergency department of the Royal Sussex County Hospital in Brighton, a patient who had arrived in a wheelchair dared to ask the porter who had come to help him, 'Where is your name tag?' 'What's it to you, mate?' 'You're supposed to wear one. It says so in the patient's charter.' 'F*** off!'
>
> But this was no ordinary patient. He was John Spiers, chairman of the Brighton Health Care NHS Trust (slogan: 'Putting Patients' Interests First'), who... had decided to borrow a wheelchair and pose as a patient who had suddenly lost all feeling in his legs. He wanted to find out about the 'invisible hospital' that management usually chooses to ignore.

It is in the brutal impersonality of the Welfare State that its fundamental inefficacy inheres – since genuine help must always be offered to *this* person, for *these* particular situational reasons, with *these and these* concrete costs and consequences for his or her future life. This same impersonality is also the primary source of that cruel lack of humanity which is the fifth and final feature of Welfare State ineffectiveness which needs to be addressed.

Since the Welfare State is inherently and in principle impersonal and large-scale, its proclaimed humanitarian philanthropy is inevitably specious. The care it pretends to offer as a rational, modernized alternative to the genuine, voluntary, local charitable endeavours which it subverts in order to sustain its own collectivist, universalist principles is entirely fraudulent. Its inhumanity is not an accident, or a product of inadequate resourcing, or the result of underdevelopment in state welfare which can be rectified by progress in the theory and practice of social administration. Just as socialist societies are inevitably authoritarian, and egalitarian systems are *ipso facto* enemies of freedom (Li, 1994), so the Welfare State is by its very nature inhuman.

Consider some examples. Where else except in the conditions of a Welfare State society would old people be left to die alone in a bleak, untended, state-provided, state-neglected flat? Where else would their kinfolk and neighbours have been so completely stripped of their natural human feelings of obligation, charity and even curiosity that a corpse can be left to rot for weeks before the death is so much as discovered? Where else except in the conditions of high civilization represented by the

Welfare State could the public response to such cases comprise nothing more than a nation-wide collective shrug of the shoulders? We expect the Welfare State to do no better.

Again, to turn from neglect to hyper-activity, consider the punitive, witch-hunting overconfidence with which social workers possessed by lunatic abstract theories have persecuted, entirely unjustifiably, innocent families and communities suspected – for no better reason than social scientists' insistence that such people must be guilty – of child abuse. Or conversely, consider the case after case after case of social workers, health visitors and even voluntary workers corrupted by modern theories of the family, all of them managing to ignore the silent pleas of little children for help in the face of physical brutality or horrific sexual abuse. How can more and even more detailed 'guidelines' serve to counteract the inherent careless lack of humanity which such cases demonstrate?

For example, according to an independent official report by Emlyn Cassam, 'Paedophiles, pimps, and drug-pushers preyed upon young people in Islington children's homes. Child sex abusers were able openly to telephone and recruit from the borough's homes, "luring" boys and girls with offers of drugs, alcohol, and money from under the noses of those entrusted to care for them' (London *Evening Standard*, 1 August 1994). Children's homes have apparently become, despite detailed regulations, despite systematic guidelines, despite comprehensive bureaucratic controls, state brothels.

Again, should we not condemn as systemic products of engineered inhumanity rather than excuse as accidental cases of mere mismanagement: the careless neglect of truancy and bullying in the schools; the hopeless innumeracy and illiteracy of so many pupils after 15 000 hours of schooling; the oafish lack of manners of many more; the hustling beggars in our streets; the schizophrenics sleeping in the rain; the male and female prostitutes escaped from children's homes; the dementing masses of elderly men and women mouldering in state warehouses; or the countless patients carelessly offered irrelevant potions by doctors who know them only as numbers?

The instances of such dereliction could easily be multiplied a hundred-fold and more by even a cursory reading of local newspapers over a one week period. The Welfare State has not proven a remedy for man's inhumanity to man. On the contrary, it has served to canalize and justify all our worst instincts in regard to our responsibilities for each other. Someone else will see to it. It's the Government's fault. The experts will know what to do. It's up to the Welfare State. Nothing to do with me.

Of course, the proponents of state welfare will claim that these and similar gross failings in the system are due to inadequate resourcing, or government cuts, or lack of training, or the excessive case-loads of burned-out social workers, or the materialist values of capitalism, or the advertising industry, or almost *anything* else except the system of state welfare itself and its culture of irresponsible generalized provision. They are wrong. These continuous gross failings in state welfare arise out of inherent, incorrigible features which guarantee that inhumanity will continue and worsen, whatever extravagant level of resourcing is achieved. To prevent such failings we shall have to remove care from the state's inhuman control entirely, and restore it to the arena where it properly belongs – to local communities where people know and care about each other; to voluntary agencies which act out of genuine commitment to providing real help; to welfare workers equipped with the discretion to make particular judgements about individual people and their varying needs, and with the common sense to understand that helping always means above all helping people to help themselves; and above all to that most derided but most effective of caring institutions – the family.

Conclusion

Suppose, for the sake of argument, that the objectives of the Welfare State were consensually and coherently agreed, suppose that our need for it were demonstrated by incontrovertible evidence, and suppose that we were entirely confident that we could afford whatever it would cost to run. Even so, I have argued in this chapter, it would not and could not work other than grossly inadequately.

The *monopolistic position* of the welfare services prevents them from learning from competition and from experience, or from attending other than trivially and inadequately to their clients' needs and concerns. Their *bureaucratic structure* consistently prevents them from operating with the adaptable flexibility and attention to changing circumstance which we take for granted from service-providers in the private sector. Their *colossal scale* inhibits innovation and encourages depersonalized routinization. The commitment of their managers at all levels to *centralized planning* stands in the way of local and individual initiative and enterprise, and precludes genuine concern with the reactions of clients and consumers. Finally, the Welfare State's adherence to the concept of generalized universalism contradicts the fundamental principles of genuine charity, which require recognition of individuality, agency and responsibility. In consequence the welfare services become more and more *inhuman* and thus more and more grossly ineffective to the point of routine counter-productivity in their operations.

Each of these five sources of ineffectiveness in the operation of the welfare services – monopoly, bureaucracy, excessive scale, planning mania, and inhumanity – are bound together and thus multiplied in their destructive effect by two distinct bonds. First, they interlock causally one with the other, excessive scale encouraging bureaucracy, for example, and monopoly facilitating futile centralized planning. Secondly, and worse, they are all conjoined as features of the state as such – an institution which in and of itself tends, except where it is vigorously controlled by the power of tradition and the force of democracy, towards these same negative characteristics.

Little wonder, given this further powerful multiplier, that, in whatever cultural circumstances, the Welfare State works with such disappointing ineffectiveness. Its gross failings are incorrigible. Its ineffectiveness in providing for those who need help is beyond reforming remedy. We must seek an alternative.

6 Moral Hazards, Welfare Dependency, and the Underclass: The Welfare State as an Enemy of Society

It might seem more than enough to criticize the Welfare State for its philosophical incoherence, its redundancy in an era of prosperity and economic progress, its extravagant cost, and its bureaucratic inefficiency. There is, however, one further charge to be levelled against it and this the most serious of all.

The most damaging impact of the Welfare State is on the character, motivations and behaviour of the individual men and women subjected to its comprehensive expropriation of their capacity for free and independent action, for self-reliance, for enterprising initiative and for moral autonomy. The Welfare State creates and reproduces dependency. 'Why', asks Myron Magnet (1993), 'when immigrants from around the globe are making American lives worthy of respect and self-respect from the humblest jobs, do the poorest Americans – the underclass – not work?' The answer he identifies is as true for Britain as the United States:

> The key to the mystery is that their poverty is less an economic matter than a cultural one. In many cases, these 'have-nots' lack the inner resources to seize their chance, and they pass on to their children a self-defeating set of values and attitudes, along with an impoverished intellectual and emotional development that generally imprisons them in failure as well.

These destructive moral consequences are apparent wherever self-reliance has been replaced by comprehensive state welfare provision. They are best characterized in terms of Hermione Parker's concept (1982) of the 'moral hazards' of the hand-out culture, and best understood in terms of a courageous *Times* leader headline (2 December 1993) to the effect that 'Social security should be a temporary crutch, not a way of life'.

These consequences have been most clearly visible where collectivist welfarism was carried furthest – in the societies of 'actually existing socialism', where deep moral corruption of whole populations was scarcely moderated even by the lingering trace effects of long-established religious beliefs. The renewal of socialist Europe is going to require comprehensive reprogramming of persons and institutions for hard work, honest effort, enteprising initiative, self-reliance and responsible concern for the local community. All this was destroyed by the nationalization of care and the expropriation of personal responsibility by the state. The situation of China, despite fashionable support for its current phase of so-called 'market socialism', is even worse (Li, 1994).

The effects are fortunately not so fearful as yet in the mixed economies of welfare in liberal democratic societies. However, as Parker has demonstrated, they are certainly already quite severe, affecting every level of society and every sphere of social life. Welfare by right and on demand inevitably destroys what free and civilized societies have always defined as the fundamental human characteristic – *the capacity to make rational moral choices as a basis for independent action* (Sirico, 1994).

Not before time, Charles Murray's enormously important work, especially *Losing Ground* (1984), is at last being brought before large audiences in Britain. Where social policy analysts were somehow able until recently to marginalize and ignore the equally cogent critiques of welfarism provided by the Institute of Economic Affairs, the Social Affairs Unit and others, Murray's writing seems at last to be compelling the attention even of our Poverty Lobbyist academics and the moguls of British media collectivism. What he has succeeded in demonstrating beyond any possible challenge is that collectivist welfare provision generates helpless dependency in its cowed clientele. While this has damaging consequences for almost the whole of the population, breeding for example irrational deference to doctors and nervousness about their children's education even among the prosperous and privileged, its major structural impact is the creation of an alienated, de-motivated underclass excluded by socially engineered incapacity from genuine participation in the mainstream of society.

With Ralph Segalman, I have explored these effects systematically in a comparative study reported in our book *Cradle to Grave* (Segalman and Marsland, 1989). The evidence is clear. However benevolent the intentions underlying it, collectivist welfare provision damages the economy, cripples the dynamism of enterprise culture, fails to help those who most need help and, worst of all, positively harms those it is most meant to help by creating out of the temporary misfortunes of our fellow citizens an underclass of welfare dependants.

As long as equality and rights are the watchwords of social policy (as they are even now, after a decade and a half of Conservative government), the moral decay of the people will continue and spread. The watchwords we need instead are enterprise and self-reliance. These are the only secure foundation of social policies appropriate to free societies. They are the only principles capable of restoring that essential moral dimension to social policy which, in the face of 'current confusion about pluralism', Basil Mitchell (1989) has urged us to retrieve before it is too late.

The Underclass

All of the other weaknesses of the Welfare State which I have examined have been recognized, and more or less candidly acknowledged, for many years, even by apologists for state welfare. The Welfare State's responsibility for generating dependency in the population and for creating a subservient underclass is rather less easily excused, even by the most fanatical supporters of collectivist welfare, than impersonality, extravagance or inefficiency. So they have preferred to deny it altogether.

Moreover, since social research in Britain is largely funded, managed and carried out by ideological adherents of state welfare, little effort has been made to investigate the morally destructive effects of the Welfare State objectively (Marsland, 1990). Such studies as have been published, notably by Parker (1982 and 1984), Anderson (1981), Green (1982, 1984 and 1993), and Dennis (1993), have been deliberately and vigorously marginalized. Indeed, until very recently the idea that an underclass is developing here as a result of the debilitating influences of state welfare was scarcely tolerated even hypothetically by social policy researchers, or by the social affairs correspondents of television and the quality press. The whole notion was taboo.

No improvement in this absurd and intolerable situation would have occurred without a remarkable study-visit to Britain in 1989 by Charles Murray. An influentially eloquent American social scientist, Murray had systematically investigated the phenomenon of welfare dependency, earlier explored by Moynihan (1969), by Segalman and Basu (1981), and by Gilder (1981), in his book *Losing Ground* (1984). During his 1989 visit, he gave a number of important seminars, carried out field research in some of Britain's poorer neighbourhoods, and wrote a report for the *Sunday Times*. The report (*Sunday Times Magazine*, 26 November 1989) was widely read and much discussed. It put the underclass firmly on the British social policy agenda at long last.

The report was re-published in 1990, together with critical commentaries and a rejoinder from Murray, as *The Emerging British Underclass* (Murray, 1990). His analysis strikes me as entirely cogent. It conforms with much of my own experience in research and in practical development work among those of our fellow citizens whom supporters of state welfare construe as 'the deprived, the disadvantaged and the poor'.

In studies of youth unemployment, I have regularly found that many young men, unemployed since leaving school at the earliest opportunity, and supported in a life of futile idleness by state benefits, family support and a variegated repertoire of scrounging skills, simply do not want to work. Even in London, with job opportunities readily available – and eagerly snapped up by foreign youngsters and by Irish youth flooding into Britain even at the depth of the recession – they turn down perfectly good starter jobs dismissively, using all sorts of implausible excuses: the pay is too low; the work is too far away; they would have to get up too early; or work too late; or work too long. Without a job, their time is their own.

The truth is they just don't want a job at all. The dole allows and encourages them to stay unemployed. The attitudes they have learned at school and especially at home towards work and money equip them for little but idle moaning, and certainly include little trace of the work ethic. A successful modern society requires the maintenance of a system of economic incentives which reward initiative, enterprise and effort, and penalize laziness and failure. This in turn implies commitment by the population at large – including the less successful and the less well-paid – to defending this reward system (Marsland, 1994).

Or again, Murray's research reminds me graphically of my experience while working on a project in one of those vast barracks-like housing estates in one of our northern cities. Thrown up with short-sighted municipal pride thirty-five years ago to house families unceremoniously tipped out of entirely adequate but unfashionable terraced houses, it has since become a squalid haven of welfare dependency, and a typical example of the habitat of the new underclass.

I talked with people there who had never been off the estate in twenty years. It includes corner shops, betting shops, a dole office, a clinic – everything its browbeaten tenants have been schooled to think they need. Unemployed men of forty, perfectly capable of work except in terms of motivation; mothers with children and no husbands, with no aspirations at all beyond passive survival; old people fed up with litter, graffiti and sub-criminal hassle, but de-motivated by state-provided adequacy from making the effort to move elsewhere; gangs of young people sponging on their families and the state, and killing time until circumstances and luck –

good or bad – should take them off somewhere else. A tragic menagerie of large-scale welfare dependency, its inhabitants as recognizable by their peasant fatalism as the southern Italians of the 1950s whose child-like resignation was reported on by Robert Banfield in his famous book *The Moral Basis of a Backward Society* (1958).

Murray's work also brings to mind a perfect icon of this peasant fatalism reconstructed in modern industrial society by the maleficent influence of state welfare. It was displayed in one of those all too typical television programmes about alleged cuts in public expenditure. It featured an interview with a council tenant whose sitting-room was being damaged by damp percolating from above. 'Look,' he said plaintively, pointing to some very modest damage to the ceiling, 'I can't use that room any more, and I've been waiting months for them to fix it.' Schooled to helpless dependency by the great state 'Them', his natural capacity for a bit of DIY well within his available financial resources had been completely paralysed.

Murray's research charts the process of this creeping paralysis, and traces its sources in the destructive influences of state welfare. It shows that in certain neighbourhoods there are very high concentrations of illegitimate births, crime and unemployment. In these neighbourhoods he discerned in 1989 the beginning of a new and deadly social problem. 'I am not talking here', he says (*The Emerging British Underclass*, p. 4), 'about an unemployment problem that can be solved by more jobs, nor about a poverty problem that can be solved by higher benefits. Britain has a growing population of working-aged, healthy people who live in a different world from other Britons, who are raising their children to live in it, and whose values are now contaminating the life of entire neighbourhoods.'

Even moderate socialists have begun to acknowledge that there is an underclass problem in Britain, as Frank Field's *Losing Out* (1989) demonstrates. However, they mostly still prefer to believe (Norman Dennis is a notable exception) that the sources of the problem are to be found in poverty and inequality (Wilson, 1987; Macnicol, 1994; Kellner, 1994). Although the arguments and evidence are complex, Murray's work strongly suggests that this cannot be true. He locates its causes instead in the development during the 1960s and 1970s of a permissive moral climate backed up by over-generous and misdirected welfare support. Punishment, and even public shame, for delinquent and anti-social behaviour has been reduced. Social stigma has been withdrawn almost entirely from illegitimacy. New benefits for the homeless, including single mothers, were introduced, and levels of welfare support in general were considerably improved – to the point where employment makes little rational sense to hundreds of thousands of people.

Murray emphasizes the inter-connectedness of a whole series of factors in the causation of welfare dependency (ibid., p. 31):

> These changes in the law enforcement and benefit systems are not occurring in isolation. State education was a lively topic of conversation among people with whom I talked everywhere: the stories sounded depressingly like the problems with urban public education in the United States. Drug abuse in Britain is reported to be increasing significantly. Everything interacts. When one leaves school without any job skills, barely literate, the job alternatives to crime or having a baby on the dole are not attractive. Young men who are subsisting on crime or the dole are not likely to be trustworthy providers, which makes having a baby without a husband a more practical alternative. If a young man's girl friend doesn't need him to help support the baby, it makes less sense for him to plug away at a menial job and more sense to have some fun – which in turn makes hustling and crime more attractive, marriage less attractive. Without a job or family to give life meaning, drugs become that much more valuable as a means of distraction. The cost of drugs makes crime the only feasible way to make enough money to pay for them. The interconnections go on endlessly, linking up with the reasons why community norms change, the role of older adults in the community changes, community bonds change.

He doubts, I think correctly, that here in Britain we can learn much from the American experience that could help (ibid., p. 33):

> The central truth that the politicians in the United States are unwilling to face is our powerlessness to deal with an underclass once it exists. No matter how much money we spend on our cleverest social interventions, we don't know how to turn around the lives of teenagers who have grown up in an underclass culture. Providing educational opportunities or job opportunities doesn't do it. Training programmes don't reach the people who need them most. We don't know how to make up for the lack of good parents – day-care doesn't do it, foster homes don't work very well. Most of all, we don't know how to make up for the lack of a community that rewards responsibility and stigmatises irresponsibility.

However, since the causes of the problem are moral decay and collectivist welfare, it is on these difficult and challenging fronts that changes are needed if solutions are to be found. What we need, in Murray's striking phrase, is *'authentic self-government'* – by local authorities, by families and by individual people.

Unless the general line of social policy established during the post-war period is changed radically – including a fundamental restructuring of welfare provision, and of the philosophy of 'rights without responsibilities' which underpins it – welfare dependency will expand beyond the inner city and into the suburbs, and the whole fabric of civilized life in a free society will be threatened.

Petrol on Troubled Waters

Murray's analysis has not yet been widely accepted. John Moore lost his political credibility, and eventually his ministerial position and his place in the British cabinet, because he had become convinced by the evidence that state welfare is destructively counter-productive and chronically damaging to the very people it is supposed to help.

A large part of what the chattering classes held against Margaret Thatcher was her brave determination to arrest the moral and economic damage done to the British way of life by collectivist welfare. Her successors are being powerfully tempted by electoral and media pressure to revert to the pre-Thatcherite folly of seeking remedies to the destruction caused by welfare with – more welfare!

In attending to this organized opposition to good sense on welfare, *The Emerging British Underclass* incorporates four critiques of Murray's thesis by a team of socialists ranging from the moderate to the quasi-Stalinist. Murray is a good deal more patient and generous with them in his rejoinder than I would have been. None of them addresses his arguments or his evidence squarely. Each of them prefers to peddle his own personal version of denial and re-interpretation of the problem, and his own more or less collectivist remedy. One line, however, is common to them all. Each of them accuses Murray of 'blaming the victim', and each interprets this as a sufficient condemnation of his analysis. They could not be more wrong. Murray's plea for self-reliance, like mine, is precisely a condemnation of specific members of the governing élite for what *they* have done, and for what they are *still doing*, to hurt and damage ordinary, capable, British people.

It is socialist politicians, academics and journalists who invented and imposed the Welfare State. It is the fanatical ideologues of collectivist welfare who have undermined the good sense and sound moral values of ordinary people with their 'sophisticated' permissivism. It is the over-privileged intelligentsia who subverted the family, the neighbourhood and the police, and thus sabotaged the normal, natural and necessary process of social control which every community needs (Berger and Berger, 1983; Segalman and Himelson, 1994).

It is our political élite – until 1979 willingly or unwillingly socialist, and since then hardly less unremittingly collectivist – who have heaped up state welfare provision, and distributed it like a drug to more and more people as their 'right'. The source of welfare dependency, the origin of the underclass, is not the British people, but corrupted democracy and its cowardly leadership. Who else has an interest in subjugating the population, in destroying the British people's native capacity for self-reliance, in undermining their traditional determination to be their own master? What more powerful instrument for the attainment of these purposes do the enemies of freedom have than the Welfare State?

Murray Returns

As I was drafting this chapter, the British media announced two highly germane developments. First, Government plans for the introduction of workfare for the long-term unemployed were reported in the press; somewhat prematurely, as it happens, more's the pity. Secondly, a new, updated analysis by Murray of the underclass in Britain was reported in the *Sunday Times* and published by the Institute of Economic Affairs as *Underclass: the Crisis Deepens* (1994).

In one of the four critical commentaries generously appended by the IEA for the sake of supposed 'balance' to Murray's essay, at least one true word is spoken – by the brilliant and courageous, if occasionally wrong-headed, journalist Melanie Phillips. Before going on to criticize him, she makes the telling admission (p. 59) that 'it is impossible to shake off Murray's analysis of Britain's underclass because it has exposed *a decay at the core of our society which most of us would prefer to ignore*' (my emphasis).

To this Murray might reasonably respond 'I rest my case.' For if it is once admitted that there are grave and unacknowledged, not to say denied, problems with British society, it would seem foolish or worse to refuse to admit that the person who has managed to identify a problem that escaped the rest of us might also be right to some significant extent in his account of the nature of that problem and of its causes. Moreover, he provides in *The Crisis Deepens* both evidence and argument which support his case powerfully.

In the five years since *The Emerging British Underclass*, rates of illegitimacy have worsened substantially, the relevant crime rates have escalated dramatically, and, even as normal unemployment has declined, that most destructive component of unemployment which represents permanent or semi-permanent self-exclusion from genuine concern for self-reliance has continued to grow inexorably. Besides objective indications of the emergence of the underclass into substantial reality, the period since 1989 has also seen a significant shift in the more subjective domain of what Murray calls 'the public mood' (*The Crisis Deepens*, p. 3):

> Five years ago, the idea that England was developing an underclass attracted harsh scepticism. I had failed to make my case with 'scientific evidence', as one academic critic put it. My thesis was not only 'misleading', but 'perhaps wilfully so'. By autumn 1993 when I visited, the idea of an underclass got a more sympathetic hearing. As I talked to people around the country, there still existed an obvious split between the intellectuals and the man in the street, with many intellectuals continuing to dismiss problems of crime and single parenthood as nothing more than a 'moral panic'. But [Secretary of State] John Redwood's Cardiff speech in July had brought the debate about illegitimacy into the open. The day I arrived in London in September, I turned on the television to find Panorama running an unsympathetic portrait of a single mother and the BBC's Breakfast News beginning a five-day examination of British crime that, unlike five years ago, did not reflexively assume that the public was getting excited over nothing. Among intellectuals and politicians alike, the larger meanings of crime and illegitimacy were being taken more seriously.

The Crisis Deepens capitalizes on burgeoning acknowledgement of the severity of the underclass problem and on dawning awareness that its roots reach deep down into long-running cultural changes initiated by state welfare to strengthen and extend Murray's case. By his unapologetic use of the concept of the 'New Rabble' to characterize the distressed condition of the underclass, and the term the 'New Victorians' to describe the values and life-style of the mainstream majority, he points up the polarization of British society which is going on more and more rapidly right across the country.

By the same token he identifies the primary source of the problem in misconceived welfare provisions and their destructively disincentive effects. We are actually paying people to avoid marriage, to neglect fatherhood, to avoid work and to enter on lives of petty crime.

By way of remedy, he urges the necessity of radical reform of the Welfare State to address the problem of dependency and its anti-social effects on morality and behaviour. Thus (p. 31):

> The state should stop intervening and let the natural penalties [of unmarried parenthood] occur. The penalties may occur in the context of a welfare state. It is possible to have a social safety net that protects

everyone from cradle to grave, as long as a social contract is accepted. The government will provide protection against the vicissitudes of life as long as you, the individual citizen, take the responsibility for the consequences of your own voluntary behaviour... Many will find even this level of restraint on the welfare state unacceptable. But as you cast about for solutions, I suggest that one must inevitably come up against this rock. The welfare of society requires that women actively avoid getting pregnant if they have no husband, and that women once again demand marriage from a man who would have them bear a child. The only way the active avoidance and the demands are going to occur is if childbearing entails economic penalties for a single woman.

The argument is unassailable. Moreover, even Murray's coy apology for the supposed 'sexism' ('It is all horribly sexist, I know') of his proposals is, in my judgement, unnecessary, a product of the hysterical feminism which has seized the intelligentsia of the United States rather than a rationally justified qualification of his argument. For his analysis quite plainly involves an entirely even-handed criticism of selfishly irresponsible young people of both sexes, and beyond this a thoroughgoing condemnation of a welfare system which facilitates and encourages their irresponsibility.

Murray's analysis is by no means generally accepted yet, even by conservatives, as Simon Jenkins's predictable critique indicates ('But there is no underclass', *Times*, 25 May 1994). 'Mr Murray', he says, 'sees a widening moral divide between the New Victorians and the New Rabble. I do not. I see poor people who would like to be rich and respectable and enjoy a stable domestic life.' It seems to me this is a grossly over-sanguine view, and a product of suburban short-sightedness. Jenkins's rose-tinted perspective is a privilege denied both to researchers like Murray, whose trade exposes them willy-nilly to the savage realities of modern urban life, and to politicians like Frank Field, whose constituents no doubt report to him more accurately than *Times* columnists. According to a newspaper report of Field's views (*Sunday Times*, 27 May 1994) Murray has 'got half of the truth' and his analysis shows 'the need to be tough both about morality and about reducing unemployment'. Well, we all knew about the damage done by unemployment long ago. What is new about Murray's analysis, and what is acknowledged even by sceptics like Field, and by more and more people in all parties and none, as true and important, is its recognition of the key role of moral attitudes in social decay.

Uncivil Society

Lest anyone should think that this analysis can be dismissed as a typical product of the American right-wing (not that Murray, as an advisor to President Clinton, is in any simple sense right-wing), one should consider an influential account of these problems which is very similar to Murray's, at least as trenchant, but prototypically British in its assumptions and style, and which comes with a bona fide left pedigree. This is Norman Dennis's *Rising Crime and the Dismembered Family* (1993). This remarkable study, written by the joint author with A. H. Halsey of *English Ethical Socialism* (1988), should be read in conjunction with *Families without Fatherhood* (Dennis and Erdos, 1993), to which *Rising Crime* is the sequel, and Kiernan and Estaugh's study for the Family Studies Centre (1993) of cohabitation and its negative effects.

Dennis demolishes once and for all the carefully crafted lies of our post-war intelligentsia about crime, about the family and about the connections between them. Sociologists and social policy analysts have sought to per-suade us, in despite of the evidence and quite contrary to common sense, to accept three bizarre propositions. First that the apparent and alleged increase in crime is a fictional product of moral panic encouraged by the 'gutter press' and 'reactionary politicians'. Second, that the manifest decay of the normal family is really a positive development in the quality of domestic arrangements, more compatible than the traditional system with the liberated spirit of modernity. And third, that if there is after all any increase in crime, it is to be explained in terms of unemployment, or poverty, or deprivation, or oppression, or indeed in terms of almost any factor *except* family breakdown.

Dennis's historical and statistical analysis gives short shrift to the liberal myth – the staple orthodoxy of the criminal justice and social work estab-lishment – which is constructed out of these fallacious propositions. Crime has been and is increasing. The family is in an escalating state of decay. The former is explicable to a large degree in terms of the latter, with the isolated and fractured family increasingly incapable of socializing and controlling male children.

Dennis insists that there can be no remedy to civil disorder unless a stop is put to the decay of the family. This in turn will require changes in élite and public attitudes – in the direction of greater support for the family as an institution and reduced tolerance of moral deviance – and a transforma-tion of social policy designed to reverse current disincentives to family stability. In short, the worsening chaos of underclass criminality will con-tinue unless and until we restore to children stable and supportive social environments such as only self-reliant families and self-managing local communities can provide.

Tales from the Dependency Culture

Welfare reform is firmly on the agenda at last, as media and political reactions to the Adam Smith Institute's 1994 book (*The End of the Welfare State*), Charles Murray's renewed influence, and Government initiatives on workfare and single parent families unambiguously demonstrate. The grave deficiencies of state welfare – long denied, even longer ignored – are becoming widely acknowledged, even on the left of British politics. Even, indeed, among academic social policy analysts, whose stock in trade has for decades consisted of unthinking apologia for the Welfare State and the collectivist values which it enshrines, there are faint signs of recognition that reform is unavoidable.

We should not, however, count our welfare reform chickens before they are hatched. *Soi-disant* social affairs experts in the universities and the media remain at heart bitter opponents of the principles which underpin any genuine alternative to state welfare. They are implacable enemies of the family, of competition and of traditional British concepts of respectability, pride and shame, and right and wrong. The Labour Party, despite current pragmatic adjustments shaped by electoral considerations, remains as prejudiced against the market as ever, and just as much committed as it was before 1979 to collectivist remedies for every problem. In particular, the opponents of welfare reform remain implacably blind to the evidence about welfare dependency and the role of state welfare in creating the underclass.

The Welfare State is not the pinnacle of modern civilization, as the Hampstead Catechism and the Gospel According to the *Guardian* would have us believe. On the contrary, it is outmoded, ineffective and destructive. It is philosophically incoherent, unnecessary, expensive, inefficient and worst of all it harms rather than helps its clients by creating welfare dependency and sustaining a self-excluding underclass. In the most cited sentence I have ever written – in the *Guardian, The Times*, the *Sun*, the *Morning Star*, and the *Kentish News*, just by way of example – 'It is turning neighbourhoods and estates all over Britain into factories of crime and arbitrary violence' (Coad, 1990).

In relation to this last and worst weakness of state welfare, I turn next to some examples of what Digby Anderson has called 'open secrets' – well-known facts about abuses and follies in the Welfare State which are routinely suppressed or politely hushed up. I begin with some examples of underclass effects on the mainstream population, and turn thereafter to the dependent population narrowly defined.

Upper-Class Dependency

My first example concerns, with credits to Peter Greenaway, a judge, his wife and health care reform. He was actually a retired judge, and I met him recently with his wife at a social occasion. We got onto discussing reform of the NHS, and it very quickly became apparent that despite their otherwise consistently conservative opinions, they were ferociously antagonistic to health-care reform, especially to closure of a certain well-known hospital close to their home. Debate flowed furiously, but with little rational effect.

Despite their general political stance, they believed, as absolutely as any Islamic fundamentalist believes, in the preservation of the sacred and unimprovable purity of an unreformed NHS. Despite their income – a judge's pension is about five times the national average salary, and I imagine they had capital too – they had never taken out private health insurance, and saw no reason why they should have done. As far as they were concerned, they were being robbed by a hard-hearted and incompetent government of their inalienable rights.

Moral: why bother to look after yourself if the Government promises, however implausibly, to do it for you?

Autistic Undergraduates

With this sardonically intended concept, I am referring to the tendency of the well-heeled, Conservative-voting, middle classes to resist their obligation to support their children's involvement in higher education. Already annoyed by being forced to pay for part of their maintenance, they are currently up in angry arms at the prospect of having to pay tuition fees as well.

But why? A large proportion of the young people in question go to university only because that's what people like them do. They have no idea of why they are studying, and little commitment to the discipline involved. Many of them are following courses in spurious or instrumentally useless subjects. They lend themselves by default to bizarre campaigning by their unions on behalf of collectivist missions which make it even more difficult for their fathers to afford to educate them properly.

Why not change the whole system? Let parents who wish to do so pay for their own children's education (in the Sixth Form as well as at college), with state and private scholarships available on a meritocratic, competitive basis to those whose ability and effort justify them.

The Child Benefit Scandal

I can see no reason why anyone except possibly the very poorest should expect to be paid for the privilege of having children. Whether or not it is taxed, child benefit is an absurdity which only the logical dialectics of the Welfare State could justify. Yet Conservative Ministers who so much as suggest getting rid of it are labelled by the media as cruel monsters.

I was encouraged by the finding reported in a recent ICM national survey that a larger proportion of people believe child benefit should be restricted to low-income families than insist on universal payment regardless of need (*Daily Express*/ICM, March 1994). But support for the welfare status quo is as much as 43 per cent, and only marginally lower than this at 42 per cent among the higher social classes. Before long, no doubt, we should expect a campaign in the Home Counties for dog and pony benefits.

Entertainment on the Rates

One might have dealt next with the escalation of public expenditure on legal aid, and the whining demands of the more litigiously inclined among the middle classes to have their barristers' fees paid by you and me and by those with less money and more sense than themselves. This is a large and complex issue, however, which is better left to be analysed fully and in its own right. Instead I turn, for my last example of shameless abuse of state welfare by those who should know better, to libraries.

I spoke recently to a meeting of the Royal Society of Literature about the future of public libraries. Mr Yeltsin could hardly meet a more dogmatically close-minded response from his die-hard Stalinist enemies than I found in an audience of London litterateurs challenged to contemplate the ultimate capitalist threat of – library charges!

Yet the libraries are increasingly in the entertainment business. Why should we not expect those who can afford it – the large majority of the population and the huge majority of library users – to rely on privatized commercial libraries? Why should the poor pay from their taxes and their improved benefits forgone for the well-heeled to have free access to detective stories, thrillers, science fiction, travel and cookery books, down-market audio-cassettes, and Hollywood videos?

Indeed, even the proper and traditional business of public libraries – education, scholarship, art, high literature and science – could also be handled perfectly well, and more efficiently, on an entirely commercial basis – a niche-market in quality reading, as it were.

The real cost of both the artistic and the entertainment functions of the libraries should be carried by those who benefit from them. A free library service is at one and the same time a guarantee that standards will be diluted, and a calculated insult by the over-privileged to those among the disadvantaged who might prefer their money spent in quite other directions.

The Welfare State has thus, as these examples suggest, gradually but inexorably corrupted the whole nation, the prosperous majority included. Its destructive influence is at its worst, however, on precisely those it is intended to help – the poor, the weak, and the unfortunate.

The Benefits of Unemployment

Benefit fraud of £5 billion per annum has been officially identified. We can be confident there is at least as much again going unnoticed, much of it in unemployment benefit. Just talk around any council estate, any inner city area. Criminal fraud is wholesale, and has been for years, as was demonstrated by Robin Page's *The Benefits Racket* (1971), a study of 'exploitation, graft, determined cunning, and even violence' which got the author the sack from his job at the National Assistance Board. All the supporters of state welfare come back with is the trite and irrelevant claim that tax fraud is even worse – yet many benefit frauds are vast – such as a recent case involving a £1 billion swindle! (Hussey, 1994). Some 2700 false claims were made, and 2000 different names were used, netting the perpetrators (including 'the daughter of a wealthy Nigerian chief') £250 000 per week.

If unemployment support were handled on a local basis, officials would know who the half to three-quarters of a million professional criminals and prostitutes who claim benefit were, and stop them. They would know which feckless families routinely swing the lead, and stop them too. The unemployed should surely not have time or energy to work as well as claim. The Government's recent cautious moves towards introducing workfare are to be welcomed.

In a film I made about welfare reform for BBC2 (*Let's Kill Nanny*, 4 August 1994), we included a reconstruction of an interview with a not untypical 'scally' or scalliwag from the North West:

'Course I sign on, yeh. You can buy identities like from the lads. Passports an driving licences an the like. Then you go to Chester on the train or whatever an tell the Sosh yer homeless. They give yer thirty quid an a place ter get an address from. So yer can claim down there or in Birkenhead or anywhere really. But if it's too far I don't bother... too much hassle ter get up specially if it's early morning signing on, yer know.'

Invalid Benefits?

Fraud and waste are probably almost as bad in this sphere as in unemployment. As we get healthier and live longer as a nation, we apparently have more and more chronic invalids! This nonsense is perpetuated by socialist and sentimental doctors who, despite their scientific training, fail to recognize the sociological law demonstrated unequivocally in Holland and Scandinavia: the uptake of invalidity benefit and the prevalence of sickness absence from work is a function of the accessibility and generosity of benefits, entirely regardless of the objective condition of the population. In Britain the number of people receiving Invalidity Benefit has increased, according to research by the Policy Studies Institute, from 600 000 in 1978/9 to almost one and a half million by 1993/4. Increasing numbers are stuck permanently on benefit once they have accepted its definition of them as dependent and helpless.

Research by the Department of Social Security confirms that – surprise, surprise – we are not becoming less healthy. 'It suggests', according to Grice and Nelson (1993), 'that people are merely staying on invalidity benefit for much longer periods and that it has become an unofficial form of early retirement which boosts the income of the jobless' – boosts it very substantially, one might add, in some cases by 100 per cent. The *Sunday Times* quoted a Glasgow GP as saying: 'There is no incentive to be rigorous. The certification system is lousy. A doctor is more likely to give a claimant a certificate than not.' A BMA spokesman is quoted as saying: 'There certainly is potential for collusion between doctors and patients. Doctors feel very sympathetic for unemployed patients, who stand precious little chance of getting a job. They are trying to do their jobs and follow the rules, but they are human beings.'

The system has been tightened up to some degree since 1993, but the scope for abuse remains enormous. Perhaps we could make a useful concrete start on the massive task of sorting out the widespread misuse of support intended to protect the genuinely sick by insisting that employing organizations, especially state agencies such as local authorities, British Rail and London Transport, should produce sickness absence data on a league table basis. Unless the problem is addressed seriously, the long-term worsening in commitment to work will continue. Annual sickness absence among male employees of the Post Office, one of the few public sector organizations to have kept systematic records over a long period, rose from 7.6 days per employee before 1914, to 10.0 days between the wars, and up again to 13.1 days – almost double the Victorian and Edwardian rate – in the era of the fully developed Welfare State (Taylor and Burridge, 1982).

Education Squandered

According to the same recent ICM national survey I mentioned earlier, barely half of parents check that their children have done their homework! Not many more than this claim to listen to them reading when they are young and learning; and only about four in ten control their television viewing – barely a quarter in social classes D and E. Less than half insist on a set bedtime for young children.

Would they thus squander a costly investment in their children's education if they were paying for it directly themselves? Can we imagine that those hundreds of thousands of the poorest in England who paid for their children's education out of their own pockets in the decades before education was nationalized in 1870 by the Forster Act, can we imagine that *they* would have been so irresponsible? I rather think not, and nor would they have tolerated routine truancy (West, 1970 and 1990; O'Keeffe, 1988; O'Keeffe and Stoll, 1995).

Housing Benefit

There are still absurdly too many people living in council houses – the tied cottages of socialism. But there is not much point keeping up the pressure for a shift to Housing Associations and the private sector if we tolerate an escalation in parallel of housing benefit.

So much is this largesse taken for granted in recent years, that people are allowed to complain about their supposedly inadequate benefit support without being challenged to admit they are having their rent paid as well. We are supposed to sympathize with people who prefer to run a car, take a holiday, smoke and drink to paying their own rent. The concept of housing rights, which is ludicrous in principle, becomes positively lunatic when it is carried to its contemporary extreme as meaning the right to demand exactly the sort of residence in precisely the place that one would ideally wish for. It will be thatched cottages all round 'on the rates' before long, no doubt.

By the same token, I fail entirely to understand how we can tolerate the absurd sentimentality about the so-called homeless which is paraded daily on our television screens. A large proportion are mentally ill and handicapped people who were much better and more economically served in asylums. Others are young people who have left home inappropriately and unnecessarily on the expectation that the state will provide for them what their own prudence, planning and patience has not. Many more than is officially admitted are illegal immigrants and fraudulent refugees. We should attend urgently, making maximum possible use of a liberalized housing market, to the causes of homelessness, instead of allowing ourselves to be distracted by superficial symptoms.

We should address fraud in this sphere too. Pensioner council tenants routinely hide their savings in the working-class equivalents of Swiss bank accounts in order to minimize their rents and to avail themselves illegitimately of benefits to which they are not entitled (see Appendix 3). And here is the 'scally' from my television film *Let's Kill Nanny* again:

> 'It's not just me, like. Everyone's at it. You get another address, see, with a mate or someone, an you claim the rent from the Sosh. They send you a giro like to that address an you split it with the guy who owns the house... or yous let him use your address for the same thing like.'
>
> 'Doesn't anyone check up on you? To ensure that you are living at this false address?'
>
> 'Sometimes. But they tell you. They write and say they'll be calling, so I turn up don't I.'
>
> 'And you have a false address at present?'
>
> 'I got three at the minute an they bring me a hundred quid a week near enough. I got some others lined up.'
>
> 'How many more have you lined up?'
>
> 'Another three.'
>
> 'So together they could bring you in £200 a week?'
>
> 'Bout that, yeh.'

Fraud aside, there is enormous abuse of housing benefit, with assistance intended to help the disadvantaged serving routinely, in the words of a *Sunday Times* analysis (2 October 1994), to keep wealthy families 'in the lap of luxury'. A landlord in Haringey collects cheques on behalf of tenants, according to the same report, "worth nearly £1m a year". From top to bottom, housing benefit is a destructive underclass racket. It should be stopped.

Home Alone?

Apparently we have to rely on a Democratic President of the United States for honesty about young lone parents and welfare. 'We will say to teenagers', Mr Clinton said recently:

'if you have a child out of wedlock, we will no longer give you a cheque to set up a separate household.... We want families to stay together.... People who bring children into the world cannot and must not walk away from them.'

Britain, by contrast, has become so much a haven of fraudulent welfare-speak that even allegedly right-wing Ministers respond to the shameless, bitchy demands of Lone Parents Incorporated in the fawning, honeyed tones of ideological surrender. In yielding thus cravenly to the campaigning bluster of collectivist ideologues, we are denying common sense, betraying rational political principles, and subverting the family (Berger and Berger, 1983; Davies, 1993).

These enemies of the family have become more and more powerful in recent years, and are now out of control. It seems to have occurred to none of the supporters of what one might call either 'modernized domestic arrangements' or 'the continuing decay of the family' that the reason for fewer divorced women remarrying may be the forfeiture of benefits and housing costs involved. Yet the damage done to the family by welfare is admitted even by its supporters – and without the slightest trace of regret.

For example, a correspondent writing to the *Sunday Times* to criticize Charles Murray's latest examination of the underclass (29 May 1994) calmly suggests that:

couples do not get married for the sound economic reason that with children their social security and housing entitlements improve if they stay single with separate addresses.

Again, the Director of the National Council for One Parent Families, Susan Slipman, was able to take it entirely for granted that the Broadcasting Complaints Commission would back her in her criticism of a penetrating BBC Panorama investigation (*Babies on Benefit*) of "young never-married mothers". Yet, as the *Observer* journalist Melanie Philips has established (11 September 1994 [2]), the case is arguable:

Ms Slipman is understood to have claimed to the Commission that she was only interested in fairness and balance. Phooey. Her allegations against Panorama simply don't stand up to serious scrutiny. Some of them misrepresented what the programme actually said and she apparently retracted them in subsequent correspondence with the Commission. Her allegations formed a nit-picking miasma which ranged from the misleading to the bizarre. She claimed that the programme had failed to distinguish adequately between young never-marrieds and the majority of lone parents. False. It did so on a number of occasions. She accused it of giving prominence to right wing or 'predictable' opinion, naming among others Professor A. H. Halsey.

Halsey is, of course, the renowned ethical socialist; but since his thought-crime is to have pointed out some home truths about family breakdown, who cares about a little detail like that?

We should all care – but those claiming to represent one-parent families won.

Young lone parents need a home: but they are better off in a supervised institution in the countryside than in a flat of their own in the inner city. They need money: but the father of their child or children should be paying up, as should their current boyfriends – who trade in their tens of thousands on the credulity of social workers to obtain free lodging. They need above all wise adult support and training: but of this we provide, out of deference to their spurious rights, almost nothing. As a recent report (Whelan, 1994) has conclusively demonstrated, child abuse is concentrated overwhelmingly among single parents – particularly those involved in casual serial relationships. The risk of fatal abuse is almost twenty times greater from cohabiting than from married parents!

According to Whelan, summarizing the findings of the four-decade, nation-wide National Child Development Study, which provides the most trustworthy longitudinal data available anywhere: 'At every stage at which the follow-up interviews have been conducted it has been found that children from broken or incomplete homes do significantly worse than the children of intact homes by every indicator of educational and social status.' As Dennis and Erdos (1992) put it, making the connection between family decay and welfare: 'Young men who are invited to remain in a state of permanent puerility will predictably behave in an anti-social fashion.'

Tom Sackville, junior health minister, should be allowed the last word on this crucial topic, since he spoke so wisely on it that his words won him an award for Political Incorrectness in the *Guardian* (9 November 1993). These were his – judged by the liberal progressivist criteria which have destroyed the family – reprehensible words:

> We have to expect people to see that there needs to be a contract between a father and mother to stay together to bring up the child they created.... The existence of a very comprehensive benefits and free

housing system has reinforced the conclusion that anyone can have a baby at any time, regardless of their means and of the circumstances in which they can bring up their babies.

These are Victims – Who are the Villains?

I have spoken less than tenderly about some of these denizens of the underclass habitat. I make no apology for that. If we want to help them, it is truth we are short of. But they are in part victims of something larger and worse than their own saddening inadequacies:

- Opposition politicians who defend the welfare status quo at all costs.
- Academic social affairs experts, so-called, and social researchers, who ignore what they don't want to see, and at the taxpayers' expense draw a completely phoney picture of social conditions in Britain.
- Collectivist ideologues in the corrupted voluntary organizations which have given up their great tradition of service for a place on the Welfare State gravy train.
- Journalists and television pundits who prefer embarrassing a Minister to pursuing the truth, and are so much lacking in common sense that they could as much tell a train-driver from a train-robber as they can distinguish a genuine plea for help from the charm and bullying of professional welfare conmen.

As I write, the latest in a long line of tragic social work scandals is breaking in the news. A man and his wife, both of modest capacity and supposedly under the tender care of Social Services, have been found guilty of the manslaughter of their infant child, neglected and starved to a cruel death in conditions not fit for pigs. Yet the house had been specially provided for them and their innumerable offspring by the authorities of the caring Welfare State, and totally refurbished and re-fitted at a cost of more than a hundred thousand pounds! This is a sadly typical case of Welfare State intervention in the lives of vulnerable people. It is typical in three senses. First, extravagant public expenditure has been squandered. Second, extreme harm to an innocent victim has not been prevented – and may even have been facilitated. And third, the real needs of the primary clients have been neglected as a result of two characteristic features of state welfare agencies: their bureaucratic inefficiency, and their domination by outlandish, unrealistic theories inimical to practical common sense.

There will be more and more such cases unless we initiate radical reform of the Welfare State urgently. Until reform is carried through, the size of the underclass and the scale of hopeless vulnerability in the population will continue to increase. They are increasing daily as state welfare works at its practised art of creating and re-inforcing incompetent dependency. Peasant fatalism is being anachronistically resurrected in modern society by the malign influence of state welfare. We outlawed slavery and stopped it. Now we must liberate the new serfs of welfare dependency.

Laying Waste the Temple

Collectivist state welfare, in combination with unthinking liberal policies on divorce and on 'rights' so-called more generally, is undermining the family by making fathers redundant (Morgan, 1995). With the family destroyed, its essential role in the socialization of children goes by the board. In consequence, the attitudes and skills required of independent adults in a free society are progressively attenuated. Commitment to self-reliance and the capacity to achieve it and maintain it are sabotaged (Segalman and Himelson, 1994).

A swelling population of welfare dependents is thus created. Economically supported outside the labour market, they have little interest in work, and are thus deprived of the psychological support and discipline which work provides (Marsland, 1994). Inhibited by central state welfare from developing any real stake in the neighbourhoods in which they live, they watch their local communities decay around them. Appropriate remedial action is sometimes – but sadly rarely – taken, as a report by Geraint Smith ('Estate's "Terror" Family Evicted', *Evening Standard*, 15 November 1994) about violence, burglary and drug dealing indicates. More commonly the problem is allowed to fester, and gets progressively worse.

Educational, health care and housing programmes in the inner cities are close to collapse in consequence. Employers are frightened off by environmental conditions, by the costs required to maintain extravagant welfare provision, and by the lack of skills and work commitment in the demoralized population – and so establish their new businesses elsewhere. Crime escalates. The life of welfare dependency is institutionalized and normalized, and the fractured family re-creates new generations of children incapable of disciplined and independent lives.

The outcome is graphically decribed in Theodore Dalrymple's reportage (1994) from the underclass conditions – which were supposed to be improved, but have actually been grossly worsened, by state welfare – where he works as a doctor: 'for sheer apathy, spiritual, emotional, educational, and cultural nihilism and vacuity, you must go to an English slum'.

For a typical instance of this general case, consider Roy Greenslade's (1994) description of life in his childhood home area of Barking in East London:

> the high-rise Gascoigne Estate, whose lifts stink of urine and break down too often, where obscene graffiti are daubed on filthy walls and where the stairwells are covered in rubbish. I ask one resident about a cleaning rota. 'No, mate,' he says, 'they have a peeing rota in this place.' The council is spending millions on landscaping, but these homes need good management, not shrubs.

This destructive process is apparent in the United States, in Britain, on the Continent, and wherever welfare state policies have been adopted. Unless some radical alternative is found which gets 'Big Government' off the backs of the people, an increasing proportion of the population will be sucked into welfare dependency. The underclass will inexorably expand.

Democratic societies cannot afford the financial costs of state welfare, which drives up taxes, rates and inflation, and squanders resources which are needed for productive investment. How much less, however, can we afford the *socially destructive effects* of excessive state welfare. 'Unless we can restore a moral perspective to the lives of the poor', argues Gertrude Himmelfarb (1994 [2]), 'the alienated underclass will grow larger.' Unless social policies are radically changed, we are embarked, as a result of the long-run shift from 'Victorian virtues to modern values' (Himmelfarb, 1995) on nothing short of cultural suicide.

It is a little reassuring in this saddening context to note that even among influential supporters of state welfare the dangers of dependency, and the resultant damage to individuals, to families and to communities described in this chapter, have been more and more widely recognized in recent years. Foremost among these realists is Frank Field MP, who, as Chairman of the Parliamentary Social Security Committee and as a writer and commentator in his own right, has consistently emphasized, even at the risk of unpopularity, the moral dimension of welfare provision. A second notable example is the distinguished American social scientist Amitai Etzioni – the more notable in this regard because he is generally seen as being on the left or liberal side of American politics, and is reported to be an advisor to or to have influence on both President Clinton in the USA and the Leader of the Opposition, Mr Blair, in Britain.

In a recent article (1994), Etzioni urges the application of a principle of subsidiarity to welfare provision. The first line of responsibility for welfare, he argues, lies with the individual, adding that '*Nobody is exempt*'. The second line of responsibility belongs, he proposes, to the family, to which he would thus restore many duties of which it has in recent decades been stripped. The third line of responsibility falls, on Etzioni's analysis, to the local community, a proposal which I take up in Chapter 9 below. It is only when and where these three front lines of welfare provision fail or otherwise prove inadequate, that Etzioni would cede responsibility to what he calls 'society at large'. His analysis merits detailed consideration:

> Society has a responsibility to help those least able to help themselves, to share unexpected calamities, and to attend to *the few services* [my emphasis] that the community agrees are best discharged via the state. There is no contradiction between demanding that everyone will do their share and realizing that some still will need to be assisted after and as they discharge their duties.

This concept of welfare is incompatible with the universalist approach which has done so much damage in the post-war period. By emphasizing the duties of the individual and the family and the key role of the local community, it introduces a powerful barrier to the dependency-creating tendencies of state welfare. It cuts at the roots of dependency by focusing public welfare provision on the minority who cannot help themselves, and by demanding even in these cases active, responsible involvement by individuals, families and local communities.

If we could move the Welfare State sharply in this direction, we could save ourselves most of the grievous problems of the currently still expanding and worsening underclass phenomenon.

7 The Benefits of Consumer Sovereignty: Trusting the Market

In Chapters 2, 3, 4, 5 and 6 I have examined the five main deficiencies of the Welfare State. I have argued in turn that:

- The concept of the Welfare State is philosophically incoherent.
- Economic progress has made comprehensive state welfare redundant.
- The extravagant costs involved in providing it are driving Britain towards bankruptcy.
- The Welfare State is bureaucratic, inefficient, and inhuman.
- State welfare is responsible for manufacturing dependency and creating a deprived and dangerous underclass.

I turn now to an examination of the market as an alternative to monopoly state supply of welfare and as an antidote to the several deficiencies of the Welfare State.

The collapse of world socialism has demonstrated, concretely and definitively, the inadequacies of unmitigated state monopoly provision of goods and services. The plan has been vanquished by the market. There are two strategies for reforming failed state monopolies. These are what the Public Choice school of economists call 'voice' and 'exit' (Hirschman, 1970), or what I prefer to call *voice and choice*.

The first strategy involves organizing the consumers of collectively provided goods and services, and enabling them to challenge monopoly providers in respect of quality and (where relevant) price. This is the fashionable way of the consumer movement. The second strategy requires privatization, and the installation of genuine markets, with quality optimized and prices minimized by competition between producers. This is the route which has been successfully adopted in relation to nationalized industries and public utilities. It has not so far been tried in the welfare sphere.

No doubt consumer organizations have some significant beneficial effects. However, I have a good deal of sympathy with Brian Torode's critical analysis (1990) of the tendency for the concept of 'the consumer' to be made over into a basis for political organization, and even manipulation, by the media, by partisan pressure groups, and by other special interest lobbies.

A typical instance of the dangers of corruption of the concept of the consumer is provided by a recent report by the Association of Community Health Councils (1989). A fundamental aspect of the current reforms of the National Health Service is a strong emphasis on the patient as consumer, and a powerful programmatic commitment to quality in the health care services provided by the state (Marsland and Emly, 1996). This consumer focus is crystallized and definitively specified in 'The Patient's Charter' (Department of Health, 1991). Yet spokesmen for the Association and for individual Councils have been consistently critical of the reforms almost in their entirety.

In its report 'Quality Assurance and the Role of the Community Health Councils', the ACHC witheringly rubbishes the attempts of NHS managers to introduce competition and the sort of quality assurance systems which have long been taken for granted in profitable private businesses. Rather than welcoming these consumer-oriented reforms, ACHC – the supposed champion of health care consumers' interests – seeks to undermine their validity. Instead of pressing for more competition backed up by stronger consumer-oriented management, ACHC cavils about imaginary deficiencies in the new customer focus, tediously extends its long-standing defence of the health care status quo, and devotes much of its energy to shrill insistence that a key role in consumer protection should be reserved – for itself!

This exemplifies perfectly the dangers of reliance on organized consumerism as a strategy for countering monopoly provision of goods and services. Any organized pressure group represents primarily – by definition and regardless of its auspices – its own special interests. Moreover, given the establishment of such groups (whether specialist organizations such as the Community Health Councils, or general bodies such as the Consumers' Association, or organizations with a brief as extensive and elastic as the Citizens' Advice Bureaux), the scope for infiltration and take-over by sectarian interests is considerable (Seldon, 1994 [3], pp. 80–3, 'Best Friends of Shoppers: *Which?* or Competition?', and *passim*). It would be interesting, for example, to see some systematic critical research undertaken on some of the recently established 'Green' pressure groups and food quality protection groups (Whelan, 1989).

Again, despite criticisms in the ACHC report of the methodologies of quality assurance currently being adopted in the reformed NHS, their own methods hardly inspire one with overflowing confidence. Thus they say (p. 1, my emphasis):

Since 1979 over 1000 CHC surveys have been completed, the vast majority of which are independent assessments of the quality of service being provided in local hospitals, clinics and family practitioner services and how these services meet the expectations of the users of those services. *CHC research is not and does not have to be of the same sophistication as academic papers or surveys produced with all the resources of commercial companies.* It has to be good enough for its purpose....

Practical objectives and modesty of ambition such as this may seem attractive, but they can serve terribly easily as a cover for partisan manipulation of the evidence and political distortion of the truth. Another example, a 1993 report by the National Consumer Council called inauspiciously 'Paying the Price: a Consumer View of Water, Gas, Electricity and Telephone Regulation', represents the epitome of counter-productive consumerist naïveté. Absurdly, given the unregenerate line of opposition to Government policies which it adopts, it was published by HMSO.

It demands comprehensive, intrusive controls which would return the utilities to the condition of paralysed bureaucracy from which privatization was supposed to rescue them. It proposes a high-security regulatory regime which is an impertinent and ignorant challenge to the sensible proposition neatly and persuasively put by Michael Howard as Secretary of State for Trade and Industry: 'Competition is all the protection the consumer needs.' Indeed, 'Paying the Price' explicitly argues *against* introducing competition, preferring instead reliance on bureaucratic controls. Thus (p. 132):

> The regulators should, in our view, carry out proper cost/benefit analyses of the effects of introducing competition into these services. These analyses must include the implications for domestic consumers. We also need much more information from the regulators about how competition will work in practice and what it will mean for consumer protection.

The report also, as one would anticipate, grossly over-emphasizes the significance of so-called 'social policy', devoting a whole chapter to the topic, and exaggerates absurdly the numbers of those who 'cannot afford' these 'essential services'. The following paragraph (p. 141) is typical of the consumer lobbyists' fussily ignorant approach to business in general, and of their tendency to assume that markets and prices are inherently suspect. The authors' neurotic hankering for wartime planning and controls is palpable:

It is very evident from the experience of price regulation so far that it is very much more complicated than was envisaged when these industries were privatized. The thorny questions relating to social, health, and energy policy issues which are all inevitably linked to the provision of these essential household services go beyond the regulators' limited terms of reference.

How they long for the regulators' brief to be extended, and for the newly commercial enterprises to be de-commercialized! Yet all their anxieties and the whole complex tissue of their proposals for elaborated state regulation and political interference are postulated on trivial price rises occasioning little real concern to the public. A national survey, commissioned by the authors themselves at the taxpayers' expense from MORI, reveals an increase of only 9 per cent since their previous study in the number of people concerned about water prices, while there has been 'little change in people's views about gas and electricity prices since 1990' (p. 2)!

Consumerism and its correlative of extended regulation certainly cannot provide an alternative to markets, competition and consumer sovereignty. It may offer a useful complement, but that is the best that can be hoped for, and consumer organizations themselves need policing by competition. Regulation is better handled with the light and intelligent touch recommended in Colin Robinson and his associates' *Regulating the Utilities: the Way Forward* (1994) than the ham-handed, pseudo-democratic bureaucracy of the consumer movement.

Consumer organizations are unlikely, then, even in the form of a powerfully organized consumer movement such as Ralph Nader has sought to develop in the United States, to provide better than a very modest antidote to the penalties and pains inflicted on consumers by collectivist provision. The only genuine alternative is provided by real markets, with the state's enlarged domain rolled back, monopoly broken, and consumer sovereignty enthroned by permanent struggle between competing suppliers.

Despite the continuing prejudice of social scientists, the grounds for further enlarging the sphere of competitive markets are many and powerful. Certainly they have been acknowledged in Poland, Hungary, and most parts of the former Soviet Union, even if they sadly continue to be denied and traduced in the liberal democracies by academics, journalists and trade union leaders, by politicians in all parties and even by businessmen. Thus, to judge by reactions reported in the press, a recent vigorous address (1990) to the Institute of Directors by its then Director General, Peter Morgan, seems to have been altogether too resolutely enthusiastic in its commitment to the Enterprise Culture for some of his business colleagues!

In a further address on the topic of 'The Morality of Wealth Creation' (1991), Morgan provides a persuasive critique of the anti-capitalist prejudice which still prevails in Britain, explaining cogently why competition is necessary, addressing intelligently the ethical issues involved in business, and illustrating perfectly, without even trying, the spirit of creative innovation which our public services so much lack.

Arguments for the Market

The main arguments supporting the role of markets can be summarized in the following terms (Marsland, 1988):

- Consumer *tastes and needs vary* over a wide range and unpredictably. Only markets, that is to say mechanisms specifically answerable to consumer demand, can address this variety effectively (Friedman and Friedman, 1980).
- Consumer tastes and needs are subject to rapid *unpredictable change*. Only markets can adjust with reliable rapidity to such change.
- Entrepreneurs and technologists, in the social field as much as in any other, tend – unless they are prevented – to produce *innovations and improvements*. Only a market answerable to consumer preferences allows reliably for effective testing and implementation of such improvements (Diebold, 1987).
- Only those forms of organization of the production of goods and services which are oriented to consumer preferences and subject to consumer sovereignty are likely, through competition, to *minimize costs and prices* (Seldon, 1990).
- Only supplier organizations which are consumer-oriented are likely, again as a result of competition and the effects of prices, to *reduce waste and, more generally, to maximize efficiency.*
- Only consumer sovereignty is capable of determining *optimum levels of investment and expenditure.* In its absence, investment and other expenditure is likely to be artificially and damagingly either held down, as in health care, or exaggerated, as perhaps in education (Hayek, 1982).
- Only consumer sovereignty within a competitive market *prevents the need for excessive and dangerous political controls*, ramifying regulatory bureaucracy, and rationing in one form or another.
- Only organizations which are answerable to competitive markets and consumer choice are capable of *resisting excessive trade union wage demands* (Marsland, 1991[4]; McKinstry, 1995).

These arguments in favour of the market and competition – by comparison with centrally planned administrative systems – as the best source of
protection for the interests of consumers apply as cogently to what we
have come to call 'welfare' as to other types of goods and services.

Markets for Welfare

There is no reason at all in principle, and none that is evident in practice
either, why – except in relation to a tiny proportion of the population,
certainly less than 10 per cent in normal circumstances – the whole range
of welfare services should not be provided through the market, with
clients, patients and users transformed into paying customers and genuine
consumers. Education, health care, community care, housing, pensions,
income support, transport, cultural facilities and the rest could perfectly
easily be transferred out of the hands of the state and administered far
more efficiently by market and quasi-market voluntary institutions (Green,
1991).

Indeed, what the ongoing revolution in the old socialist world seems to
suggest is that the the concept of the 'consumer' should be restricted to
situations where:

1. There is genuine choice between two or more alternative suppliers;
2. Suppliers are competing in a market which is genuinely free; and
3. Competition in terms of price and quality is measured by profit and
   loss, success and failure, on the part of suppliers.

Otherwise what we get is – no bread, no sausages, no cars, no health care
worth the name, and no consumers: just sullen, dissatisfied subjects of
bureaucratic monopoly machinery. Neither the concept of the 'subject',
nor even the concept of the 'citizen' can be stretched to do the cultural
construction work of the concept of the 'consumer'. *The concept itself
implies and necessarily entails markets and competition.*

There is a telling and interesting passage in Herbert Spencer's analysis
of 'the relief of the poor' (1893) which graphically illustrates the absurdities and incompetencies of attempts to avoid the beneficent and efficient
services of the market. He takes, as he often does, a hard case, that of
health care (pp. 385–6, my emphases):

> Nor is it otherwise with institutions thought by most people to be indis-
> putably beneficial – hospitals and dispensaries. The first significant fact
> is that 30% of the people of London are frequenters of them; and the
> largeness of this proportion makes it clear that most of them, not to be

ranked as indigent, are able to pay their doctors. Gratis medical relief tends to pauperize in more definite ways. The out-patients begin by getting physic and presently get food; and the system 'leads them afterwards openly to solicit pecuniary aid'. This vitiating effect is proved by the fact that during the 40 years from 1830 to 1869, *the increase in the number of hospital patients has been five times greater than the increase of population*; and as there has not been more disease, the implication is obvious. Moreover the promise of advice for nothing attracts the mean-spirited to the extent that 'the poor are now being gradually ousted out of the consulting room by well-to-do persons'. People of several hundreds a year, even up to a thousand, apply as out-patients, going in disguise: *20% of the out-patients in one large hospital having 'given false addresses' for the purpose of concealing their identity*. Swarming as patients thus do, it results that each gets but little attention: a minute being the average for each, sometimes diminished to forty-five seconds – thus those for whom the gratis advice is intended get but little. Often 'the assistance given is merely nominal'; and 'is both a a deception on the public and a fraud upon the poor'. These gratuitous medical benefits, such as they are 'are conferred chiefly by the members of the unpaid professional staffs' of these charities. Some of them prescribe at the rate of 318 patients in three hours and twenty minutes – a process sufficiently exhausting for men already hard worked in their private practice, and sufficiently disheartening to men with little private practice, who thus give without payment aid which otherwise they would get payment for, very much needed by them. So that the £600,000 a year of the metropolitan hospitals, which, if the annual value of the lands and buildings occupied were added, would reach very nearly a million, has largely the effect of *demoralizing the patients, taking medical care from those it was intended for, and giving it to those for whom it was not, and obliging many impecunious doctors and surgeons to work for nothing.*

Thus free provision produces welfare dependency; it allows the poorer and more needy to be driven out by the greedy well-to-do; it squanders the scarce skills of the professionals involved; and it provides at best a second-rate service which ignores almost entirely the real needs and varied preferences of its clients.

These same weaknesses, identified a hundred years ago by Spencer, continue as viciously in the NHS today, as Green (1985), Gammon (1987) and Redwood (1988), among others, have demonstrated. Without genuine markets, serious competition, prices which signal costs accurately, and active, choosing customers – which is to say without consumers *tout court* – these deficiencies cannot be overcome (Whitney, 1988). Nor will the equivalent weaknesses in our other collectivized services be overcome without similar radical reform. Only markets can provide effectively for the range and ambition of human wants and needs (Berger, 1987; Gilder, 1984).

The Market and the State

Reporting on a visit to the planners' paradise not long before it was lost to ruin and chaos, Ralph Harris (1990) remarked on the contrast between market and state provision thus:

> It was a strange, almost eerie sensation to return from a week of meetings in Moscow and Leningrad where all the economists I met were enthusiastic about Mrs Thatcher's philosophy and policies only to arrive in London where most papers seemed to be preparing her political obituaries. Of course, my new-found Russian friends do not have to pay the poll tax or 15% on mortgages! Instead they have savoured the full impact of state socialism, including appalling housing conditions (with one room for a family of four sharing kitchen and bathroom), poor public services, shortages of consumer goods, endless queues for essential supplies, and periodic rationing alternating with the total absence of such household goods as soap.
>
> True, inflation is hardly openly admitted in the USSR. But when price-controlled meat, vegetables, and other necessaries are not available, housewives have to go to the free market, where supplies are abundant at prices that are much higher – due not to capitalist exploitation but to the absence of subsidies that keep down the prices of non-existent goods in the drably ubiquitous state shops.

Meanwhile, back in Britain, he found:

> widespread discontent, principally over schools and the National Health service. Yet the undoubted shortcomings of both these pillars of the Welfare State owe nothing to market forces. Objective analysis points the opposite way. The provision of state education and medical care reflects all the worst features of the same nationalization which Government apologists have never ceased denouncing in telephones, shipyards, airlines, motor cars, steel, gas, even water and electricity.

He might also have mentioned what John Tusa, presenting a programme about Prague (BBC2, 28 May 1994) called in a memorable phrase 'those special characteristics of socialist service – surliness and resentment'. In every case, state provision is subject to the failings associated with monopoly supply: politicized control, financial laxity leading to over-manning, chauvinist trade unions, national wage-setting, inadequate and misdirected investment, and almost total indifference to consumer choice and convenience (Eberstadt, 1989; Matthews, 1987).

Arguments against the Market

Three distinct sorts of arguments are typically used by those proponents of the Welfare State who, while acknowledging the benefits of consumer sovereignty, seek to ignore the wisdom of Lord Harris's analysis, and to preserve 'welfare' from the supposedly negative impacts in this sphere uniquely of market forces.

First, it is argued that, while market provision may be appropriate for many, it is bound to be inadequate and unfair in relation to the poor and deprived, or to lower income groups generally (Wicks, 1987).

Second, it is argued that 'two-tier systems' – with the market providing for a prosperous majority and the State providing special schemes for the minority excluded from the market as a result of low income – must necessarily result in damaging stigma attaching to the latter (Gough, 1979).

And third, it is argued that the Welfare State is not and should not be intended merely to 'provide services', and that libertarian welfare policies such as those proposed here would prevent the attainment of the new levels of 'justice', 'equality', or 'citizenship' which the Welfare State is properly in the business of initiating (Lee and Raban, 1988).

The first of these arguments is an expression of the long-standing liberal plea on behalf of 'the poor', for whom it presumes market mechanisms cannot adequately cater (Le Grand, 1991). This argument has been a major source of support throughout this century for those intent on supplanting the market by state organizations. I find it difficult to conceive how it has ever managed to win the slightest credibility. After all, if it were suggested that cars or clothes or food should be removed from the market and supplied by the state because of income differences, the idea would be regarded as absurd and rejected out of hand even by socialists. Yet many besides socialists apparently accept the same argument unhesitatingly in relation to libraries, hospitals and schooling.

There are two distinct sorts of answers to this argument. First, to the extent that it may be judged politically that some groups are inequitably disadvantaged in economic terms, their situation is likely to be much more effectively remedied, with less damaging effects on them, on the economy, and on the population as a whole, by fiscal means, or more generally by monetary transfers, than by state take-over. In Eamonn Butler's words (1994, p. 14): 'If a minority of the population were too poor to afford proper food, we would not think of setting up state kitchens to provide a free but nourishing standard menu for us all; so why provide free healthcare, or free education?'

Secondly, historical analysis reveals increasingly persuasively that much larger proportions of the so-called poor are capable of taking advantage of market systems than apologists for paternalist state control have generally claimed. Thus, for example, E. G. West (1970) has demonstrated that large numbers of ordinary people, including the poorest, were successfully and contentedly paying for their children's education before the Forster Act of 1870 killed off private educational development in Britain for all except the wealthy.

Again, David Green (1985) has shown that a combination of market and mutual systems was providing health care for the poor at least as good as the nationalized Health Service has managed since, until doctors noticed the syndicalist advantages to themselves of monopoly control. And again, John Benson (1983) provides in his study of 'penny capitalists' a vivid account of the wide range of personal and financial services used routinely by the poor in nineteenth-century Britain.

The 'Two-tier' Calumny

The second argument for resisting the natural extension of markets into spheres reserved still in Britain and other welfare state societies for state mercantilism urges the damaging effects of two-tier systems, with the prosperous taking advantage of private sector provision, and the minority poor restricted to inadequate public services. There is certainly some validity to this argument, as is evidenced by the fact that people of all sorts do opt out of public provision in education, health care and housing whenever they can afford it, even at the cost of paying twice over – once in fees, and a second time in taxes. However, to that extent it collapses into the previous argument, about income differences and their impact on access. It is answerable in the same terms.

For if second-tier provision is inherently or generally inadequate, it is manifestly preferable to shift as rapidly as possible to first-tier provision for all through the market, with those on lower incomes assisted in taking advantage of it by monetary rather than administrative measures. After all, no one to my knowledge has complained about 'private squalor and public affluence', and there is no evidently plausible argument, except in terms of political dogma, for a movement in the opposite direction – with two-tier systems unified by outlawing entirely all market provision.

Moreover, there may be positive advantages in the apparent weaknesses identified by opponents of two-tier systems. Provided the lower quality public provision is small in scale compared with the totality – in the proportion we find in housing in Britain, for example, of 30/70 or better, rather than in education where it is 90/10 – then the dissatisfaction and stigma associated with public provision can serve as a dynamic motivator for the aspirations of even the poorest. Just this effect seems to be common in the United States and especially in Switzerland, where the statist and collectivist assumptions of welfarism are relatively weak and commitment to the work ethic and to self-reliance is particularly strongly entrenched in the national psyche (Segalman and Marsland, 1989).

Where the tilt is in the other direction, however, the psychological effect is also in the contrary direction, gradually reducing incentives and motivation for self-help and progress on the part of consumers, and destroying all commitment to standards of excellence on the part of producers. This seems to be the main lesson we should learn from the failure of Eastern European socialism (Conquest, 1980 and 1986; Goldman, 1983).

'Idealists' against the Market

The third argument commonly deployed against extension of the market into the welfare sphere acknowledges in principle that welfare services, like others, *could* be provided entirely effectively by market and other non-state mechanisms. Its supporters – in Britain most notably Richard Titmuss – insist, however, that this is not the point. It is, they argue, a criterion of a decent, civilized society that such services are rights rather than mere commodities and are provided not merely adequately but equally for all.

The case is thus transformed from an economic and sociological argument to a philosophical debate. As such it has been answered more than adequately in my judgement by critics of socialism such as Hayek and Nozick and by historians of socialism such as Kolakowski and Conquest. The onus of proof now rests with socialists, who currently show no great ability to discharge it (Commission on Social Justice, 1994, which I examine in Chapter 10 below).

No doubt socialists will remain unpersuaded, but that is not my concern here. If the only remaining defence of State monopoly welfare provision rests entirely on a commitment to socialism, it is not one which need much concern rational analysts of welfare provision as such, even if they happen to be socialists. Nor need it concern democratic politicians, provided they are neither knaves nor fools. If there is not a better argument for resisting the disestablishment of state welfare than socialism's need for it, then – given the evidence about the inevitable deficiencies of monopoly provision of any goods or services, and the manifest incapacity of state welfare to answer consumer needs – so much the worse for socialism. There is real scope for a genuinely 'New Labour' party here.

Natural Monopolies and the 'Public Good'

Sometimes exponents of this third argument seek, illogically, to strengthen it by linking it to distinct arguments in terms of 'public goods' and 'natural monopolies'. The illogicality of this step should be evident. Both the public-good argument and the natural monopoly argument presuppose market failure. Our third argument against marketizing welfare – the idealizing case of Titmuss – presumes on the contrary that effective welfare markets are feasible, but that they are none the less wrong and unacceptable because welfare simply ought not, *qua* welfare, to be involved in market relations at all.

Thus these further arguments, in terms of public good and natural monopoly – both of them, be it noted, general economic arguments rather than arguments about welfare specifically – stand or fall by themselves and should be addressed separately from any consideration of welfare as such. Both arguments are of long standing, but they are much weaker than is commonly acknowledged. Cowen and his associates (1992) and Cheung (1981) have separately disposed of the public-good argument pretty conclusively.

The argument has tended to be considered in theoretical and abstract terms, with inferences about the supposed 'third party effects' of private bargains, about the presumed 'social costs' of individual choices, and about alleged 'externalities' drawn largely deductively rather than on the basis of empirical evidence. As Arthur Seldon (1994 [3], pp. 314–21) has shown, the grounds used by exponents of the public-good argument for determining social costs and externalities are typically vague and subject to easy political manipulation. They might as easily be used to justify the maintenance of slavery and the restoration of public executions as the continuance of free public libraries and the introduction of comprehensive, taxpayer-financed child care. The only coherent grounds for tolerating state monopolies in such limited spheres as government itself, defence and criminal justice are political rather than economic in nature. Even in these sectors, Seldon argues, we pay a heavy price in terms of economic inefficiency for the privilege of avoiding social conflict. The case against extensions of the public-good argument such as might provide intellectual backing for supporters of comprehensive state welfare is evident in the fashionable sphere of environmental problems.

Faced with the global, regional and local threats to the environment occasioned by the massive historical and international forces of industrialization, population growth and urbanization, the Green Movement is deploying arguments in terms of the public good to support substantial extensions of state control and bureaucratic regulation (Whelan, 1989). In the light of experience in the USSR, graphically laid out as long ago as 1972 in Goldman's *The Spoils of Progress*, these arguments should be resisted. For state control more comprehensively formidable than could conceivably be tolerated in democratic societies, and more confidently justified in terms of arguments for the public good than even our most avid supporters of state welfare can manage, did not reduce environmental problems one whit.

On the contrary: by eliminating the innovative power of the market and its responsiveness to consumers' rising expectations, by sabotaging the moderating effects on industrialists of competition and of an independent legal system capable of challenging the state, by subjugating to state control the independent initiatives of individual citizens and voluntary pressure groups, and by preventing the testing of environmental claims in free media, socialist planning – speciously justified by appeals to public-good arguments – delivered not an environmental paradise, but the nearest approximation to an environmental hell on earth that humanity has yet devised.

We should be vigilant in ensuring that environmentalists' claims are not exaggerated or even wholly fallacious. We should be circumspect in the extreme about allowing genuine anxieties about environmental damage to be used as an excuse for yielding yet more control to the local and national state and to international bureaucrats, however seemingly benevolent. We should instead bend the institutions we know we can trust – the market, the law, science and open debate, and their competitive interaction – to addressing these new environmental problems with the same realistic effectiveness they have demonstrated in other spheres.

The political 'Greens' seek to undermine our confidence in the established institutions of a free society by reliance on exaggerated claims which are not easily challenged in the short term, and by specious appeals to a fictitious public interest supposedly threatened by personal choices. If the solutions they prescribe require substantial further reductions in our freedom and enormously increased state control, we should be thoroughly sceptical.

The Green Movement is now the primary arena for the anti-democratic activities of the extreme left world-wide. 'Friends of the Earth' they may be, but even that remains to be demonstrated, and enemies of Britain and of other free societies they certainly seem to be. Their equivalents in the international campaign for entrenching and expanding collectivist state welfare should be resisted no less vigorously. The argument in terms of purported conflict between individual choice and open competition on the one side and state control and public good on the other is equally fallacious in both spheres.

Natural Monopolies?

A useful arena for rational critique of the second argument, with its appeal to the concept of 'natural monopolies', is provided by a recent defence of public ownership by Hutton (1995). On the one hand he admits that 'the wholesale nationalization implied by Labour's Clause IV and western communist parties was absurd and a menace to economic and political freedom'. On the other hand he insists, following and citing Tawney, Crosland and other supporters (including Conservatives such as Harold Macmillan) of the so-called mixed economy, that:

> Where there were natural monopolies – such as railways or water – there had been enough failed attempts at regulation to know that public ownership was the only way of reconciling the logic of monopoly with public interest. And who in 1995 is prepared to argue that they were completely wrong?

Using the topical example of rail privatization, he argues that such self-evidently natural monopolies should be brought into public ownership as the only way of ensuring effective and equitable operation. 'Private ownership and the price mechanism', he suggests, 'cannot capture all the benefits not just to individual rail users but for everybody else of having a functioning transport system.'

At the same time he interprets public ownership thus justified in terms of efficiency and equity as serving in addition as a symbol, as it were, of commitment to progressive ideals and a marker of a modernizing, progressive government's insistence on keeping the market within bounds. So confident is he of the validity of his analysis that he actually proposes that the Labour Party should announce to the investment funds its definite intention of re-nationalizing the railways in order thereby to prevent privatization in the first place.

The argument turns first on whether there are such things as natural monopolies, and on whether, if there are, they can be consensually or reliably identified, and secondly on judgements about the optimum strategy for dealing with near-monopolies.

On the first issue there is surely considerable room for doubt. The strong programmes of comprehensive nationalization which Hutton rejects out of hand were themselves justified by their supporters in terms of the supposedly natural and inevitable inclination of capitalism towards monopoly. This long-fashionable judgement has proved wholly mistaken. As a result, competitive markets are being introduced throughout the socialist world. Why should we imagine that Hutton is any more likely to be correct in his assumption that railways and water are natural monopolies, and as such immune to competitive structuring? Why should we believe his relatively moderate diagnosis rather than the analyses of rather bolder supporters of the mixed economy, for whom the Post Office, the other privatized utilities, and some key manufacturing industries such as the mines and defence are equally self-evidently natural monopolies, ripe for incorporation into public ownership as soon as a sufficiently progressive government is at hand to do it?

How, moreover, can we assume other than that, on his analysis, the same argument for public ownership applies *a fortiori* to the whole welfare sector? Yet, as we have seen, the arguments for state monopoly welfare are weak in the extreme. There simply *are* no natural monopolies. There are a few politically essential monopolies, notably law making, law enforcement and defence. But beyond and outside this narrow realm there is neither in principle nor in practice any sufficient reason for organizing things other than competitively.

Furthermore, where temporarily monopolistic tendencies are found, the case for much stronger trust-busting mechanisms than we have ever yet tried in Britain remains much stronger than Hutton allows. Given all the demonstrated deficiencies of nationalization or of public ownership in any form, even an inadequate private market is preferable, provided that an appropriate regulatory regime is deployed toughly.

In short, none of the commonly used arguments for resisting the marketization of welfare is telling. Neither income differences, nor the supposed dangers of market tiering, nor the philosophical claims of idealistic principle, nor the demands of the public good, nor the threat of natural monopolies provide either singly or in combination any sufficient reason for avoiding or postponing liberal reform of the Welfare State.

Socialism and Markets

Naturally, market provision of welfare services, as with market supply of other goods and services, is unequal. What matters for this analysis, however, and what matters most to all except to fundamentalist egalitarians, is that it appears to be the only mechanism capable of answering reliably, effectively and at reasonable cost, consumer needs in all their variety.

Only in the market is the consumer sovereign and protected from abuse by monopoly exploitation. This is no less true in relation to welfare than to other goods and service. If, from time to time, this leaves some consumers too much disadvantaged in terms of disposable income to take full advantage of the market and of their normal rights as consumers, then this is a case not for limiting the market's operations, but in the short term for adjusting the tax and benefit system, and in the longer term for pressing ahead with economic policies designed to secure economic growth and increased prosperity.

In recent years, even diehard socialists have apparently experienced Pauline conversions in large numbers in relation to the role of markets. *Market Socialism*, edited by Julian Le Grand and Saul Estrin (1989), is just one influential instance of the growing tendency for socialist academics to acknowledge, after decades of indignant denial, the efficiency of markets and the benefits of consumer sovereignty. Their commitment to markets, even in the sphere of welfare, is indicated plainly by their support for vouchers as a means of allowing consumers a real choice in education and health care. That theirs is not an unusual or eccentric conversion is indicated by a growing tolerance for markets – appropriately 'managed', of course – among social scientists, and especially by the current policy upheavals in the 'New' Labour Party.

Just how powerfully the pressure of dissatisfaction with state services is being felt is indicated by the urgency with which, never mind academics, even local councils – currently havens of unresponsive bureaucracy – are turning their attention to 'customer care'. According to a report by Bill Taylor (*Sunday Times*, 19 August, 1990):

> A rapidly growing number of councils are viewing quality of service as a key strategic issue for the 1990s. This for many people may seem a remarkable turnaround, for local councils have in the past tended to focus on the concept of client, not of customer. This is an important distinction, because it moves away from a take-it-or-leave-it standard level of service to one that seeks to tailor services to the requirements of both individuals and local communities.

This is at least a start in the right direction, as are similar customer-focused initiatives in the NHS, in the education system, and in the public services generally. However, if my overall analysis in this chapter is correct, bureaucratic perestroika is likely to prove insufficient and, in the last resort, impossible. A monopoly bureaucracy simply cannot 'incorporate the marketing and customer-relations skills that are used by quality-oriented companies such as M and S' (ibid.).

Only competitive markets provide the incentives and sanctions which guarantee that producers and suppliers have no choice – except bankruptcy – but to attend to consumers' wishes. Only competitive markets can reach the parts which state machinery necessarily, in its very nature, fails so much as even to notice. If the multifarious services we have been schooled to classify as 'welfare' are to be provided efficiently, without excessive bureaucracy, at a reasonable cost, and in ways which successfully answer people's varied needs and tastes, only real markets will bring it off.

Prejudice against Markets in Welfare

There remains, none the less, in the most surprising quarters, considerable prejudice against private sector provision of welfare. A revealing example was afforded by my own experience of working as a consultant in Taiwan in the mid-1980s (Wiseman and Marsland, 1985), where, as part of a research project for the Government, we were asked to examine the island republic's training and employment services.

We found in the official report which provided our starting point numerous negative references to the private sector. For example, it claimed that 'private employment agencies are in a state of chaos', and argued that while 'the existence of private employment services is still worthwhile', on the other hand 'the [state] authority should take them under the national employment service system, and give them technical assistance to keep them normal'. No doubt the report's authors meant by that insouciant 'normal' nothing more sinister than 'up to standard'. In the context, however, one could not help but be reminded of the process of 'normalization' in post-1968 Czechoslovakia, with all its ghastly connotations of central control, state policing and enforced conformity.

The report was similarly dismissive about voluntary, non-governmental efforts, which in the sphere of training were described, in a more than somewhat cavalier fashion, as short of man-power and lacking in professional expertise. We were not in a position to challenge the validity of these or other such criticisms of the independent sector decisively, but we had sufficient evidence to be sceptical. We advised the Government that the approach taken in its report, in relation to other spheres of welfare as well as employment and training, could be dangerous.

First, we suggested that given constraints on public expenditure, it hardly seemed sensible to squander resources on taking over what were allegedly inefficient private agencies. Better to invest positively in improving government agencies, and let the private sector sink or swim as a result of natural competitive forces. If they were indeed inefficient, they would soon be bankrupt.

Secondly, however, we argued that it was in the Government's interest to have a flourishing private sector in employment and training services, operating in co-operation *and* in competition with state agencies. This would provide both variability, in itself to be positively valued in a free society, and competition, which would keep both sectors up to the mark.

Our third argument addressed the evident statist prejudices of the report directly. The more services are provided in the private sector, we argued, the more money would be saved for essentials: defence, law and order, social assistance and some parts of education in particular. The more that unnecessary state expenditure could be restricted, the greater the likelihood of containing inflation and unemployment, and therefore of maintaining economic growth and prosperity. The appropriate general principle in a free society, we found ourselves having to remind the leaders even of this supposed haven of unfettered capitalism, was 'if the market can do it, the state should keep out'.

In the light of these arguments, we advised the authorities that they should endeavour to improve the quality of private training and employment agencies. They should institute necessary registration, licensing and inspection systems, certainly, but beyond that they should positively encourage private agencies to succeed and to manage without state help or interference. There was no reason at all that we could identify why Chinese entrepreneurial skills, triumphantly successful already in manufacture and trade, should not serve the Republic equally effectively in training, job placement and for that matter every other sphere of welfare.

The Taiwanese Government Report which we criticized was not unique in – nor by any means the worst example of – a fundamental confusion about the modernization of public services arising out of prejudice against the market. Consider the diagram opposite.

In relation to this diagram, presumably professionalism, in the sense of appropriate expertise, skills and intelligent, adaptive organization, is generally positively valued. Presumably bureaucracy, in the sense of rigid, large-scale organizations staffed by rule-bound personnel, is to be nega-

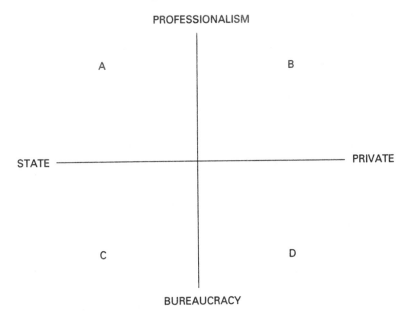

Fig. 7.1   A typology of organizations

tively valued. Neither state organization nor private enterprise need in principle be valued other than neutrally: both are needed, with a general tendency none the less in free societies for preferring the latter to the former, other things being equal.

There seemed to us to be some danger in the report on employment and training that attempts to shift services and programmes towards a more modernized, better administered condition at A or B in fact tended to push things, by an elision of logic, towards C. In our view, even primitively underdeveloped conditions such as Taiwan has long outgrown provide no adequate justification for multiplying instances of category C. Videlicet the former USSR, and Wilhelm Roepke's analysis (1992) of what he calls the Nazi and Communist collectivist malformations of economics.

As between A and B, there is certainly in every society a need for both. I would be immensely surprised, however, if the economic conditions and broad thrust of social policy in Taiwan, let alone the UK, did not favour B over A in the field of welfare as much as any other. Beware those who advise that modern welfare presupposes state professionalism. It drifts away all too easily from professionalism into state bureaucratic welfare, which is, alas, a contradiction in terms.

The Role of Markets in Society: Neglect and Misunderstanding

Reviewing Keat *et al.*'s *The Authority of the Consumer* (1993) in the official journal of the British Sociological Association, David Chaney (1994) claims that 'Although consumerism and consumer culture are necessarily key themes in the sociology of modernity, they have been relatively neglected.' While accurate and timely, this judgement seems to me a considerable understatement. Modern sociology has grossly neglected and almost wholly misunderstood the role of markets, consumption, consumers, sales and shops in free societies, as I have shown in Chapter 5 ('On Industry, the Market, and Enterprise') of my book *Seeds of Bankruptcy* (Marsland, 1988). This grave flaw has been worsened rather than corrected by the recent flood of books by sociologists prompted by their dawning realization – after ten years of Thatcherism – that the market has triumphed over the plan. Despite overdue attention to the market and consumption by Keat, Warde (1994), Giddens (1991), Bauman (1988), Beck (1992) and others, including analysis of the potential market in welfare specifically (Burrows and Loader, 1994), the condition of academic analysis of the market remains primitive and negative.

This is just too bad for social scientists, since in the meantime the intensity of market relations and the pitch of competition – globally and domestically, in relation to welfare services as much as in other sectors – has been rapidly increasing. The market simply will not be bucked, and the advantages of competition for consumers cannot be denied or prevented. Those individuals, organizations and nations which stubbornly opt to stand out against this flooding tide of competition will lose out all round. Tom Peters (1993) has grasped better than most writers the severity of the demands we shall all have to make of each other and of ourselves: 'In short, there is no place to hide. To survive economically as individuals and as a society, we have little choice but to apply the perform-or-else dogma to everyone and every enterprise.'

In the sphere of welfare, no less than in industry and commerce, competition is the order of the day. We expect the advantages it brings in the way of efficiency, innovation, flexibility and quality, and we must pay the price a competitive world inevitably exacts in terms of enterprising initiative and courageous self-reliance (Gilder, 1988). The connections between welfare spending, taxes and competition are brought out graphically by Norman Macrae (1994):

> All successful countries will need vastly to reduce government expenditure, more moderately cut taxes... and bring back more family-based

entrepreneurialism and values. If you doubt that, note how savagely last week Sweden's newly re-elected and rather Blairite Social Democrat government had to slash the land's old welfare state to keep its budget deficit below 13% of GDP and unemployment below 12% of the potential labour force... As Sweden flees from its failed welfare state, one of its newspapers comments: 'We are having to move care of our old from socialist bureaucracy to conservative family love.'

There really is no alternative to the market. History is littered, in Brigitte Berger's words (1991) with 'failed schemes of forced economic growth through enormous state enterprises'. Achieving and sustaining prosperity depends entirely on that 'culture of entrepreneurship' which provides the title of her important book. This law applies as much in the sphere of welfare as in industry and commerce. Effective welfare provision is as unlikely as economic growth in the absence of a free market, competitive choice and entrepreneurial innovation.

Norman Barry (1990, p. 128) provides a useful formulation of what a more individualistic welfare system might look like. Although he is sceptical in the extreme that welfare reform can be successful, going so far, indeed, as to claim – quite implausibly as it seems to me – that 'it is fanciful to suppose that there will be substantial changes in the welfare systems in the UK or USA', his sketch of a possible liberal welfare future is none the less a helpful bridge between the analysis in this chapter of the benefits of market systems and the detailed account in Chapter 8 following of plans for wholesale reform. Thus he suggests that:

> the growing recognition that well-being is an individual phenomenon which is not necessarily advanced by a state apparatus that is as sensitive to electoral pressure as it is to the demands of a rational welfare ethic indicates that the times are propitious for a fundamental reexamination of the whole issue. The return of education, health, pensions and so on, to individuals through various methods of empowerment, such as the voucher scheme, mark the beginnings of a new consensus. The decentralization of welfare services to smaller political units would be a more feasible way of advancing the moral claims and the attendant social obligations associated with communitarian and citizenship theories than is the method of national legislation. Again, the re-activation of a genuine insurance principle for such things as retirement pensions would prevent the burdening of future generations with debt.

For reasons less than compellingly specified, Barry claims that such eminently sensible reforms of the welfare system as these are 'not likely to happen'. I think he is wrong. I turn in the next chapter to an attempt at sharpening up and detailing a welfare reform programme, and at explaining why it is necessary and how it can be achieved.

In concluding my effort in this chapter to explain the benefits of markets and competition, I must stress that if liberal reform of welfare is to be successful, we shall need to act boldly and to keep our nerve, Markets are not for the neurotically insecure, as recent hysterical reactions in the media and in Parliament to the success, and to the concomitants of success, of the privatized utilities suggest.

In the face of substantial but quite proper and entirely justified salary increases awarded to senior executives of British Gas – designed appropriately to reward strategic leadership in a competitive environment, and systematic down-sizing of the labour force, intended to reduce unnecessary costs – there was a sudden spasm of envious guilt among our chattering classes during the early weeks of 1995. As often in Britain, they got more attention than they deserve. Such episodes will recur as marketization progresses, and we need to be armed to address them. Fortunately, a very good answer to the panic, which can serve usefully for future instances, was provided by an editorial in the journal *Business Money* (January 1995). Salaries of company executives, the editor reminds us, are a matter for the elected Board. Government interference is a contradiction of free enterprise. We must also keep in mind, he suggests, the cultural transformation and the improved efficiency which privatization assures:

> the ludicrous notion that the utilities operated for the benefit of the nation while under public control is one of the recurring myths to resurface on such occasions. The fact that they were over-manned, featherbedded, thought they existed for the benefit of the workforce, and, above all else, received huge subsidies from the taxpayer is too easily overlooked...

Every word of this analysis is true *a fortiori* in relation to the agencies of state welfare. We shall need to be as clear and tough as *Business Money* about *their* operations if, Norman Barry's scepticism notwithstanding, reform of the Welfare State is to be carried through successfully to the point where, in Arthur Seldon's words (1994), 'the British will be one nation of consumers in buyers' markets in welfare'.

8 Towards the Disestablishment of State Welfare: A Free Market in Real Welfare

'The expectation that society, the state, the government... will look after our problems tricks us into abdicating from self-reliance and social responsibility' (David Marsland, 1989).
Assess this New Right perspective in terms of what you know about the Welfare State.

University of Oxford Advanced Level Sociology Examination 1992.

The modest celebrity occasioned by figuring in an examination paper alongside Titmuss, Townsend, Halsey or Donnison is flattering. Consider, however, its real meaning and its implications.

First, it is a rare and token appearance compared with regular stardom for the left in such settings. Second, I am labelled explicitly as belonging to some curious political faction – whereas committed, and even fanatical, socialists are allowed political anonymity. Even scholars (naming no names) who belong to real extremist factions of the left for whom public support can be counted on the fingers of one hand are referred to in examination papers and textbooks simply as 'sociologists' or 'social policy analysts'. Third, the correct, high-scoring answer to the question is transparently clear: 'it is a right-wing over-simplification or exaggeration or error which fails to take account of poverty and deprivation and equity, etcetera'. In short, the question is a set-up which trades disingenuously on orthodox assumptions and routine prejudice about welfare. The orthodoxy is strong. The prejudice is ubiquitous. Together they powerfully inhibit rational analysis of welfare needs and welfare reform.

Not long ago, Professor Bosanquet, then an advisor to the House of Commons Social Services Select Committee, suggested that the burden of care for the elderly, due to double in number over the next thirty years, could not be supported 'without extra insurance-based funding' (*Observer*,

12 August 1990). This undeniable claim, and accompanying proposals by Commercial Union to mount and market community care policies, was greeted by the welfare lobby as if what was intended was compulsory euthanasia.

Thus Jill Pitkeathly, Director of the Carers' National Association, was reported as saying (ibid.) that 'Those able to afford it will be able to buy their own future care, while the rest will be dependent on dwindling state-funded services.' Eric Reid, Director of the Association of Retired People, called predictably for 'increased income for all elderly people to guarantee a dignified old age', spluttering anxiously to the effect that: 'These insurance policies look a very uncertain risk to me. People do not know in their middle years what their needs in retirement will be. They could well be wasting their money.' Melanie Henwood of the King's Fund Institute reacted rather more realistically than Reid to the unchallengeable demographic and financial facts presented by Professor Bosanquet. She managed, nevertheless, to lament the development of the dreaded 'two-tier system'. The introduction of long-term care insurance marked, she claimed:

the end of the cradle to the grave cover of social insurance envisaged by Lord Beveridge. Clearly, the cost of paying for the grave has been deemed to be too great for a publicly-funded system. Private insurance based solely on people's ability to pay can only accelerate the growth of two nations in old age.

Despite these wearisomely predictable reactions from the welfare lobby (Bytheway and Johnson, 1990), Bosanquet is right, as a later study by Taverne (1994) amply confirms. In the sphere of pensions and health care for the elderly, demographic and economic pressures are combining to make established social policies ineffectual. They necessitate innovative approaches and radical reform. Related causes are likely to produce similar effects within a very short time in health care generally, in education, in housing, in income support, and indeed in the whole range of state welfare benefits and services built up since the 1940s.

Added to the pressures for reform occasioned by demographic change and escalating costs, further compelling reasons for radical change spring from the several grave problems with state welfare examined in earlier chapters. Existing social policy rests on hopelessly confused philosophical assumptions. Economic progress and improved standards of living have rendered comprehensive state provision otiose. State provision is increasingly viewed as incompetent, by comparison with the market, to answer varying needs and tastes flexibly, dynamically and efficiently. State welfare is manifestly costly and wasteful of scarce public financial resources. It unavoidably brings in its train all the problems associated with monopoly and bureaucracy, including especially the danger of distraction of help from those who genuinely need it to those who manifestly do not. And last but not least, existing policies and structures encourage welfare dependency, and weaken the basic institutions of a free society: the family, the local community, voluntary associations and the market.

For all these reasons, radical reform is essential. Recent reforms, designed to target assistance more effectively, and to introduce competition, local management, and consumer choice within the existing state monopoly framework, may secure some real improvement in the wasteful extravagance, gross inefficiency and bureaucratic sclerosis of the Welfare State. They are unlikely, however, to provide adequate long-term, permanent answers to the deep-seated problems of state welfare. For example, even after the implementation of radical structural reforms in education and health care, it seems certain that pressures for yet bigger increases in resources will continue, and even escalate. Standards are improving, but they are a long way short of adequate. Nothing less than the disestablishment of state welfare, it seems, will suffice to produce the levels of efficiency and effectiveness we have the right to expect from these crucial services.

Principles of Reform

Even in the face of predictable media misrepresentations, and even at the cost of seeming in the short run to present political opponents with a gift-horse which they will certainly not look in the mouth, I suggest that all those who are committed to freedom and to genuine improvement in the real welfare of the British people ought to speak up unapologetically for:

- A gradual but substantial expansion of the area of freedom and choice in welfare.
- A diminution of local and central state control in education, health, pensions and housing.
- A serious effort at targeting welfare help more purposefully and precisely.
- Measures designed to strengthen the family, and to restore to it those rights and responsibilities for looking after its own which the Welfare State has expropriated.
- A continuing campaign to present to the public the positive attractions of enterprise, initiative and self-reliance, and to scotch the enervating influence of the Poverty Lobby and other friends of state power.

In the context of these objectives, welfare reform should be guided by three working assumptions. Together they define a principled approach to progress beyond state welfare.

First, genuine welfare depends entirely on economic progress and national prosperity. This is turn requires hard work and enterprising attitudes on the part of the population, and constant revivification of a dynamic enterprise culture. Anything which hinders economic progress, threatens prosperity, or stifles enterprise is an impediment to genuine welfare. These impediments include: the remaining nationalized industries; bureaucratic big business; anti-competitive professional associations and trade unions; excessive tax levels; wage regulation; local government extravagance; and egalitarian social policies. No one who defends any of this collectivist baggage can be genuinely concerned about welfare, whatever they may pretend.

Second, any compromise with the Poverty Lobby has to be avoided. Its arguments and influence have to be faced and answered. This largely state-financed network of academics, pressure groups and media operators is a powerful negative factor in any attempt at improving real welfare. Its spokesmen constantly exaggerate the extent of poverty. They disseminate misunderstandings of its nature and its causes. They deliberately paint the bleakest possible picture of social conditions. They peddle outdated bureaucratic-collectivist remedies to largely imaginary problems. I sometimes find it difficult to be sure whether they are being less than honest or worse than stupid. Unless their power, here at home and especially and increasingly on the European front, is controlled, we shall be dragged down before long to the levels of beggary from which the socialist world is only now seeking escape.

My *third* basic assumption involves trusting the British people. For despite what is often alleged, the British much prefer self-reliance and self-help – and the independence which accompany them – to state hand-outs. *They* know, even if the intellectuals and the mandarins do not, that socialism with a human face is a squared circle, that the Welfare State is a treacherous, if tempting, snare, and that the world is a tough sort of place, with free lunches about as common as wasps that don't sting. Polling research which apparently reveals widespread support for state welfare and economic equalization is highly suspect, to put it no more strongly (Saunders and Harris, 1990; Harris and Seldon, 1987).

Beyond these three assumptions – no progress, no welfare; treat the poverty lobby with contempt; trust the people's independence of spirit – there are a number of further principles which should guide the tranformation of the Welfare State into a genuinely free society.

First, welfare services should be provided by independent, competing suppliers – schools, colleges, doctors, clinics, hospitals, pension and insurance companies, building societies and so on – to the choice of consumers, and paid for either directly out of consumers' pockets, or by means of commercial insurance. The Welfare State has done much to destroy the British people's traditional prudence. It will have to be restored, and linked to life-time planning for self and family. The insurance industry and voluntary mutual associations will need encouragement to provide the essential mechanisms of self-reliance in a free society (Green, 1984). Why should not most people be responsible for their own insurance against unemployment, sickness and so on, and provide for their own positive needs, for education and housing for example, by the same means (Bell *et al.*, 1994)?

Second, if the people are to take back responsibility for their own and their family's welfare, they will need relieving of a substantial proportion of the tax burden to which they have been unjustly subjected for fifty years to pay for the wasteful machinery of the Welfare State. This has to mean serious reductions in income tax across the board, promised clearly and definitively beforehand, and delivered on time. It should also involve, on top of this, substantial tax rebates along the lines of the allowances introduced as part of the current health care reforms for private insurance of elderly parents. This aspect of welfare reform is necessary, and at the same time a source of potentially powerful support for its effective implementation. Real tax cuts could be even more attractive to voters in large numbers than were council house sales discounts or privatization share sales – both of them big vote winners.

Third, timing and phasing of the introduction of such radical reforms will be crucial to their success or failure. No one currently protected – or rather apparently protected – by state welfare provision should be compelled to exit, or find a service he or she has been taking for granted suddenly withdrawn. Detailed planning will be required, indicating plainly the phasing-in of the various alternatives over a period of years.

Fourth and last, but by no means least, the principles governing social assistance for the – mainly temporary and fluctuating – minority of those needing special help will require very careful elucidation. It was to help this minority that the Welfare State was first established. We have let it expand absurdly for no good reason at all, considering that standards of living have been improving rapidly and consistently during the period of its growth. We must at all costs prevent this recurring, or the whole reform process will be undermined. The crux is to avoid confusing disadvantage with inequality. There is no adequate reason for believing that even the relatively disadvantaged necessarily need long-term assistance. What they want is positive support, designed to restore them to self-reliance expeditiously. On this crucial issue, see Chapter 9.

The command economy of socialism is almost everywhere regarded today as an impediment to progress and prosperity, and a threat to freedom. Yet its precise equivalent in the sphere of those services we have been encouraged by socialists to define as 'welfare' remains entrenched in Britain and in much of the otherwise free world. We should let this 'command society' of the Welfare State, this spurious community of bureaucratic rules and mechanically routinized practices, go the same way into the dustbin of history – and for the same reasons. It doesn't work, and it enslaves the people. We have to shift beyond 'welfare' towards a genuinely free society of self-reliance and enterprising initiative if real welfare is to be assured.

Strategies of Reform

Whatever is claimed by the Government (by any reforming government) about its intentions in the field of welfare, the Opposition parties and the media will insist that it will be cuts and injustice all the way. Whatever further increases in resources over and above the expansion of the past fifteen years the Government continues to pour into education, health, pensions and social security, the lobbyists and the unions will clamour – and the public will listen and half believe them – about the imperative moral and practical necessity of expanding public expenditure still further again. The secret slogan of the Poverty Lobby and all the other paid agents of state welfare seems, as far as resources are concerned, to be 'Double the number you last thought of'.

Since there is no way they can ever be persuaded that enough is going to be spent on welfare, and since in any case general elections appear to be won or lost mainly on the state of the economy rather than on policy issues, supporters of welfare reform might reasonably ask the following questions. Why not risk being clear and principled by openly preparing the way now for purposeful movement over the next ten years towards the disestablishment of state welfare? Why not aim seriously at creating a free and self-reliant Britain by the turn of the century, and make it thus a millennium indeed? Why not actively seek to win the people's support for this further bold extension of liberty, as the Conservative Government has already done earlier – against the apparent grain of public opinion – over union reform, tax cuts, council house sales and privatization?

If this ambitious task is to be successfully addressed, serious precautions will need to be taken on several fronts. First, reform should not be presented merely, or even primarily, as a means of saving money, but positively, as a key dimension of general progress towards freedom and prosperity, and as a principled goal of any modern democratic society. At the same time, the instrumental benefits of reform should be unapologetically emphasized: benefits for consumers liberated from monopolistic restrictions and bureaucratic inefficiencies, and for genuinely professional welfare personnel, such as nurses, doctors, teachers and social workers, afforded opportunities for improvements in salaries, conditions of work and career structures. Only state monopoly is preventing real advances for consumers and producers alike.

Next, the contraction of state welfare services should be handled with the same pragmatic mix of strategies as was successfully employed in relation to steel, the mines and the print industry. Privatization is preferable to closure. Manpower savings should be achieved by carefully planned and gradual voluntary redundancy. Recalcitrant workers should be bought out expeditiously. Luddite unions and professional associations should be fought hard and defeated, with effective use made of the law and of public opinion.

Again, the arguments of the enemy will have to be addressed seriously and vigorously. In particular, the tissue of lies and half-truths busily disseminated by the Poverty Lobby will have to be demolished systematically. We must have an end to *ad hoc* concessions, made for the sake of seeming nice on television, to transparently spurious claims about poverty and inequality.

The British people sometimes seem – although no doubt the opinion pollsters exaggerate the extent of the impression by the way they frame their questions and interpret their responses – almost as nervous about the prospect of real freedom as Poles or even Russians, exposed for the first time by the collapse of communism to the rigours of self-reliance. This danger will need to be handled extremely carefully if welfare reform is to succeed. We must learn the right lessons from the Community Charge débâcle. The people will have to be persuaded patiently and thoroughly that real security in the long term requires us to throw off the cocoon of state welfare. We will all need to be fully convinced of what is after all a commonsensical truism constantly rediscovered, that genuine welfare can be provided only by individuals and families for themselves, and from their own moral and financial resources.

Lastly in this list of strategic precautions, the pace of change is of the essence if reform is to work. It must be neither too fast, so as to produce bewilderment and incoherent resistance, nor on the other hand too slow, allowing vested interests and extremist factions time to organize. To hit a deadline in the year 2000, careful planning should be starting now.

In their important study of public attitudes to welfare, Saunders and Harris (1990) have demonstrated that latent demand for independence from state restrictions on welfare choice is substantial, and likely to grow rapidly as prosperity and standards of living continue to improve. We need to be ready to answer the demand for freedom and higher standards as it swells over coming years. It may turn otherwise into an uproar of dissatisfaction with state monopoly provision which could threaten the stability of civil order.

Practicalities of Reform

One can understand the hopeless perplexity of Eastern and Central Europeans in the face of political demands for movement towards a market approach to the organization of their societies. It is two, three, or even four generations since they have had any experience of capitalism. The market has long been outlawed. Prices bear no relation to supply or demand. Socialism has made of the pursuit of profit a capital offence. Provision of commodities and services of every sort is controlled by state bureaucrats. The efficient, enterprising effort required, on pain of bank-ruptcy, from producers in capitalist societies, the straight-dealing expected from traders, and the purposeful, actively selective behaviour natural to consumers in free societies – all these have been suppressed under social-ism by the full force of state power (Seldon, 1990).

The phoney shock-horror evinced here in Britain and elsewhere in the free world by socialists and other supporters of the Welfare State at pro-posals for liberalizing social policies and welfare services is more surpris-ing. All around them, in almost every sphere except welfare, commodities and services are provided through market mechanisms. Profits, costs, prices, supply, demand, effort and incentives shape much of their lives. They take advantage daily of the efficiency and consumer-responsiveness of capitalist forms of organization in the production and distribution of commodities and services ranging in price from a few pence to thousands of pounds, and varying in importance from balloons for children's parties to central heating systems, from packets of elastoplast to thousand-acre farms. All that stands between their socialist perplexity and the satisfac-tions provided – for consumers and producers alike – by capitalism is the artificial barrier, the ideological Berlin Wall, erected by the Welfare State.

Moreover, the disestablishment of state welfare is not in principle an especially difficult task. We have all around us in the real economy the models we need. All that is required, in the sphere of welfare so-called, as in the broader realm of goods and services, is competing suppliers, demanding consumers, free markets, genuine prices and a framework of legal regulation, including in particular securely established institutions of property and contract (Berger, 1987).

Furthermore, the monopoly in most welfare services is already, fortunately, less than total. In housing and pensions the extent of the free market is considerable. In insurance it is extensive, but chronically limited by state expropriation of large sectors. In education and in health care it is, alas, minute – but none the less very important because most of the best 'brands' are in the private sector. Indeed, even in these pre-eminently state collectivist sectors, the extent of market provision is much larger than appears because of the snobbish way in which down-market products – such as driving instruction, language schools, dance academies, chemists' shops, health-food stores, and so on – tend to be excluded from normal definitions of education and health care.

The Welfare State mentality apparently cannot imagine how efficient, independent suppliers of the whole range of welfare services could spring into dynamic operation. It is the same blinkered dogmatism as prevents the curiously labelled 'right-wingers' of Russia from envisaging steel, cars, clothes or food being produced and distributed other than by bureaucratic committees of party functionaries in Moscow. Given a clear decision, a positive government lead, and legislation designed to free-up the market, we could have education, health care, housing, pensions and insurance industries operating competitively and efficiently in Britain in short order. Michael Bell (1994, p. 31) describes the way ahead:

> The availability of a safety-net of benefits for the incapable and unlucky is, of course, one of the redeeming features of our sometimes nasty civilization. But the completely unnecessary extension of this principle on ideological grounds to attempt to compel equality of provision across the population simply serves to reduce choice and dull incentive. It flies in the face of human nature and economic development, and it is wasteful even in delivering benefit to the very people for whom it exists in the first place. It is time to begin to plan the wholesale removal of pensions, perhaps followed by health and education, from the public sector.

Alleged Difficulties

It has to be admitted that even if they reluctantly granted that liberalization might be feasible in principle, Welfare State loyalists would nevertheless point to practical problems which they imagine would prevent privatized welfare from working successfully (Walker and Walker, 1987). Three such alleged problems merit particular attention.

First, the intolerably high costs, which they anticipate would leave most people preferring tax-funded state provision. Second, the incoherent patchiness of provision, which they imagine is the best the market could manage, with the planning supposedly essential in a 'national service' precluded by the 'chaos' of competition. And third and worst, the cruel injustice of the situation of the poor, excluded by their inadequate incomes from participation in markets supposedly reserved for the prosperous majority, and restricted to the apartheid conditions of 'residual welfare'.

Concern about prices is exaggerated. State welfare lobbyists deliberately distort the analysis by quoting extreme and irrelevant examples: the fees at Eton, despite the certainty that demand for boarding education will be slight; the cost of heart transplants at London teaching hospitals, despite the minute number of such exotic operations ever likely to be needed. Consumers cannot be expected to pay twice over as at present, and reduced taxes will substantially increase disposable income available for personal provision. Moreover, current costs in state welfare – in so far as they can be identified at all through the fog of administration, subsidy and complex paper transfers – are much increased by monopoly, bureaucracy, centralization, union power and the errors in investment and other expenditure which always characterize command economies by comparison with markets.

Privatization would substantially reduce costs on all these counts. It would reduce them still further by its stimulation of technological and organizational innovation. Best of all, prices would respond very positively to increased real demand from genuine consumers with competitive choices available for the first time. As in other markets, one would expect 'luxury', 'mainstream', and 'downmarket' providers to appear, with competition consistently making yesterday's luxuries available today to mass markets, combining high quality with sharp prices. Imagine the exorbitant price – and squalid quality – of television sets today if production had been nationalized in 1948 and foreign competition outlawed!

I recall my father telling me in the 1950s about his workmates' amazement when, after careful reflection and thorough discussion with my mother and with friends he trusted, he was almost alone in the big organization in which he worked in taking on some voluntary occupational pension contributions to provide substantially improved retirement income for himself and my mother. The payments involved were modest in the extreme (his peak earnings never reached twenty pounds a week), but his colleagues preferred to have the money available in the short term to spend on beer, cigarettes, and other such daily 'necessities'. As far as they were concerned, they couldn't possibly afford extra pension payments, and this is no doubt what they would have told an opinion pollster or a BBC interviewer had they been asked.

Thus the acceptability – indeed the meaning – of costs depends crucially on consumers' preferences and priorities. According to Williams (1994), a Mintel report suggests that 'the cost of individual health insurance remains high'. Yet for a married couple aged thirty with two children, it quotes a range from as low as £90 to a ceiling of £260 per month for comprehensive cover in a Band A hospital. Is this really expensive in relation to average income? Moreover, all the evidence suggests that a mass market in all the diverse segments of welfare would provide good quality services at very reasonable prices, well within the reach – directly or through insurance – of more than 80 per cent of the population.

The Welfare State lobby's second criticism of liberalization is that the 'chaos of the market' – that old socialist bugbear challenged so effectively long ago by Max Weber (Roth and Wittich eds, 1978, p. 1403) – will prevent comprehensive planning of essential services and condemn people to patchily inadequate and unreliable care. Coming from champions of the supposed triumphs of state welfare, this plea seems to me about as plausible as the ludicrous claims of Kremlin hardliners about the Soviet Union's glorious heritage of state planning. Most ex-Soviet citizens more accurately conclude that it has produced seven decades of chaotic inefficiency, hopeless shortages, and titanic economic and industrial errors – a catalogue of disasters for which the Russian people are paying a heavy price today.

For none of our established welfare services can it be reasonably claimed that planning has been effective or beneficial. The health service and education have both lurched violently between over-supply and gross shortage of manpower, plant and investment. Attempts at harmonizing supply and demand have regularly involved vicious political wrangles, occupied considerable time and wasted much money. London hospitals are a case in point. Despite continual reorganization and frequent alterations of the criteria determining resource allocation, we still have health and educational facilities in the wrong place, in the wrong form, at the wrong time (Enthoven, 1985).

Higher education provides a case study in the inefficiency of central planning. The relevant authorities have floundered hopelessly for years between contradictory objectives, shifting decision-criteria, and mutually exclusive planning data. Little wonder if there is gross over-supply in some subjects, desperate shortages in others, and no way of knowing for certain which is which! Again, state pension contributions have had to be changed frequently and arbitrarily to adjust to gross errors in earlier estimates of need – and this in relation to demographics, one of the very few aspects of social change about which social science is able to provide central planners with any reliable knowledge at all (Marsland, 1990). In most other spheres, reliable knowledge is so scanty, and in any case so much subject to unpredictable influences, that the planning process is more nearly equivalent to a rain-dance ceremony than to the rational procedure which central planners and policy specialists like to pretend it is (Hayek, 1975 and 1982).

Central planning has proved a complete failure, in welfare as much as in the industrial sphere, as a means of securing a reliable supply of the diverse services required by differentiated populations in changing circumstances. If state monopoly is to be retained, it is much better if planning decisions are made locally rather than centrally. Even more flexibly adaptive provision, adjustable to changing patterns of demand rapidly and cheaply, can be made by competing suppliers operating in a free market. From profit levels and prices they know where the demand is and precisely what for. Because of their competitive situation, they have unavoidable incentives to adjust their products, product range, prices and market coverage as market information – infinitely more accurately than bureaucratic planners – advises them. Enemies of the market seem to have no idea at all about how it works: the Social Security Advisory Committee apparently objected (*The Times*, 15 September 1994: 'Private Welfare Schemes Unlikely') to private insurance against unemployment, sickness, and disability on the ground that 'premiums would vary widely' – as if this were not the whole point!

In short, there is no reason to believe that replacement of 'planned' state provision of welfare by a welfare market would have any deleterious effects on coverage. Indeed, there is every reason, to judge from the sophisticated, comprehensive coverage of the whole range of needs and preferences in the consumer goods market, to suppose that market welfare would be considerably more efficient than state welfare in providing the diversity of services which people of all sorts want (Marsland, 1991).

The third and most serious criticism of welfare reform, in terms of the hurt it would supposedly do to the poor, reflects the most fundamental principles – or certainly the most dogmatic prejudices – of the Welfare State's most enthusiastic supporters. When every other argument has failed them, they return again and again and in the last resort to the plea that without the protection provided by the Welfare State, the disadvantaged sectors of the population would be exposed in all their vulnerability to the full destructive force of 'unfettered capitalism', and would be gravely harmed as a result.

This is a curious argument, and, despite the popularity and apparent plausibility suggested by its regular use even by Conservative MPs and by journalists and academics otherwise sceptical of collectivist social policy, remarkably unconvincing. Consider the strongest possible version of the argument, which might go along the following lines:

> 85 per cent of the population may be reasonably prosperous, and better than adequately served by market welfare, thank you very much. But the other 15 per cent are all desperately poor; they cannot afford to avail themselves at all of market provision; and they have no other recourse for support whatsoever. Remove the Welfare State and they are doomed.

Despite its regular deployment, this case is highly inaccurate and exaggerated. The size of the prosperous majority capable of self-reliance is probably higher than 85 per cent. Far from being homogeneously disadvantaged, some of the minority are quite close to the level of the self-sufficient majority – the 'margins of poverty' are also, after all, from another perspective, the margins of prosperity. Very few are permanently in absolutely desperate straits, and most are somewhere in between. Some proportion of them are at least as capable of making some use of market welfare as the genuinely poor of the nineteenth century who saved to pay for their children's education (West, 1971).

Again, very few indeed are entirely without alternative sources of help. Charity provides more effective help than the Welfare State for many of the most deprived already. It could help many more if social policy thinking were not dominated by socialists who regard the concept of charity as scarcely less outmoded by the onward progress of history, and barely more compatible with civilized morality, than slavery or even human sacrifice (Bracewell-Milnes, 1989; Chodes, 1990; O'Keeffe, 1994).

The family is also capable of providing more help, without the damaging side-effects of state welfare, than it does currently if only similar 'sophisticated' prejudices against that maligned institution could be overcome. Is there any reason, for example, why fathers should not be obliged, as effectively as they manage it in Switzerland, to support their abandoned children? Is the Child Support Agency really the best we can manage? Is there any good reason for our current practice of absolving parents of all responsibility for supporting their adolescent children just because they have left home? Should we really be discouraging grandparents and uncles from helping their kin by buying out their obligations with state benefits? Certainly the Swiss and the Germans continue to maintain family obligations for support of the indigent (Segalman, 1986; German Employment and Social Order, 1990). Indeed, as recently as 1930, British legislation stated unambiguously that 'It shall be the duty of the father, grandfather, mother, grandmother, husband or child of a poor, old, blind, lame or impotent person... if possessed of sufficient means, to relieve and maintain that person' (Poor Law Act, Section 14).

These necessary corrections to its underlying assumptions aside, let us consider the 'minority poor' argument on its own terms, in the extreme form in which it is commonly used – what one might call 'the Richard Titmuss ploy'. Suppose, for the sake of argument that 15 per cent of the population is indeed in abject poverty. How does this prevent thoroughgoing disestablishment of state welfare?

Why not make special, effective provision for those who need it without altering at all the self-sufficient, self-reliant arrangements of the 85 per cent majority? What is wrong with a safety net, which protects those in helpless need without interfering at all with the lives of those who have no need for it? All that is required is adequate transfer of resources, via the tax system, from the majority to the minority to provide the necessary help. Furthermore, why not spend at least some of this transferred income in enabling as many as possible of the disadvantaged minority to join the majority in the normal self-service system of welfare? Why pretend that there is anything positively praiseworthy or attractive at all in needing help?

Again, why not take every possible precaution to ensure that the help provided for the remaining minority-within-a-minority is supplied – at state expense, be it emphasized – exclusively by efficient non-state organizations; to guarantee that the help provided includes measures designed to return as many as possible to self-reliance as rapidly as possible; and not least, to make certain that the extent of tax-derived expenditure required is kept to a minimum by the fullest possible use of charitable and family resources?

These issues are dealt with in detail in the next chapter. As regards welfare reform in general, I conclude this part of my analysis as follows. The Titmuss ploy is unworkable, unnecessary and quite literally a red herring. The situation of a disadvantaged minority, however desperate, provides no argument at all against radical welfare reform. The Welfare State began as a safety net for the disadvantaged few. It swelled to become an all-encompassing spider's web, entrapping the whole population in a poisoned snare of financial extravagance, bureaucratic incompetence, and suffocating collectivism. It should be urgently restored to its proper role as a temporary support for the less fortunate minority by legislation which liberates the prosperous majority from compulsory participation in state services.

Disestablishing State Welfare

I visited the Slovak Republic recently for the first time, to lecture and to discuss welfare policy with academics and officials involved in the reconstruction of a free society out of the ruins left behind by communism. I found much interest in the commercially financed social and market research I have undertaken over the years in Britain. Their interest was combined, however, with deep puzzlement. Even highly intelligent people, deeply committed to reform and thoroughly convinced of the evil of state domination, were nevertheless incapable for the most part of understanding how social research could possibly be financed other than by the state. 'But where does the money come from?' I was asked time and time again.

They have grown up from childhood under socialism, with no experience at all of independent businesses, including commercial research companies, which make a profit. Accustomed to bureaucratic monopoly which restricts the initiation of activity exclusively to the state, they are unfamiliar with the idea, let alone the practice, of individuals freely entering into contracts to answer one another's needs at a price which is at the same time fair and profitable. Little wonder if they find it hard to comprehend how business might have a real interest (in both senses) in information which improves its understanding of consumers' characteristics and preferences, or of patterns of social change which marketing needs to take account of, and might be willing and able to pay for such information.

A similar puzzlement in the face of equivalent radical changes in the direction of freedom occasioned by the disestablishment of state welfare in Britain would not be at all surprising. After all, as far as welfare is concerned, we too have grown up under socialism since the 1940s. We too have come to take for granted, after almost five decades of centralized collectivism, the habit of state monopoly and bureaucratic domination. Scarcely less than the wretched heirs of Lenin's poisonous testament, we find it hard to understand how subservience can be replaced by self-reliance, or how clumsy but familiar state organs can make way for independent, enterprising businesses providing quality welfare services tailored to consumers' varying needs, preferences, and pockets.

They will find a way in Bratislava, Warsaw and even Kiev, nevertheless, to transcend socialism. We ought to be able to do at least as well here in Britain. After all our socialism, by comparison with theirs, has fortunately been no better than half-baked. Unlike the people of Eastern and Central Europe, who must start almost from scratch on the road towards freedom, all we have to do is to translate and transfer our readily available experience of successful enterprise from the business and commercial world into the decaying pseudo-socialist realm of welfare. This will require careful, patient, radical reform along the following lines.

Practical Plans for an Alternative to Planning

We should extend the local management and grant-maintained status of schools and colleges introduced by recent educational reforms into genuine privatization. Parents, independent adult students and employers would pay for education and training to their choice, in the first instance by vouchers. These could be topped up out of current income or via special savings and insurance schemes (Flew *et al.*, 1991). This transitional system would subsequently be phased out, except for people needing special assistance, and replaced by fully marketized, genuinely independent and properly regulated provision. Schools and colleges can be released from state control just as easily and effectively as industrial monopolies, using a mixed strategy of sales to existing independent educational institutions, to other companies, to co-operatives of staff and/or parents, and to newly established profit and non-profit educational companies (West, 1994).

Similarly, the recent establishment of independent hospital trusts and the devolution of budgets to GPs provides a sound basis for gradual movement towards full privatization. Here, too, a combination of vouchers, real money and insurance offers a practical mechanism which could make quality health care available rapidly to most people. Again, ownership would be transferred from the state to a variegated alternative economy. This would include larger and smaller specialist health companies; other companies within whose larger portfolio health care would be one segment; insurance companies and provident associations; independent hospitals and clinics; professional partnerships of doctors, dentists, nurses and other health-care specialists; and charitable foundations. Poorer people would be provided for through vouchers and social assistance (Whitney, 1988; Green and Lucas, 1993).

An increasing proportion of pension provision is made year by year through occupational schemes and by means of independent, personal retirement insurance. By the end of the century, almost no one will be dependent entirely on state pensions, which will comprise for most people a bonus at best. Both the basic state pension and of course SERPS should be gradually phased out, with a very small reserve system maintained to cover unpredictable emergencies and the needs of the small and decreasing number of people incapable of providing for their retirement during their working lives. Recent scandals in connection with personal pensions should not be allowed, as the champions of state monopoly desperately hope, to discourage rapid movement in a liberal direction (Vinson, 1994; NOP, 1994). The taken-for-granted scandal of state pensions is infinitely worse, and the advantages of personal pensions in terms of flexibility are very considerable (de Soto, 1994). The fiftieth anniversary of the Beveridge Report in 1992 ought to have signalled the initiation of a serious review of its paternalistic prescriptions for pensions (Marsland, 1992 [2]). The analysis should be taken up and pushed through vigorously as soon as possible, along the lines which Michael Bell (1994) has recently proposed.

Supporters of welfare reform have perhaps been too glibly self-congratulatory about the success of council house sales. Millions still live in state-owned property. Radical steps should be taken urgently to sell off all council housing to individual tenants, to tenants' co-operatives, and to private landlords (Thurnham, 1993). Rent controls should be lifted to allow the resurrection of the private sector, which remains at present far too small as a result of unfair competition by the state, inadequate returns to landlords (especially small landlords), and counter-productive tenant 'protection'. As D. J. Lewis, Chairman of Molyneux Estates, succinctly put it in a letter to *The Times* (22 December 1994): 'The history of efforts to impose rent controls repeatedly demonstrates that they merely distort the market, reduce supply, remove the incentive to invest, arbitrarily pass value from landlords to tenants, and inevitably increase underlying rental values as a result of the creation of scarcity.'

Rents should float free, then, but housing benefits should be brought ruthlessly under control. State housing expenditure should be limited to tax rebates for first-time buyers only, to encourage home ownership, and to the provision of cheap, modest, temporary accommodation for the genuinely homeless and for emergency social assistance. In relation to this latter purpose, maximum use should be made of the private rented sector. No new council housing should need to be built ever again (Minford *et al.*, 1987; Ricketts, 1994).

Beveridge was as gravely mistaken about unemployment benefit as about pensions. There is no reason at all why insurance against unemployment should be so largely monopolized by the state. Commercial insurance companies do the job more cheaply and more effectively. The state should restrict its role in this sphere to compulsorily requiring insurance, as with motor vehicles, leaving the insurance industry to provide unemployment protection for individuals and for companies with the flexibility of which the state is incapable (Beenstock, 1994). In this area it is amusing to note that Barr's tabloid-titled 'The Mirage of Private Unemployment Insurance' is listed in the STICERD (LSE) catalogue as 'out of print'. It is the argument against independent unemployment protection which comprises the mirage. No doubt special measures may be required for the long-term unemployed and for people with permanent employment difficulties. These are discussed in the following chapter. For most people, private provision would offer a better deal than current arrangements, at lower cost to the insured, and with the disincentive effect of state benefits markedly reduced.

One more major sphere of liberalization demands urgent attention, as the failed reform of local rates and the Community Charge débâcle demonstrate. We should privatize social and community care, refuse collection, leisure provision, libraries and other services currently controlled and provided by the local state, restricting the primary responsibility of the local authorities to regulation, inspection and quality assurance.

Over and above this, they should be responsible for organizing – but emphatically not for delivering – social assistance for local residents in temporary need. The local state has hypertrophied even more extravagantly than the central state, and it should be cut back hard to size. Thus reduced in its pretensions, it could provide for itself out of its own local resources and thus reclaim the useful and honourable role it long claimed before it was tempted by the sirens of government grants and ideological ambitions (Forsyth, 1986; McKinstry, 1995).

Thoroughgoing but gradual and careful privatization in these six spheres – education, health care, pensions, housing, unemployment protection and local government – is necessary and feasible. By introducing competition and consumer sovereignty, it will produce cheaper, more effective and more flexible services (Seldon, 1994). By shifting the dead-weight of bureaucratic state monopoly off the backs of the people, it will liberate their natural spirit of self-reliance and energetic enterprise. By breaking up the huge welfare monopolies, it will reduce the excessive power of 'public service' unions to reasonable levels. By demonstrating the folly and redundancy of the concept of welfare rights, it will stop the development of dependency in its tracks, and halt the growth of a subordinated, fractious underclass (West, 1990; Seldon, 1994).

Financial Parameters of Reform

To achieve these essential objectives, a number of financial measures will be required to underpin and facilitate the comprehensive disestablishment of state welfare.

First, income tax must be reduced substantially and other taxes significantly to enable most people to afford privatized services without putting established standards of living under pressure. Privatization will produce a huge one-off injection of income for the state, continuing new income from services previously untaxed, and enormous savings in public expenditure. Very substantial reductions in taxation are therefore entirely feasible, with the possibility of abolishing income tax altogether for a large proportion of the population.

Secondly, the Treasury's prejudice against tax rebates should be ignored. If a radical shift from state monopoly to self-reliance is to be successfully accomplished, special encouragements will have to be offered in the first instance. Temporary tax rebates for participants in newly privatized services, offered for fixed terms to families on lower incomes, should do the trick.

Thirdly, producers as well as consumers will have to be given special support in the early stages of the transition. Here, too, generous tax incentives have a crucial part to play to encourage staff buy-outs, new cooperatives and so on. A positive tax environment should also be provided for the insurance industry and for new forms of mutual aid, to stimulate the vital efforts of the intermediary institutions linking suppliers with consumers of education, health care, pensions and the rest. The voluntary organizations, released from the dead-hand of the state, could flourish again.

Real Welfare

In the socialist world, they have realized at long last that there is another and a better way of organizing the production and distribution of goods and services than the state monopoly model prescribed by their long-established official ideology. They are struggling hard to shift about towards a more liberal, market-oriented system. Here in Britain, and throughout the free world, we have learned this lesson long ago, and succeeded in liberating most of the industrial and commercial sector from state domination.

Somehow, however, even enthusiasts for industrial privatization seem incapable of recognizing that welfare is the free world's secret sphere of hidden socialism (Wilson and Wilson, 1991). The same principles and practices as previously crippled British industry – state bureaucracy, competition-resistant monopoly, destructive subsidies, and studied inattention to consumers – are still producing the same damaging consequences in the welfare sphere. They will not be remedied until a reforming government turns its energies unflinchingly to radical reform (Ashford, 1995).

9 A Programme for Special Needs: Effective Social Assistance for the Helpless

Eamonn Butler (1994, p. 19) provides a telling transition between the considerations of Chapter 8 and the issues to which I turn now. 'What', he asks, 'of those people':

> whose needs are correctly categorized as welfare needs, including people who will never be able to provide for themselves? In simple terms, *welfare provides benefits based on needs, regardless of contributions; while insurance provides benefits based on contributions, regardless of need.* But our welfare state tries to combine the two.

With the large majority of the population of all ages catered for by a newly liberated independent sector, an effective programme of special assistance will need to be organized for the minority of people who are temporarily (or in a very small number of cases, permanently) incapable of self-help. This might appropriately be called the *National Special Assistance Programme* in order to symbolize unambiguously its mission of providing help for those in real and unusual need. It should have the following features:

- It should be based on needs, not rights.
- It should be delivered entirely by genuine voluntary agencies, with state involvement restricted to funding and regulation.
- All assistance should be temporary and conditional.
- To avoid disincentive effects, assistance should be set at the minimum necessary level. It should normally take the form of loans rather than grants.
- Effort should be required in return for assistance; for example, workfare should be instituted for the unemployed, and training schemes, where appropriate, for young lone parents.
- The system should be administered on a local basis by Special Assistance Staff (not social workers) familiar with the neighbourhood and its people, and authorized to treat individuals and families with

discretion appropriate to their circumstances, attitudes and behaviour. No more anonymous giros through the post, or straggling queues of 'claimants' at Post Office counters.

- The fundamental mission of the Special Assistance Programme would be to shift people out of state dependency and back into the normal self-provisioning system as rapidly as possible.

Socialists and other supporters of collectivist welfare will no doubt argue that these are 'Gradgrind' principles, and that any welfare programme defined by them is likely to be mean-spirited, hard-hearted and ineffectual (Walker, 1993).

The argument should be taken up resolutely. For too long people of good sense and charitable intent in all parties and none have allowed themselves to be bullied by the welfare lobby and its academic and media allies. It is *their* system of collectivist state welfare which is ineffectual – and worse. It is unreconstructed welfare state social policies – spend more money, legislate more rights – which encourage abuse; which provide extra benefits for people who have no need of them while depriving those who genuinely need it of the help they deserve; which harm those they are supposed to help by encouraging their worst characteristics and denying their real capacities. By contrast, a radical programme such as that suggested here will provide for all except criminals the real help they need and want: support for becoming their own best selves, and for finding their own way back to the autonomous self-reliance appropriate to free people.

I must emphasize that the fundamental reason for instituting a programme of this sort for those in special need is *not*, repeat *not*, to save money. Indeed, I would anticipate that some of the huge amounts saved by widespread opt-out from the generalized Welfare State would be available for *extra* spending, compared with current levels, on those in genuine need. Certainly money would be saved, even in relation to people with special needs, because reform would return them rapidly to the general, normal, independent sector, and prevent the current remorseless escalation in their numbers. But this would be an incidental side-effect. Its real justification is that it is essential if we are to reverse and prevent the major destructive effect of the Welfare State as currently organized – its moral and psychological impact on the character of free people.

In the following sections I examine in turn the several distinguishing features identified earlier as essential in an effective Special Assistance Programme. I spell them out again here in order to emphasize the stark difference between this proposed enterprise and our current confused and sloppy arrangements. Thus: it must be based on needs, not rights; it must be delivered by voluntary agencies; assistance must be temporary and conditional, with effort required in return for assistance; loans should be preferred to grants; it should be local; and discretionary; it must on no account employ social workers as such; and its sole mission should be to restore clients to self-reliance as quickly as possible.

Needs not Rights

Enough has probably been said on this topic already in Chapter 2 above and in the analysis of dependency in Chapter 6. Rights without reciprocal responsibilities, which is what the Welfare State promises, are either fictitious (the 'right to a job'), or destructive (the right to unemployment benefit), or both (housing rights). Moreover, rights are inevitably resistant to clear definition and subject to contentious challenge. The concept of rights offers at best an incoherent and insecure foundation for an effective, practical welfare system. Worse than this, rights-based welfare provides continuing, explicit, almost irresistible encouragement to clients to demand more and more by way of fulfilment of the state's irresponsible promises, while giving nothing in return.

Within a mere twelve-month the new South Africa has recognized the dangers associated with an over-emphasis of rights. Speaking on the anniversary of liberation on 17 February 1995, Nelson Mandela insisted that 'It is important that we rid ourselves of the culture of entitlement.' In the advanced societies we have rather more evidence available about these dangers. We should address them, therefore, at least as honestly and courageously as President Mandela, and turn the cultural spotlight away from rights and onto prudence, patience and self-reliance (Willetts, 1993).

The concept of need offers a more rational and a more practical basis for a Special Assistance Programme designed to offer effective help to those with real problems. Its primary advantage is that it presumes, as the concept of rights does not, that the help required will vary from individual case to individual case. This in turn entails – instead of irresponsible handouts determined by general and vague criteria – careful judgement on the part of welfare workers, and continuous monitoring of the impact of the help offered, with adjustments as and when appropriate. This approach will limit fraud, save on unnecessary expenditure, and – most important of all – discourage dependency.

Delivery by Voluntary Organizations rather than State Agencies

Even if the development of large-scale state welfare during the twentieth century was inevitable, which is doubtful (Seldon 1994), there was certainly no necessity whatsoever that it should have been the state itself which took on the responsibility of delivering it (Leat, 1993 [2]). On the grounds of its bureaucratic inefficiency, its corruption by collectivist ideology, its monopolistic incompatibility with competition and its amenability to political interference, the state should be excluded entirely from any role in the delivery of Special Assistance.

The state's role would be restricted to the provision of funding and, through arm's-length agencies, the regulation of delivery by companies, mutual associations and voluntary agencies. These latter – chosen on the basis of competitive tendering by price and quality – would be entirely responsible for the delivery of Special Assistance. Compared with state agencies they are likely to be less bureaucratic, more resistant to political interference and control, happy with competition, and committed to individualist rather than collectivist principles – and as such, better attuned to the Special Assistance Programme's fundamental mission of restoring those in need of help to self-reliance (Yarrow and Lawton Smith, 1993; O'Keeffe, 1994). On this last crucial point, however, there is a serious problem.

Transferring the delivery of welfare assistance from state agencies to companies and voluntary organizations should certainly improve substantially the quality of the service provided and reduce significantly the current absurd level of wastage and fraud (Leat, 1993). We shall also need, however, a programme of development and monitoring for the voluntary sector, which over recent decades has itself been damagingly influenced by the normalization of the hand-out culture.

For example, there are few agencies in the field of homelessness which are more widely respected by the public than Crisis. Making efficient use of volunteers, it has for twenty-five years provided food, clothing, warmth and comfort for single homeless people. Yet even Crisis has turned increasingly to campaigning and to that species of research whose primary use is as an instrument of campaigning persuasion. Thus *Falling Out: a Research Study of Homeless Ex-Service People* (Randall and Brown, 1994), comprises a glossy brochure reporting a re-analysis of a published DoE study and a survey of an entirely inadequate 'sample' of just seventy-three people. As genuine research in any strict sense of the term, it seems highly unlikely that it would have been published in any academic or professional journal. Yet its sponsors saw fit to publish it for sale, and to accede to the active dissemination of its 'findings' in the media. The aim seems to have been primarily to focus the public's attention on allegations about the inadequacy of help made available to people leaving the Armed Services, and to lay a basis for claims to MoD housing stock for the homeless. This is certainly partisan, if not quite actually political, campaigning of the sort which has increasingly distracted many charities from their proper purposes in recent years.

Another, more influential, instance is provided by Shelter. An interview with Sheila McKechnie, ten years a trade union officer, Director of Shelter from 1985 until 1994, and now Director of the Consumers' Association – a whole career devoted to special pleading – reports as follows on her 'achievements' at Shelter (Norridge, 1995). When she was appointed to Shelter:

> She did not like what she found. Her sense was that Thatcherism had created so many holes in the welfare safety net that charities were being swamped by the level of need. They had to start campaigning for different policies if they were ever going to solve the problems. She felt Shelter wasn't doing this. 'It was an organization that has turned in on itself. It wasn't really trying to re-establish itself as a national campaign.'

So general and so serious have such problems with the voluntary sector become, that the Duke of Edinburgh was led recently to make a special address to deal with them (1994). Calling attention to the radically changed social conditions in which charities and other voluntary organizations operate in modern Britain, he proposed a fundamental re-appraisal of their purposes, their *modus operandi*, and the tax regime which, almost more than anything else, determines the pattern of development of voluntary and charitable efforts.

In this regard, he referred to 'a whole spectrum of bodies, intent on providing various kinds of benefits for the community' being encouraged 'to seek to gain the tax advantages of charitable status'. Again, he suggested that while 'Some [charities] are undoubtedly fulfilling the original humanitarian purpose of helping the relatively poor, deprived, or disadvantaged to enjoy a better standard of living', on the other hand, '*Most of the others* [my emphasis] are providing non-vital services of all kinds for people who are unable, or do not wish, to pay for them themselves.' He also argued that, since poverty 'is no longer absolute' but 'has become relative', charity is as a consequence 'no longer a matter of providing for people who have no resources at all', but 'has become a matter of helping those who are relatively deprived'.

Little wonder that his speech provoked incoherent frenzy rather than any rational response on the part of influential spokesmen for some of our most spoiled and self-indulgent voluntary organizations. No doubt their annoyance at being called on for the first time in years to think through their basic philosophy was further aggravated by the Duke's challenge to the sub-fusc political presumptions which have been allowed to become dangerously influential in the voluntary movement as a whole since the 1960s. 'Every pound spent', he said, in a truism which voluntary welfare agencies need to take on board if they are to avoid being seen by the public as alternative agencies of a collectivist state, 'on private education, private health, personal pension schemes and care in old age, is a net saving to the state.' And again: 'private enterprise does not lead inevitably to personal greed and selfishness.'

Another instance of the difficulties with the voluntary sector is provided by a reply given by the Home Office to an enquiry about the prospective appointment of a director of research to a large national voluntary body whose research might seem to some a little one-sided. The ministerial response acknowledged that departmental funding for the body ran at some one million pounds per annum, but claimed that 'it would not normally be appropriate for officials to be involved' in such an appointment. Pipers only call the tune, apparently, when they are not already satisfied with the tune currently being played.

Provided that the voluntary agencies can be 'disinfected', as it were, to clear them of these recent accretions of collectivist habits and inclinations which are alien to their traditional and proper ethos, they should play a central role along with commercial organizations in a competitive network of welfare delivery on behalf of the Special Assistance Programme (Allen and Leat, 1994). There seems little doubt that such a system would serve its clients more efficiently, more effectively, and more humanely than even the best state agencies are managing currently (Yarrow, 1994).

Most countries make more use of voluntary agencies in the provision of welfare than we do in the UK. The Swiss, above all, maintain a serious commitment to the voluntary principle which produces real success in practical terms and might serve usefully as an exemplar for us as we move away from our current overdependence on state agencies (International Expert Meeting, 1989):

> There is a powerful consensus in Switzerland that it is better to promote (and finance) private organizations than to extend public welfare services. We think that the state should not take over these responsibilities from society. In Switzerland, family, neighourhood, associations, private institutions and the church have their function in this sphere, and they are supported by the state in this role. (Declaration of the Swiss Delegation)

Assistance to be Temporary and Conditional

If dependency is to be avoided, no assistance should be offered to those seeking help which does not have a terminal date attached. People cannot reasonably be expected to make the necessary effort to do whatever it takes to change their behaviour, and shift themselves towards autonomy, if they are presented with an unconditional guarantee of permanent assistance. It is simply too much to ask of them.

Similarly, assistance should be conditional on successfully fulfilled obligations, such as involvement in relevant training or further education, participation in appropriate counselling or therapy, or engagement in some useful community activity. We cannot simply demand self-transformation from those who need help: opportunities, arenas and incentives for change have to be provided, and fruitful engagement in them by those offered help has to be effectively assured. Effort should always be required in return for assistance. For far too long the welfare system has operated on the basis of a naïvely idealistic model of the human psyche and of social behaviour, entirely ignoring well-established knowledge about the social psychology of motivation, control, maturity and autonomy (Segalman, 1978; Hanson, 1994).

As the 'scally' in my BBC2 television film *Let's Kill Nanny* said, admitting that he had never worked and boasting about his smart flat and his BMW paid for out of benefit fraud: '*Who wants ter work these days eh?*'

There is considerable prejudice in Britain against workfare. Yet it has been operating successfully in France, in Sweden and elsewhere for many years. Extensive experience and evaluation in the United States, which may have encouraged the sensible proposal by Mr Lilley to replace Unemployment Benefit with a Jobseeker's Allowance in 1996, unequivocally suggests that it is not just a mechanism for cost saving. It is positively beneficial to those who engage in it (Howell, 1985 and 1991). This is because it provides relevant and appropriate incentives. As Robert Rector (1992) puts it:

incentives matter. Any attempt to reform the current structure of public welfare must begin with the realization that most programs designed to alleviate material poverty have led to an increase in behavioural poverty. The rule in welfare, as in other government programs, is simple: you get what you pay for. For over forty years *the welfare system has been paying for non-work and single parenthood, and has obtained dramatic increases in both.* But welfare that discourages work and penalizes marriage ultimately harms its intended beneficiaries. The incentives provided by welfare must be reversed [my emphasis].

The disincentive effects of the Welfare State are apparent not just in relation to those most immediately amenable to recruitment into the underclass, but throughout the working population at all levels – and in all sorts of political contexts, as de Soto's analysis in *The Other Path* (1990) of Third World problems has shown. In a powerful plea for initiative and enterprise, Tom Peters (1994) sings the praises of independence of spirit in the following terms:

> Independent contractors, such as freelance journalists, software programmers and gardeners, wake up knowing that before sunset they must (1) prove themselves again with their clients, and (2) learn a new wrinkle to improve their odds of survival. Today the self-employed are no longer alone in this: I contend, in fact, that everyone – bellhop, scientist, boss – had best achieve the mind-set of the independent contractor.

He concludes, despairingly in relation to the culture of enterprise and service we need, with an apposite anecdote which provides a powerful challenge to the enervating spirit of state welfare:

> Contrast the mind-set of the independent contractor with this common experience. Following a last-minute change of plans, I telephoned a hotel early one morning for a reservation. First I was disconnected, then put on hold, and so on. Finally I reached a living person at the front desk. He flatly declared he couldn't help me. When I asked why (calmly), he responded (calmly): 'I'm not a reservationist'. Nor is he long for the world of the employed.

Thus neither in the open space of independence outside state welfare, nor in the temporarily protected arena of Special Assistance, should anyone be able to take artificial security for granted. Offers of help and the promise of success must always be conditional on initiative and effort on our own autonomous part. Eamonn Butler (1994, p. 13) spells out the dangers of disincentives compellingly:

> Knowing more today about the power of incentives, we can well ask whether we are actually breeding more problems for ourselves. Are we not subsidizing, and so encouraging, the very things we seek to eliminate? By providing money to everyone in disagreeable circumstances, are we simply making such conditions more bearable and so reducing the incentive for self-support? Are we tempting people at the margin to

adjust their affairs in order to qualify for this support? And is the existence of that option not ethically corrosive?

And again at p. 17:

It is also a fair question whether our net effect is to subsidize the things that we are trying to alleviate or reduce. If teenage pregnancies, single parenthood, divorce, unemployment and profligacy are so bad, do we simply increase them by cushioning their effect? And do we meanwhile strangle the opposite values by taxing people who save, people who maintain stable relationships, and people who do everything they can to keep themselves in work?

In Madsen Pirie's graphic formulation (Bell *et al.*, 1994, p. 25): '*Anything you do to relieve distress will instigate more of the behaviour which caused the distress... This problem lies at the heart of every welfare policy.*' It has to be dealt with.

Loans Should be Preferred to Grants

Nothing makes the established state benefit system so destructive of self-reliant autonomy as the character of 'the dole' as a mere 'hand-out' (Parker, 1982). Cavalier, anonymous dispensation of gifts in money, however modest, is more appropriate to some despotic autocracy intent on keeping its people subjugated than to a modern free society committed to optimal autonomy. Behavioural conditionality is not sufficient in itself to answer this problem. Assistance should be provided wherever possible in the form of loans, to be repaid, at moderate interest and over a reasonable period, once self-reliance has been restored. Only thus can clients of the Special Assistance Programme be enabled to construe themselves as genuinely autonomous from the very start of the process of assistance. Nor should we be dismissive of a valuable side-effect of transforming benefits from grants into loans: it would reduce fraud very considerably, and thus free-up resources to improve the quality of training and other developmental assistance which could be provided.

Supporters of the status quo in welfare are virulently resistant to the replacement of grants by loans – even in relation to the funding of university students, who are likely to be able to manage repayment without difficulty. The Government's modest attempts to introduce loans into the heart of the social security system, particularly in the case of the Social Fund, have met much worse obstruction, accompanied by frenzied campaigning in the media and on the streets. This is not a mark of the oppressive injustice of loans, as the campaigners spuriously claim, so much as an index of the symbolic and practical leverage which the replacement of grants by loans provides for transforming the welfare system as a whole. By the same token, if supporters of the reform programme yield on loans, they are likely to fail altogether. The Welfare State and its hand-out culture will have been saved for another generation of destructive expansion.

An alternative or a complement to loans which might be considered carefully and monitored on a pilot basis would be tapering benefits. Starting at a point modest enough to prevent work avoidance at prevailing local rates, benefits would be systematically reduced towards zero, week by week or month by month, over a six-month period. The effect would be to focus claimants' attention on finding legitimate means of survival on their own account, and to galvanize them out of dependent despondency and lethargy into urgent action to seek and seize opportunities for work.

It Should be Local

The Welfare State does much of its damage because it is state-wide, surveying (blindly) and controlling (ineffectively) the behaviour of its clients across the nation from the distant vantage point of Whitehall. The problems it seeks to address are individual, particular and local. The remedies which are most likely to work require intimate local knowledge about the culture of particular housing estates and specific streets, about the condition of local labour markets, about the reputations of this family and that. The Welfare State denies itself the benefit of all this essential local understanding by its centralized administration and by its reliance on generalized criteria of rights and needs.

When Ralph Segalman and I emphasized the importance of localism in effective welfare provision in our book *Cradle to Grave* (1989), pointing to its crucial role in Switzerland, this provoked more criticism than almost any other aspect of our analysis. Experts on welfare apparently take it entirely for granted that to allow even the slightest degree of local discretion involves a contradiction of the whole spirit of the Welfare State, and condemnation of the disadvantaged to mean-spirited exploitation by provincial and small-town burghers.

Since 1989 there has been some acknowledgement of the value of localism in welfare provision, including some overdue recognition of the fact that we might learn more from the Swiss than from the Dutch and the Scandinavians. Thus in a recent article, Norman Macrae (1994) says:

Switzerland does not have a national welfare state. Some 3000 local communes are responsible for deciding on benefits for their poor. Intriguingly, they have just about Europe's lowest rate of unemployed, lowest rate of welfare dependency, and lowest number of people genuinely poor. The communities decide which of their poorest to chivvy into jobs, and to which of their deserving local poor they should give generous and diverse aid.

Localization of welfare is on the cards in the United States too, as a report by Irwin Stelzer (1994), which interprets recent developments as 'the culmination of the Reagan revolution's attempt to scupper the Welfare State introduced by Franklin Roosevelt at the depth of the Great Depression in 1932', quite clearly suggests:

> The welfare system, too, is unlikely to survive in its present form. For one thing, rather than attempt to 'micro-manage' these programmes from Washington, the Republicans intend to hand over broadly defined block grants to the states, and let the local folk devize programs best suited to their specific areas. The goal is to encourage experiments, with everything from workfare to, dare I say it, orphanages. Indeed, the Clinton administration was forced, on persistent congressional questioning, to concede that even its milder plan for welfare reform – cobbled together in a hasty effort to offer something by way of competition with the Republicans' more radical plan – will include orphanages, derisively dismissed as cruel, Dickensian institutions by the now-ignored First Lady.

Even in Britain, where the Welfare State is bigger, more all-enveloping, and more centralized than anywhere else in the free world, and where belief in the necessity of mandarin planning from national HQ is a matter of cross-party faith, there are signs of tentative interest in the benefits of localized welfare. In a speech in January 1995, demanding bigger savings in the £85 billion budget of his Department, Peter Lilley, Secretary of State for Social Security, stated that he did not 'conclude that the whole benefit system should be localised, but whenever changes are made in future, I will consider cautiously whether some greater degree of localisation could bring improvements'. He went on:

> Britain has one of the most centralized and uniform benefit systems in the world. This has many advantages: economies of scale, avoiding disparities and inequities, and preventing internal benefit tourism. But it means local provision cannot be tailored to local circumstances. It becomes harder to bring local knowledge to bear on the delivery of

benefits. It is harder to mobilize local pride to generate positive alternatives to welfare dependency... There could be advantages in some circumstances in devolving responsibility to a local level.

It is perhaps not altogether surprising that an important official statement by the Cabinet Minister explicitly responsible for the core services of the Welfare State should cling to the old-established faith in economies of scale and bureaucratic equity, despite mounting evidence about the excess costs inflicted by scale and the extent of fraud encouraged by over-regulation (Bishop *et al.*, 1995). This aside, however, it is a remarkable acknowledgement of the advantages of localism, which promises serious attention to one of the major sources of inefficiency in the Welfare State.

Mr Lilley even went so far as to cite, with some degree of approval, the Swiss system. He pointed out – again with approval – the localist discretion already available in relation to housing benefits and community care, and he identified accurately a key advantage of localism: the scope for experimentation and testing which it allows. Above all, his reference to the mobilization of local pride in creating positive alternatives to dependency represents a very important step forward in public and official appreciation of the communitarian commitment and energy of which the disadvantaged have been robbed during four decades of centralized, homogenized welfare (Shrimsley, 1995).

A reformed Special Assistance Programme should be localized at least to Borough and District Authority level, and perhaps to some even more intimate scale. The closer the relationship between those helping and those helped, the more likely is it that judgements of need will be made accurately, that appropriate discretion will be brought to bear in the determination of the assistance offered, and that monitoring and control of clients' responses will be effective. Hysterical responses to recent official attention to the possible benefits of localizing welfare (Charlesworth, 1995) are a measure of its potential positive role in genuinely radical reform, rather than an indication of real difficulties with the proposal. A modernized and reformed Welfare State should be thoroughly localized. Real help starts with friends and with neighbours.

It should be Discretionary

In a careful analysis of the neglected moral dimension of welfare, Digby Anderson (1993) suggests that:

> what distinguishes those families that manage to escape from poverty from those that do not is not how much the Government throws at them

but the character and behaviour of the parents... what keeps many families in poverty is not so much low incomes as incompetent or no budgeting, careless borrowing (not finding out interest rates or repayment intervals), inefficient expenditure on food (a substantial proportion of low income expenditure) and male irresponsibility, largely husbands keeping too much money for themselves.

The distinction between the deserving and the undeserving poor, between those whose lives demonstrate prudence, thrift and responsibility on the one hand, and those whose behaviour is typically impulsive, profligate and irresponsible on the other, has long been resisted and lampooned by proponents of universal, comprehensive state welfare. Yet it represents a real and important disjuncture in values and life-styles. Anderson again:

'Ordinary people know about these differences. They know careful poor families and careless ones. They know unemployed people who seek work and others who do not. They know building workers who, in boom times, save some of their income for the inevitable rainy day and others who blow it all. A social security system that denies this moral dimension to poverty and need is divorced from the interests and sentiments of the vast majority of the population.

Because of its incapacity to take account of any differences among clients, however manifestly influential they might be in causing problems and in inhibiting solutions, the established welfare system is indeed divorced from the commonsensical views of most ordinary people. It is also by the same token divorced from the benefit of well-established knowledge about the dynamics of personality and social behaviour. A reformed Special Assistance Programme will reproduce these errors unless genuine discretion – which identifies and takes practical account of differences between positive and negative attitudes, and between sensible, effortful behaviour and its contrary – is built into its culture and its day-to-day operations.

Nor should we be shy of making positive use of shame and stigma, where it is appropriate, to encourage people to shift into self-reliance. It is absurdly naïve – as anyone with children of their own must surely acknowledge – to assume that positive sanctions alone can be sufficient to motivate human beings to address difficult tasks, and to keep on with them until they are at last successfully accomplished. We need rewards certainly, we need support and guidance, if we are to achieve anything, but except for angels amongst us we need from time to time a tougher (but never arbitrary) approach as well.

It Should Not Employ Social Workers as Such

Aside from and on top of the influence of the structure and ethos of the whole state welfare system, the personnel of state welfare, and especially social workers, play a significant role on their own account in creating dependency. In a reformed system we would be better not to use social workers as such at all. Highly trained specialist social workers would no doubt still have valuable work to do in significant numbers in the health, education, housing and employment sectors of mainstream, privatized 'welfare', where they would be subject to normal market disciplines. In the Special Assistance Programme, however, the dangerous temptations of social work should be avoided altogether.

Its first-line personnel would be simply welfare workers. Moreover their training (as of social workers in the mainstream sector) would need to be transformed as radically as the communist systems of training for teachers in the former German Democratic Republic and Czechoslovakia. There should be a decisive shift away from the current emphasis on 'rights' to education in the practical skills required to help people to help themselves and to inculcation of values appropriate in a free society. Useful reforms are currently underway, led by the new Chairman of the Central Council for Education and Training in Social Work, Jeffrey Greenwood, but they do not go anywhere near far enough (CCETSW, 1991 and 1995, and a press release on requisite 'competencies' issued on 1 March 1994). *The Times* (10 September 1994) has it right: 'There is now little or no public support for the social orthodoxies of the 1960s which still hold sway in social work training...'. The prevailing attitudes of social and welfare workers, in particular their simplistic and exaggerated conception of rights and their impertinently anti-democratic commitment to 'liberating' their clients from 'oppression', are a major impediment to genuine welfare.

Instead of Income Support, Restoration of Self-Reliance

The sole mission of the proposed Special Assistance Programme is to restore clients to self-reliance as quickly as possible. It is in order to accomplish this mission that the Programme has to look to needs rather than rights, rely on delivery by commercial and voluntary agencies instead of organs of the state, provide only temporary and conditional assistance, offer loans rather than grants, operate locally, maximize discretion, and rid itself of social workers.

One other key characteristic should distinguish the reformed Special Assistance Programme from our current regime. All financial assistance should be reduced to and held at the absolute minimum which is necessary. This will require rigorous application by elected governments of effective control mechanisms carefully designed to keep the Special Assistance Programme's budget low and reducing – otherwise a bloated Welfare State will gradually be restored. It will also require of welfare delivery agencies and their staff intelligence and persistence in using their discretion toughly in judgements about the amount and nature of assistance to be offered to different people. Glib resort to generalized criteria will produce ineffective help and escalate expenditure.

Some of the substantial savings resulting from welfare reform might quite properly be used to improve the standard of support and care provided for those genuinely qualified for invalidity benefit, particularly the physically and mentally handicapped, the chronic mentally ill (three groups who are especially badly served by the Welfare State), and people seriously hurt in accidents and inadequately compensated by insurance. Some improvement in the level of pensions for those unprovided for otherwise should also be possible and, in the early years of the new system, justifiable. Even here, however, we should be careful to avoid providing a perverse disincentive to saving, such as the social security system has occasioned in Spain (de Soto 1994), and could arise here (Seldon, 1994[2]).

Beyond these groups, *the first and last criterion should be avoidance of disincentive effects*, particularly in relation to unemployment and single parenthood, and the provision of education, health care and housing. It would make a complete nonsense of reform to continue the destructive encouragement which we have tolerated for years of unnecessary unemployment, subversion of the family (Moynihan, 1986; Morgan, 1995), inadequate attention by many parents to education and child rearing (Anderson, 1988[2]), irresponsible expectations about standards of housing (Thurnham, 1993), and that neglect of simple personal and family health measures which is fostered by the NHS (Brindle and Mihill, 1991).

These unacceptable social consequences and continuing escalation of the welfare budget have been powerfully encouraged by the welfare lobby's persistent criticisms of the supposedly negative effects of means testing, and misinterpretations of so-called 'poverty traps' (USDAW, 1994). These analytical errors have regularly been taken up by the media as a basis for tendentious sob-stories designed to expand welfare expenditure even further. In recent years they have been given credit even by the Government, with even the most intelligent and radical of Ministers manipulated into yielding to pressure for allowing benefit levels to drift dangerously upwards, for introducing more and yet more benefits, and for expanding the benefit culture further and further up the social scale.

Thus increasingly extravagant benefits are provided for lone parents who should be supported by the fathers of their children, by their own effort once children are old enough, and in the last resort by their families. Family Credit (soon to be expanded, with even less justification, to cover the working single) has quite unnecessarily brought large numbers of self-reliant people within the dependency culture. It will creep higher and higher up the income scale unless the specious arguments used to justify it are addressed, creating in consequence a minimum wage in all but name which is bound to increase unemployment and stoke up inflationary pressures (Lal, 1995). Again, housing benefit is provided over and above other benefits, by the loosest of criteria, and for an escalating number of people. People 'entitled' to benefits who for some, quite possibly very good, reason of their own do not claim them are hassled at Government and tax-payers' expense and with all the energetic sophistication of a car salesman in order to 'improve take-up'. And so on.

Poverty traps can only be avoided sensibly by keeping the support provided by the Special Assistance Programme at minimum levels. The welfare lobbyists tell us that most underclass welfare dependents really want to work and to be self-reliant. We should give them a proper chance to test out this implausible proposition by restoring differentials between benefits and the lower end of wages to a proper level.

Similarly, any negative effects produced by means testing (reconstrued as careful analysis of real need) should be addressed not by a gradual drift towards extravagant universal benefits, but by effective community policing of fraud and crime, by control of the welfare lobby's distortions and lies about poverty, and by nation-wide and local community campaigns for the value of self-reliance.

Typical examples of the errors I am addressing here appear in a recent publication by the National Federation of Housing Associations (1994). Thus:

> A working parent whose income increases, loses up to 97% of their gross earnings as a result of the sharp tapers of housing benefit and other entitlements, together with tax and national insurance deductions.

And again:

> At current rent levels, a couple with two children and a single earner require an income £50 per week more than they currently receive to escape the poverty trap.

And again:

> Families with one working parent, receiving the average net income of new tenants, need to earn twice as much to get £20 a week more.

A letter which I have been shown, written from the House of Commons Library to an MP, seeks to justify these misleading statements (and their even more misleading implications) by reference to publications by the Low Pay Unit and the Joseph Rowntree Foundation. These appear to be shaped largely, as one might expect, given their auspices, by the ill-considered, collectivist assumptions about welfare which cause the problem of poverty traps and the difficulties currently associated with means testing in the first place (Brittan, 1995).

I would prefer to see these propositions re-interpreted along quite different lines. In relation to the first case, a working parent should not normally be on housing benefit or in receipt of other entitlements. Income tax could be much reduced, if not eliminated, on lower incomes if money were not wasted on unnecessary benefits. End of problem. The second case is entirely a semantic problem. The couple involved are caught in a so-called poverty trap purely and simply because of the ease with which Housing Benefit is awarded. The third case is formulated in the disingenuously misleading terms which have become routine in the poverty media. We should not be deceived. Such families only need to earn so much more for so little return because their benefits are set so excessively high in relation to prevailing and realistic wage levels.

The letter refers in relation to the first case to a '97 per cent marginal reduction rate'. This is a routine formulation, but wholly specious. We should congratulate and celebrate a person who behaves decently by working hard at a modest job even though this leaves him only slightly advantaged in financial terms compared with a neighbour in similar circumstances who prefers to stay on benefit. We should make it financially and psychologically challenging, to put it mildly, for such a neighbour to prefer a dependent life on handouts. We should certainly not encourage the unemployed and the lower-paid to stay unemployed and lower-paid indefinitely by subsidizing their situation and massaging their psyche by means of benefits. Influential arguments notwithstanding (Atkinson and Mogenson, 1993), excessive and badly targeted benefits constitute a powerful disincentive to work and to every other kind of useful, positive behaviour.

If the financial support provided by the Special Assistance Programme is even marginally excessive or even slightly inappropriate, the knock-on effect will escalate the welfare budget progressively. Worse than this, it will prevent the Programme from achieving its only rationally and morally justifiable purpose by providing an incentive for people to continue in subjugated dependency, instead of moving on and up as quickly as they can manage into self-reliant independence (Smiles, 1860). As even the political left is now recognizing, self-reliance and self-help are indispensible conditions of freedom. Thus, in *'Building Social Capital'* (1995), Mai Wann, writing for the Labour Party think-tank the Institute for Public Policy Research, argues that 'New thinking about welfare should recognize self help as a core activity. It makes a major contribution to the health and well being of individuals and communities.' A similar case is made in a recent article by Frank Field MP (1994), where he argues that 'self-help is the key to Labour's new Welfare State'.

The Special Assistance Programme should be as toughly resistant, in principle and practice, to emotional pressure to reduce inequalities as the German bankers in Frankfurt are to inflation. Specious arguments in favour of equalization, such as those unashamedly peddled in the Rowntree Foundation's latest sentimental, utopian extravaganza *Income and Wealth* (1995), should be dismissed. They would create poverty and multiply unemployment (Brittan, 1995). Similarly, the populist blandishments of the Labour Party and its trade union allies in support of a minimum wage, rhetorically plausible though they can seem in the form of televisual soundbytes, should be opposed (Transport and General Workers' Union, 1994). Even at modest levels, a minimum wage increases unemployment, reduces incentives for job-seeking, blunts ambition and subverts competition between companies (Stigler, 1946). The International Monetary Fund's Annual Report for 1994 demanded significant reductions in the level of established minimum wages and unemployment benefit to free-up the labour market and improve employment prospects. Deepak Lal concludes his recent systematic review of the best research on the topic as follows (1995, p. 31):

> The revived controversy over the minimum wage thus reflects the continuing hold of certain atavistic impulses combined with a continuing lack of understanding amongst technocrats of the workings of an actual as compared with an idealised market economy. Despite the passions aroused, the textbook conclusion with which we began – that the minimum wage is an inefficient, well-intentioned but 'inexpert interference' with the mechanisms of supply and demand – still stands.

Even more dangerous to the real interests of the vulnerable than generalized equality-mongering such as that perpetrated by the Rowntree report, even more counter-productive than the current campaign to install a minimum wage, is the influential pressure of the Citizen's Income Research Group and others for the establishment of a basic income, provided as of right by the state, regardless of need, effort or merit, for everyone (Desai, 1995). For, in seeking to find a solution to problems caused by so-called 'poverty traps' and alleged difficulties arising from the use of means testing, supporters of Basic Income would subvert the whole structure of competitive incentives and sabotage completely the cultural infrastructure of market society. Implementation of social policies based on their naïvely idealistic conception of human nature would reward idleness, penalize effort and undermine the work ethic (Marsland, 1994 [5]). Those who urge a basic income scheme as a means of dealing with fraud in the benefit system are as foolishly mistaken as those nineteenth-century socialists who sought a solution to theft in the abolition of property!

Economic equality is a destructive mirage. The minimum wage is a guarantee of permanent underclass exclusion of the disadvantaged from normal social intercourse. Basic income is a fanciful dream which would reduce prosperity all round without improving the condition of those in most need in the slightest. Avoiding all these traps and snares, the Special Assistance Programme of a reformed welfare system must stand foursquare in support of the normal work system and the established value system of free societies, and equip, encourage and chivvy temporary unfortunates to join in with the rest of us.

Conclusion

Critics of welfare reform are right to see in proposals such as those recommended here elements of the nineteenth century reformed Poor Law system and traces of even older charitable arrangements (Octavia Hill, 1883). They are quite wrong, however, in supposing that this provides grounds for rejecting them, as Lorie Charlesworth (1995) assumes in an article (entitled with dismissive intent, 'The poor laws by a modern Tory name') written in implausible rebuttal of Peter Lilley's proposals for localizing benefits. The Welfare State has proved such a triumphant failure because its utopian progressivism has led it to ignore simultaneously both the wisdom of the past *and* well-established up-to-date knowledge about personality, motivation, incentives, social control and social behaviour (O'Keeffe, 1994; Yarrow, 1994). We have much to learn again from both.

Analysis of modern research in specific relation to welfare has been presented comprehensively and cogently in his various publications by Ralph Segalman. Rather than examine them further here, I refer readers to *Poverty in America* (Segalman and Basu, 1981), to *Cradle to Grave* (Segalman and Marsland, 1989, particularly Part 1), and to *The Underclass Revisited* (Segalman, 1994). Segalman's remarkable corpus of work emphasizes throughout a single, simple truth: *loss of autonomy, and consequent descent into dependency, is socially produced by the absence of effective controls; it can be restored only by the determined application of alternative controls.*

On the basis of extensive research – some his own and some by other experts, including not least Erik Erikson (1956 and 1968) – Segalman has traced these destructive and re-constructive processes in detail. He lays bare the process of decay in the power and valency of the family, the neighbourhood and the school which generates dependency, and the structures of influence by systems of welfare which either (organized badly) reinforce dependency, or (organized well along the lines described above) restore control, facilitate thereby self-control, and establish self-reliant autonomy. A reformed Special Assistance Programme has to be shaped by the commonsensical and truthful understandings and principles which Segalman (and also of course others) are seeking to retrieve from the wreckage of individual and family life produced by the utopian heresies of modern educational and welfare theory.

A major source of these errors, strongly emphasized by Segalman (Segalman and Himelson, 1994) is the extent to which protagonists of the Welfare State ignore and scorn the accumulated wisdom and knowledge we have about the family – the best source of real welfare there is. It is no accident that Alva Myrdal, co-founder with her husband Gunnar of the intellectual infrastructure of the Swedish Welfare State, viewed 'the modern, miniature family' as 'an abnormal situation for a child', and sought to displace it with 'apartment houses with a single nursery and a single kitchen for the entire building' – i.e. collectivist and socialist provision designed to iron out individual quirks (Carlson, 1988).

By contrast David Popenoe's advice (1988), grounded in carefully collected evidence rather than derived from utopian fancies, has rather less fashionable, rather more radical, implications for the way we order welfare:

> Social science research is almost never conclusive. There are always methodological difficulties and stones left unturned. Yet in decades of work as a social scientist, I know of few other bodies of data in which the weight of evidence is so decisively on one side of the issue: for children, two parent-families are preferable to single-parent and step-families.

The family is the indispensable mechanism in the production of autonomous, self-reliant personalities, capable of resisting the blandishments of welfare dependency. It is only in the context of loving support and rational discipline which the family offers – provided it is intact and functioning effectively – that children can be reliably socialized into the values and skills which social autonomy requires (Segalman and

Marsland, 1989, pp. 121–4). The Special Assistance Programme must therefore at all costs avoid weakening the family as an institution, seek wherever possible to repair families under strain, and in all aspects of its work with dependent clients strive to reproduce the subtle mix of care and discipline, discipline and care, which distinguishes families and other natural, spontaneous systems from the empty bureaucratic structures of state welfare.

If we are to understand the dangers of misdirected welfare provision, it is not necessary to accept in their totality the arguments presented by Murray and Hernstein in their book *The Bell Curve* (1994), which has provoked hysteria among collectivists world-wide because of its honest attention to the facts about disincentives. It is not even essential to follow Herbert Spencer (1873) all the way in his more modest critique of the predictably dysfunctional consequences of ill-considered do-gooding. Nonetheless, both Murray and Spencer provide us with valuable clues to truths about welfare which have been ignored for too long. Spencer's formulation is typically clear and tough-minded:

> Fostering the good-for-nothing at the expense of the good is an extreme cruelty. It is a deliberate storing up of miseries for future generations. There is no greater curse to posterity than that of bequeathing them an increasing population of imbeciles and idlers and criminals. To aid the bad in multiplying is, in effect, the same as maliciously providing for our descendants a multitude of enemies. It may be doubted whether the maudlin philanthropy which, looking only at direct mitigations, persistently ignores indirect mischief, does not inflict a greater total of misery than the extremest selfishness inflicts.

The Special Assistance Programme must be exclusively in the business of fostering the good-for-something, of whom there are many millions currently being damaged and destroyed by state welfare systems organized on the basis of inappropriate values, erroneous understandings and counter-productive principles. What these victims of mistaken and mischievous welfare concepts need and deserve is not income support but life support, not hand-outs but supportive discipline designed to restore them to authentic autonomy and genuine self-reliance.

Indeed, in reforming state welfare, we might do worse than to look for principled guidance to the medieval Jewish philosopher Maimonides. He proposes that the highest form of charity requires that we should aim at more than merely restoring those we help to self-sufficiency. Our constant ambition should be to assist them in becoming successful competitors with ourselves.

10 After the Welfare State: Real Welfare in a Free Society

During the whole of the second half of the twentieth century the state has seized and successfully held monopoly control of all those essential services which socialists have deceitfully schooled us to define as welfare. By the end of the century, this bizarre system will have been replaced by more natural and more efficient arrangements more appropriate to a free society. We shall look back on the Welfare State with the same contemptuous amazement as that with which we now view slavery as a means of organizing effective, motivated work, central planning as an instrument for operating an efficient, dynamic economy, or feudalism as a source of reliable, legitimate political rule.

Free labour, the market and democracy have triumphed as their primitive antecedent institutions have been challenged and replaced. It remains for us to challenge the equally primitive institution of the Welfare State, and to replace it with a modern system complementary to free labour, the market and democracy, and similarly compatible with human nature and the deepest aspirations of humanity.

The Welfare State is not, as its stubborn and naïve protagonists have foolishly persuaded themselves, the pinnacle and *sine qua non* of civilized society. On the contrary, state welfare is to be faulted on many grounds, as authors as diverse in ideological and theoretical terms as Herbert Spencer, Hilaire Belloc, Arthur Seldon, Charles Murray, Ralph Segalman, Peter Saunders, Digby Anderson and Norman Dennis have demonstrated. Its major weaknesses, which provide the primary focus of this book, are clear.

First, the whole concept of the 'Welfare State' is philosophically incoherent, and inevitably productive in consequence of irresoluble operational contradictions. Second, the forward march of normal economic progress, and the massive generalized increase in standards of living which prosperity has generated, make the bloated system of universal state welfare provision entirely unnecessary. Thirdly, the costs of the Welfare State have escalated to such an extent that they threaten national bankruptcy. Fourthly, the Welfare State is in any case largely ineffective. The inevitable consequence of its monopoly power, its inherently bureaucratic character and its inattention to the varying needs of individual people, is that it fails routinely to help those who genuinely need special support. It squanders the billions of pounds which it costs every year on third-rate services delivered to the wrong people, in inappropriate ways, to little useful effect.

Finally, and worst of all, it wreaks enormously destructive harm on its supposed prime beneficiaries: the vulnerable, the disadvantaged and the unfortunate. It makes of perfectly normal, entirely capable people who happen to be in temporary difficulty, a fractious, subjugated underclass of welfare dependants. The Welfare State thus cripples the enterprising, self-reliant spirit of individual men and women, and lays a depth-charge of explosive resentment under the foundations of our free society.

A Last Chance for Reform?

In this light it might seem that the whole lunatic system should be terminated and replaced forthwith. Unless perhaps last minute remedial reform should prove somehow possible? This is just what the Labour Party's Commission on Social Justice (1994) seems to promise. Before long I expect we shall find anti-government intellectuals busily and uncritically citing the Borrie Report as if it were the Fifth Gospel. They will glibly claim that it proves this, confirms that and decisively demonstrates the other. If we are to avoid enervating entrapment in a new welfare orthodoxy so soon after we have managed to slough off the old one, we need a rigorous analysis of what the report says and what it is worth.

In my judgement, it is fundamentally misconceived. Indeed it is more gravely flawed even than the Beveridge Report, adding to the otherworldly pietism of Beveridge a measure of incoherence and illogicality which only a committee could manage. It must be allowed no influence at all on social policy, a conclusion in which, to judge by Bill Jamieson's article (1994), 'Borrie's Panacea Is a Suicide Pill', I am not alone.

Admittedly, we should be very grateful for small mercies. The Commission has managed to produce a long overdue admission by the British left that the old Welfare State is not after all the eighth wonder of the world. It has succeeded against the odds in confessing that state welfare generates dependency and that this is at least regrettable. It has screwed up its courage to recognize that the only reliable source of genuine welfare is a productive economy, and that economic progress is impossible if markets and competition are stifled by bureaucratic interference. It has dared to acknowledge the heretical notion that both taxation and public expenditure must be subject to rational limitation if national bankruptcy is to be avoided.

There are, alas, two serious impediments to interpreting these progressive elements in the Commission's analysis as triumphal achievements of the modernizing British left. First, this new wisdom has been recognized as self-evident truth by everyone outside the Whitehall opposition establishment and its academic entourage, and certainly by most of the electorate, for decades. It is hardly novel. Second, it seems highly unlikely that Labour party activists will view such revisionism as anything other than treacherous betrayal of socialist values. It is bad politics.

However, there are worse faults of the Borrie Report than its hamhanded combination of nervous challenge to outmoded socialist shibboleths and spineless refusal to contemplate a radical individualistic alternative. I will mention just four of them: the *philosophical incoherence* involved in equating justice with equality; the *implausibility of the tripartite scheme of welfare models* on which its whole argument rests; its *careless use of doubtful evidence* about the condition and prospects of the British people; and its extraordinary *failure to examine the cost implications* of its proposals.

Within its motley membership the Commission included, in Bernard Williams, at least one distingusished philosopher. Despite this, the Borrie Report manages somehow to treat as entirely unproblematical the tired notion that justice means equality. It may be sufficient for Roy Hattersley, writing entertaining articles in the *Guardian*, to elide the fundamental contradictions between freedom and equality with a mere flourish of verbal dexterity. But this is hardly adequate in providing a coherent philosophical basis for a serious analysis of welfare which makes claims to underpinning the modernization of a great party and the wholesale 'renewal' of British society. Throughout the Report, its authors trade, disingenuously or naïvely, on an unanalysed equation of justice and equality, an unreconstructed, atavistic intolerance of economic inequalities, as utopian as the adolescent scribbling in a typical sociology textbook. The Commission's social philosophy of welfare is more suitable for ex-communists struggling to come to terms with 1989 than for aspiring social democrats aiming realistically at power in a free society.

A primary rhetorical device in the Report's overall argumentation is its distinction between Levellers (bad), Deregulators (worse), and Investors (very good indeed). This reminds me of nothing so much as those futile typologies constructed in advertising agencies on the basis of dubious market research in order to classify orientations to the use of baked beans or syndromes of life-style tendencies. It is social analysis on the hoof, last thing at night, by people who think they know all the answers before they have even started the research.

The authors' analysis of the 'levelling' egalitarian socialist concepts of welfare from which they seek at all costs to distance themselves relies on an artfully constructed and wholly spurious straw-man image of collectivist ideas on which the Labour Party has been quite content to depend since it was first established. If it is to give up 'levelling', the Party is redundant. I leave the happy band of recalcitrant hardline socialists in the media, the universities and the constituency parties to take up that argument on their own behalf. And they will.

The rest of this curious model is even more specious. The 'Deregulators' are a pure invention, concocted fancifully out of socialist nightmares neurotically dreamed during the long years of Conservative success since 1979. The concept provides the authors of the Borrie Report with a pretext for denying, quite fallaciously, that genuinely radical reform of state welfare is necessary and feasible. It is a thin excuse for the Commission's wilful refusal to consider cutting the Welfare State down to size.

The 'Investors' – that is to say Messrs Blair, Prescott, Brown, and Cook disguised as d'Artagnan and the Three Musketeers – represent an equally fictitious counter-image of tender-minded welfare modernizers: tough on dependency and tough on the alleged causes of dependency, generous yet thrifty, friends of the family with helpful plans none the less for single parents, and confident in the 'dynamic market economy' as long as competition is throttled by state regulation and wealth-creating entrepreneurs are taxed to the hilt as 'social justice' demands. This is not analysis. It is argument by wish-fulfilment.

The Commission's social geography is as inaccurate as its social philosophy is incoherent and its social analysis obtuse. The authors seem to accept entirely uncritically the professional lobbyists' relativist concept of poverty. Any and every inequality is treated as an unjust social disadvantage. The extent of economic progress achieved since the War and in the past fifteen years is hopelessly under-acknowledged. The extent to which the quality of life of the whole population has improved is cloaked throughout the Borrie Report with scarcely less inventive vigour than used to be employed by Soviet sociologists in their Dickensian portrayals of post-war capitalism. Welfare reform is impossible except on the basis of a realistic and honest account of the conditions and prospects of the British people. This the Borrie Report singularly fails to provide.

Finally there are the extravagant costs of the Commission's manifold proposals and ambitions. The public expenditure implications – even granted the long time-horizons indicated here and there but nowhere specified fully explicitly by the authors, and their continual plaintive refrain about the economic preconditions of their grand plans – are patently absurd. There is no room at all for any such expansion of public expenditure over the next decade. Indeed, substantial reductions are likely to be essential, and of this a significant proportion will have to come out of the welfare budget.

In short, the Report of the Commission on Social Justice is not at all, as is being claimed, a thoughtful plan for modernizing welfare provision. On the contrary, it is an ill-conceived excuse for maintaining the welfare status quo and expanding its strangulating hold on British life and the British psyche still further. Implemented even gradually and in part by an emboldened Labour Party backed by collectivist bureaucrats in Brussels, it would reduce Britain to bankruptcy in short order, and hand the British people over to European subjection. Or, as Jamieson (1994) puts it: 'The Social Justice Commission would visit on Britain not just a pauper's vision, but an economy to match.'

After the Welfare State

Since the only available programme for pragmatic reform of the Welfare State looks to be a non-starter, a more radical approach, along the lines examined in the course of this book, seems to be essential. As of today, the whole population are – willy nilly – clients of the Welfare State. After radical welfare reform, 80 per cent or more of the population will provide for themselves out of their own resources.

As of today, the small minority who genuinely cannot fend for themselves queue up in a spirit oscillating between wearied subservience and self-destructive rebellion, for miserable hand-outs which do them more harm than good. After reform, they will be afforded real help which challengingly assists them back to dignity and self-reliance.

As of today, the state has an illegitimate monopoly of the whole huge range of services which the monstrous apparatus contructed by Christian socialism, Lloyd George, Lord Beveridge and modern socialism has appropriated to itself. After reform, the diverse services encompassed within education, health care, pensions, income support and all the rest will be provided by non-state, independent, private, voluntary and mutual suppliers competing hard in a genuinely free and appropriately regulated market for the custom of prudent, demanding, autonomous consumers.

As of today, control of welfare is exercised through a tightly centralized system which endows central and local state officials with irresponsible power over our lives. After reform, this power will be returned to individuals exercising a free choice in a dynamic, self-regulating network of competing suppliers.

As of today, decisions about resource allocation in welfare are made by planners, several levels removed from direct consumers, using arbitrary formulae defined by political deals, habit, and producer convenience. After reform, suppliers will determine investment levels, product lines, prices and service-point locations in terms of consumer preferences identified by demand, profitability and careful market research.

Thus a comprehensive transformation will be required, providing solutions to current problems arising in turn from state bureaucracy, monopoly, paternalism, politicization and the sclerosis of centralized planning. If we are to understand better than programmatically the significance for our future of this radical change in the whole culture and social structure of welfare, we need to consider it carefully from two distinct perspectives – first the perspective of social theory and ideas, and secondly the perspective of social policy and practice.

In relation to the theory of post-Welfare State society, David Green's analysis in '*Rediscovering Civil Society*' (1993) provides useful guidelines. On policy and practice, the Adam Smith Institute's '*The End of the Welfare State*' (Bell, 1994) is a helpful starting point for further analysis.

Restoration of Civil Society

Civil society – that subtle matrix of institutions intermediate between the individual and the state which is the essential seedbed of liberty – presupposes certain virtues in a people which aspires to freedom (Gellner, 1994). According to Green (1993), these include: 'Good character, honesty, duty, self-sacrifice, honour, service, self-discipline, toleration, respect, justice, self-improvement, trust, civility, fortitude, courage, integrity, diligence, patriotism, consideration for others, thrift and reverence...'.

'To the modern ear', he says with saddening accuracy, 'they have a ring of either antique charm or total obsolescence.' State power, and not least state power in the sphere of welfare, has suppressed and subverted them. It has, in consequence, sabotaged civil society, and threatens freedom itself. Welfare reform, therefore, cannot consist merely of a simple technical or political process of policy development and administrative change. It will entail, on the contrary, a cultural revolution through which the virtues will be rediscovered and reinforced, and civil society restored and re-energized. Green proposes that this will involve three major changes in our culture: de-politicization of the law-making process, strict definition of the proper limits of government, and elaboration of a 'morality of liberty'.

This prescriptive analysis, supposing it is correct, means that in post-Welfare State conditions Britain will be radically different from our present anomic, decadent society. New organizational structures and administrative procedures will be insufficient. An essential prerequisite to administrative and organizational change is transformation of three key aspects of the deep structure of our national culture. First, the constitutional structure will be amended to separate out and to protect law-making – the establishing of *'nomos'*, in Hayek's terminology – from the dross and sleaze of interest-based politics. Secondly, the orbit of government will be substantially reduced, in particular limiting the extent to which political interference with the economy is allowed (see also on the limitation of government Flew, 1994). Thirdly, and most importantly, a new ethos of personal responsibility will be initiated, underpinning social support for the key values of what Novak (1991) has called 'the spirit of democratic capitalism', and entrenching what John Gray (1992) calls 'the moral foundations of market institutions'.

Liberation of the Market

'The End of the Welfare State' takes Green's cultural analysis as given, and poses the further political and practical question of how precisely the restoration of civil society is to be achieved. Its answer is straightforward and simple: what is required is the liberation of the market in the welfare sphere from illegitimate constraints and unfair competition.

The key mechanism proposed in *'The End of the Welfare State'* for liberating the market in welfare is the 'Personal Lifetime Account', a combination of savings and insurance by means of which most people could easily provide more than adequately for themselves and their families in terms of education, health care and pensions. The PLA will represent each person's investment in his own future, and at the same time comprise a huge capital fund, administered by professional managers rather than state bureaucrats, and available as an investment pool for British industry. 'The present system', says Madsen Pirie, 'has no such funds, no such pool, and no such contribution to the economic growth of the nation' (ibid., p. 26). Among its many advantages, and over and above the crucial improvement it would bring by injecting capital growth into welfare, this system would reduce fraud enormously and eliminate current complexities (ibid.):-

> The tendency to fraud will be much diminished if it is no longer the state they are defrauding, or even other contributors. People will be

defrauding themselves, since it it is their own fund they will be drawing benefits from. The complexity will be much diminished if people draw from a single source the benefits they will need in the event of well-defined circumstances.

Michael Bell details more precisely what would be involved (ibid., p. 31):

It is time to begin to plan the wholesale removal of pensions... followed by health and education, from the public sector. It is not that difficult to imagine how a privatized system would work: education would still be compulsory, with the state maintaining standards through inspection and a core curriculum. In health and pensions there could be compulsory private insurance to give a minimum level of benefit from regulated providers. The role of the state would be to maintain standards, and safety-net provision could be achieved through means-tested state payment of insurance premiums, or in the case of education, payment of fees for a standard level of provision.

The authors systematically demonstrate, in thoroughly practical terms covering both administrative organization and costings, how the whole state welfare apparatus can be rapidly privatized, leaving the state responsible for no more than a residual safety net for the 'incapable and unlucky'. They delineate a new structure which can be built up gradually out of the decaying shell of the existing state apparatus. They demonstrate inventively how the financial difficulties involved in the transition can be successfully overcome. In announcing the end of the Welfare State, they provide a blue-print of a new and better state of welfare.

Thus, in imagining the future of Britain beyond the dark horizon of state welfare, we must envisage a society illuminated by these two powerful analyses of social theory and social policy respectively. We must reject and resist the spurious social theory which is taught as an orthodoxy in the universities and peddled with mendacious eloquence in the media. We must dismiss from our minds the powerful unconscious influence of its fraudulent characterization of man as a helpless creature of social forces, and of society as a jungle of conflicting factional interests domesticated and civilized only by the constraining powers of the state. Instead we must follow Green – and through him Hayek, Novak and Gray – towards a quite contrary sociological vision: of man as an active, enterprising agent, taking rational moral responsibility for himself and others; and of society as an arena of competitive co-operation in which nations carry human economic and social progress successfully forward.

By the same token, we must put aside the persisting influence in social policy analysis of Titmuss, Townsend and their cohorts, with their gloomy insistence on human frailty and their cowardly demand for ever-increasing control by the state. Instead we should follow Pirie and his colleagues towards a more modest and at the same time more optimistic mode of policy development, acknowledging that, freed from the unjust and unnatural constraints of state control, we can invent and successfully manage arrangements for our personal and collective welfare which really work.

The State's Continuing Role in Welfare

Even after the disestablishment of state welfare, the state's role in welfare will not – indeed it cannot, and it should not – wither away. Anarcho-capitalism is as utopian and impractical as mere socialism. The state will retain an enormously reduced, but crucial role in two spheres.

First, the state in a democratic society must, within the law and under the controlling guidance of elected governments, maintain its responsibility for defining the parameters of welfare and for regulating the operation of welfare suppliers. Secondly, the state has to address, more seriously and more effectively than it has managed during the state socialist phase of welfare development, the organization and policing of assistance to the small and fluctuating minority of people who cannot at particular times manage to cope within the normal self-provisioning system defined by prudence, self-reliance and the market.

Little need be said about the first of these functions. Disestablishment will remove from the statute book those hundreds of currently operative Acts of Parliament and lesser statutory instruments which at present in every sphere of social policy authorize state agencies, require state services and impose detailed obligations on individuals and organizations, on welfare producers and welfare consumers alike, to do this, to avoid that, and to strive for the other. The whole of this ramifying socialist rule-book will be thrown away.

It will be replaced by a single Act requiring – as insurance is currently required of the owners of vehicles – insurance cover to provide for a specified minimum standard of provision of health care, invalidity support, education for children, pensions and income protection. No state preference is needed as between comprehensive cover, along the lines proposed by the Adam Smith Institute, and more differentiated cover involving a variety of suppliers. Still less is any state interference with individuals' choices of particular insurance schemes or particular suppliers necessary or indeed tolerable. These are all properly matters of free individual choice.

Nor should regulation be intrusive or excessive. All the insurance companies and welfare suppliers will of course be subject to all of the relevant established general law in relation to contract, fraud, negligence and so on. In addition, systems of direct regulation, audit and inspection will be required. Wherever possible these should be self-regulatory systems. For example, associations of hospitals, consortia of schools, and the pensions and insurance industries will be responsible for setting, policing and sanctioning their own standards. Statutory regulation and state policing will be allowed only temporarily, where general dereliction is demonstrated before the courts and to the satisfaction of Parliament. In general, one would expect the market and the beneficent impact of competition to provide as effective a protection for consumers in the sphere of welfare as it does in the broader sphere of production, service and distribution already liberated from state control.

The State and Special Assistance

Comprehensive disestablishment of state welfare will of itself reduce significantly the numbers of people seeking last resort state assistance. Awareness of the changed ideological climate, with the shift from rights to automatic hand-outs to a presumption of self-reliance, will serve to encourage people to find some way of managing. Families will play a bigger part than they have done for decades. Charities will rediscover their traditional and honourable role and switch back away from negative whinging and collectivist campaigning to providing real help designed to get people back on their own two feet as rapidly as possible. A market in welfare, like all markets, will encourage innovations and call into being supplies of cheap, adequate versions of schooling, health care, housing, etcetera, such as the availability of state welfare has inhibited. These will answer the needs of hundreds of thousands who currently turn to the state for help.

Potential demand for special assistance could also be substantially reduced by reforms in the tax system designed to leave lower income families with more of their own money – indeed, preferably with *all* of their own money. It could be further reduced with solid, long-term effects if we could manage somehow to turn the tide on the decay of the family. A healthy family institution is the best guarantee we can have of effective socialization and social control designed to produce the attitudes and behaviours which a self-reliant life demands (Segalman and Marsland, 1989; Morgan, 1994).

Even with improvements on all these fronts, however, there will still be significant numbers of people who fall, for one reason or another, through their own fault or as a result of genuine misfortune, out of the normal system of self-reliance, and who need temporary help which neither families nor charities can provide. The state in a democratic society – I hope I have sufficiently emphasized this in the preceding chapter – must not balk at accepting its reponsibility for their welfare.

The ethos and mode of organization characterizing this important task in post-Welfare State conditions must be quite different from the bureaucratic yet casually rights-oriented approach to which we have become habituated since the 1940s. Neither central nor local state organizations will be involved in any aspect of the delivery of special assistance services. The whole service will be contracted out to commercial agencies and to genuinely voluntary organizations. The number of people being provided with special assistance will be monitored closely, and any increase accounted for carefully and dealt with appropriately. Assistance will be made available solely on the basis of carefully assessed need, with assumptions about 'rights' on the part of either clients or welfare workers strenuously challenged and officially rejected. The training of welfare workers will be carefully monitored to prevent ideological contamination by outmoded concepts of welfare which might encourage the re-emergence of dependency.

The whole system will be localized to small community patches, allowing the welfare workers involved to make appropriately discretionary judgements – about whether and how much help should be offered to individual clients and what form it should it take, and about the progress being made by clients – on the basis of detailed local knowledge. In order to encourage prudence and self-reliant life-planning, money transfers will take the form of loans rather than grants wherever possible. Clients – including not least the unemployed and lone parents – will all be required to offer some relevant, effortful return for assistance received, for example through community service or through participation in some appropriate form of training.

The whole purpose of the Special Assistance Programme is to help and encourage people back as quickly as possible to self-reliance. This involves persuading clients to believe that self-reliance is the normal and proper way to live, and that helplessness is at all legitimate costs to be avoided. Inevitably this entails the attachment of some degree of stigma to applications for assistance. In the new regime there can be no room for apologetic defensiveness about this. A major reason for the expansion of welfare dependency in recent years is the decay of shame as a mechanism of social control and positive motivation. After welfare reform, its beneficial impact will be restored and encouraged.

The state, through the elected government and through elected representatives at local level, ought to have some specific responsibility for encouraging commitment to self-reliance in the population, and for discouraging the growth of counter-productive sentimentalism in the media and the educational system. Beyond this educational role, the organization of a local monitoring and inspection system, and the provision of modest, carefully audited essential funding, the state will have no involvement at all in special welfare provision.

As of now the State is a powerful activist agency in the delivery of welfare, with its Palaces of Dependency arrogantly dominating the landcape of all our local communities, and its electronic communications network busily interfering with the lives of millions right across Britain. In post-reform conditions it will withdraw to an altogther more modest and circumscribed role, leaving agencies better equipped for the essential task of helping concrete individual people back to self-reliance to get on with the job unimpeded by state bureaucracy and collectivist ideology.

Knowledge and Wise Action

Throughout the period of Conservative government since 1979, and even while a succession of Ministers in all the relevant Departments has been struggling to effect rational reforms of the welfare system which are desperately needed and long overdue, the welfare lobbyists and social policy academics have continued with their relentless campaign to defend and entrench the status quo. Their purpose is to thwart and resist the policies of the elected government, and thus to controvert the will of the British people. A typical example is provided by the responses of social analysts and social researchers to health-care reform.

Reactions to the White Paper 'Working for Patients', to the reforming NHS and Community Care Act which followed in 1990, and to the Government's and NHS management's implementation of reform subsequently, have demonstrated that there are very few academics, social policy researchers or social affairs correspondents in the media who are not substantially prejudiced in favour of the status quo in health care (Marsland, 1989 [6]). Apart from the Health Reform Group, the Institute of Economic Affairs and the Adam Smith Institute, Secretaries of State for Health have been able to rely on precious little support from the intelligentsia in their efforts to effect reform. Even these exceptional cases are outside the universities, where the bulk of funding for research on health care is spent. Indeed, even from the sadly few centres of innovative thinking about health care in the universities (one thinks of York, for example, and the Health Services Management Centre at Birmingham), there has been very little by way of public support for NHS reform from the day the White Paper was published up to the present. Thus even Professor Chris Ham, Director of the Birmingham Centre, was reported in July 1994 as claiming that the 'NHS reforms are out of control and the Government has no clear idea of where they are going.'

Research projects in the sphere of health care funded by the ESRC, the main source of public financing for social research, have, almost without exception, produced yet more critical material, rather than any positive assistance for the implementation of NHS reform. Social scientists remain in general thoroughly sceptical about – not to say prejudiced against – any serious role for markets, external or internal, in the health sphere; about objective scrutiny of current – high and increasing – health-care costs; about strengthening the hand of devolved management; about genuine attention to consumer perceptions and dissatisfactions; or about allowing the proper emphasis on efficiency which, along with care, is essential in a modernized, dynamic NHS. Even the sociology and social policy now routinely taught to doctors and nurses in training is, if we may judge from the textbooks typically used, largely impregnated with prejudices incompatible with genuine reform of health care.

This lack of support for health-care reform from the academic community, typified by the Radical Statistics Health Group's knee-jerk condemnation of hospital league tables (Macfarlane and Chambers, 1994), cannot simply be dismissed as a predictable, trivial nuisance. The agenda of debate in the media and the atmosphere of public discussion are powerfully shaped by 'merely' academic and intellectual influences. Unless something is done to encourage a more balanced and more objective approach in research and analysis, it seems unlikely that serious reform of health care can be better than partially successful.

In the private sector, it would be considered absurd to commission studies from sources known to be opposed in principle to the service or commodity being researched, or from researchers with economic interests in competitor companies or political allegiances to a rival. It is not viewed as in any way prejudicial to place research with investigators who are believed likely to approach their task open-mindedly and in a spirit of honest practicality. Why should it be any different in the public sector?

There are two distinct constituencies with a real interest in attempting to amend and improve the one-sided character of research into health care. First there are all those many people who are concerned about current levels of costs (too high) and efficiency (too low) in the NHS. Secondly, there are those with a broader interest in welfare reform as one fundamental aspect of the modernization of Britain. If reform is blocked or delayed in health care, success in other spheres in the struggle against bureaucracy, collectivism and inefficiency will be considerably weakened. There are several important tasks which people who identify with either of these constituencies might take on:

* Monitor academic publications, especially those used in teaching health care personnel and those which are taken up by the media, for the extent of their open-mindedness and objectivity in relation to NHS reform.

* Investigate the conclusions and public statements arising from research on health care funded from the public purse, and publish the results.

* Identify researchers in higher education who are other than prejudiced against health-care reform.

* Seek ways of strengthening funding for research undertaken by such people. This will involve persuading the business community of the dangers of current social scientific prejudices, and thus obtaining private sector funding for bona fide alternative research. It will equally require breaking the stranglehold of collectivists on public sector research funding. There can be no good reason for taxpayers' money being misused systematically to sabotage initiatives taken by elected governments on taxpayers' and citizens' behalf.

* Develop networks of contact between academics of good reputation who are sympathetic to reform on the one hand, and the media and publishers on the other.

Since 1945, and more particularly since the expansion of the social sciences in the 1960s, the research community has been more than somewhat partial in its ideological inclinations. Even among economists (as evidenced by the famous or infamous letter from 364 of them to *The Times*), but especially among social historians, sociologists and social policy analysts, the tendency has been: to underplay and even denigrate the potentially positive role in welfare of markets, competition, enterprise, and incentives; to overestimate the scope for effective central planning and ignore its destructive side-effects; to lay greater emphasis on generalized principles of presumed social justice than on the particularities of individual consumers' preferences; to underestimate costs and to downplay their significance in policy development; to sympathize with the concerns of trade unions and professional associations at the cost of ignoring the requirements of efficient management; and to presume on some supposed general trend of history towards increased state control and away from active participation by private, independent and voluntary producers and suppliers of goods and services.

These tendencies have been apparent in most fields of social policy, including housing, pensions, education, training, employment advice and placement, and health care. An intellectual context shaped by these tendencies is unlikely, to say the least, to provide support for the radical reform needed as much in the health sphere as in the other sectors of social policy.

Ex-cathedra Prejudice

A second symptomatic example of the perversely partisan reaction of the social policy establishment to welfare reform is provided by Oakley and Williams' important book '*The Politics of the Welfare State*' (1994). It merits close analysis.

Written, as the blurb less than modestly claims, by 'renowned academics and policy makers, including feminist and welfare historians, highly regarded figures in social policy, influential critics of recent educational reforms, and key analysts of current reform in the health sector', it represents a quasi-official manifesto of resistance to welfare reform. It stands as a monument to the welfare lobby's inherent incapacity to learn from experience or evidence, and to adapt their ideological prejudices to changing circumstances.

Ann Oakley's introduction announces the book's pre-emptively one-sided terms of reference unapologetically. 'After 14 consecutive years of Conservative government in Britain certain policies were seen', she says, in the usual *de haut en bas* tones of patriarchal state bureaucracy, 'to be dismantling or undermining those established forms of welfare through which the national state had assumed centralized responsibility for the welfare of all its citizens.' The implications of welfare reform for service-users, she alleges – as if the claim were firmly evidenced or necessarily damaging to real welfare – are 'that disparities and inequalities are likely to be greater today than they were under the "old" welfare state'. On the welfare costs and public expenditure front, she endorses unquestioningly John Hills's question-begging and pre-eminently questionable proposition that 'there is no evidence... to support the prediction of a crisis generated by excessive spending' (see Chapter 4 above for a systematic refutation of this glibly irresponsible claim).

She continues with a categorical assertiveness belied entirely by the facts and supported only by ideological prejudice:

While both government rhetoric and welfare practice enforce the view that individualized and marketized welfare is ensuring significant gains in terms of choice and cost-containment, the evidence of the contributors to this volume points in the opposite direction. Changes in health, education, and welfare provision have introduced more choice for a few at the expense of a lower quality of service for many.

She seeks to evidence this curious proposition in a paragraph on p. 13 which comprises an official manifesto, even indeed an orthodox litany, of all the misconstrued, ill-founded, and politically slanted complaints of the welfare reform resistance movement as a whole. It should perhaps be embroidered in silk and carried as a banner at the head of the new Jarrow marches which will no doubt enliven the next general election. It warrants detailed analysis. I have itemized the several propositions in the paragraph as 1 through 9 to facilitate evaluation:

there is no doubt that in the period of significant Conservative 'dismantling' of the welfare state, social inequalities have increased significantly (*Proposition 1*). For example, although average income rose by 20 per cent between 1981 and 1987, the lowest 10 per cent experienced a rise in income of only half the average (*Proposition 2*). Against the backdrop of overall falls in mortality, the relative disadvantage of manual, compared to nonmanual, social groups increased over the period 1970 to 1983 (*Proposition 3*). The systematic nature of the links between social structure on the one hand, and health and illness on the other are well-established (*Proposition 4*); it has also been shown that life expectancy is highest in those countries with the most egalitarian income distributions (*Proposition 5*). What this means for the population of the UK is that the poor as a category have increased (*Proposition 6*); half of all British children, for example, live in poverty (*Proposition 7*); and this figure represents a two-and-a-half-fold increase over ten years (*Proposition 8*). This is a bigger increase than in any other European country (*Proposition 9*).

In the formulation which Oakley has chosen to adopt, Proposition 1 is simply false. One can think of few issues as subject to continuing contention as the effects of recent welfare reforms. To claim that the nature of their effects is beyond dispute ('There is no doubt') is therefore inaccurate and untruthful. Deny it as she may, the one-sided interpretation of the outcome of welfare reform to which she seeks to attribute by this claim a spurious legitimacy, is being increasingly resisted – by dissident social scientists and journalists, by reforming governments, and above all by ordinary people.

As to the substance of Proposition 1, a significant increase in social inequalities, even if it were demonstrated conclusively, might prove insubstantial in practical terms. Moreover, however large such an effect was, it might have been caused by factors entirely unconnected with welfare reform. In any case, this first and crucial proposition in Oakley's litany presumes in a dogmatically axiomatic fashion, that social inequality is inherently wrong and harmful. This naïve and implausible assumption is neither argued here nor in any other way coherently defended. Readers are supposed simply to take it on trust as if it were one of the Thirty-nine Articles or Ten Commandments of a religious group.

Proposition 2 can be reformulated quite easily and justifiably to produce the exact opposite of the rhetorical effect intended by Oakley. Thus: 'Even the lowest 10 per cent experienced a substantial rise in income, amounting to as much as 50 per cent of the average increase across the population as a whole.' At least Oakley has avoided here the even more dishonest, and regularly peddled, version of her story to the unblushing effect that the poor have got actually poorer. Even in her own more modest formulation, however, it remains tendentious in the extreme.

Proposition 3 is disingenuous, if not worse. The relevant fact is that throughout the arbitrary period selected by Oakley – as throughout the whole of modern British history – the mortality rates of the whole population and of all sub-groups of the population have continued to improve. If the relative rate of improvement in the mortality of manual groups did indeed worsen – which is arguable – it was certainly at most a very slight change, and probably temporary, since such figures are notably subject to short-term and largely arbitrary fluctuations. The relevant facts about trends in British mortality rates, considered dispassionately, simply cannot do the rhetorical work which Oakley demands of them.

The substance of Proposition 4 is, as formulated, a self-evident truism and as such trivial. How could health and social structure be *other* than 'systematically linked' in any conceivable society? What is at issue is precisely *how* and *how far* they are linked. On this she carefully says nothing at all, presuming that readers will accept the implicit proposition that there is well-established detailed knowledge about the nature and extent of the relationship. This is sadly untrue. All we have is a rag-bag of more or less tentative and partially evidenced theories, in large part mutually contradictory. The Black Report, which she cites uncritically, is a wholly inadequate and thoroughly suspect source of supporting evidence for this part of Oakley's socialist credo (Le Fanu, 1994).

Proposition 5 is impertinently overstated. Its claim that improved life expectancy is associated with egalitarian income distribution rests entirely on uncritical acceptance of a single study (Wilkinson, 1990). This is very recent, and therefore properly treated at best as suggestive rather than demonstrative, unsupported by any other studies and controverted by some, challengeable as to its methodology and measurement, restricted to a small number of cases representing an inappropriately narrow range of income inequalities, and argued naïvely and implausibly even by the standards usual in the collectivist literature of which it forms a part. Even given a higher estimate of Wilkinson's work than mine, the grounding of Proposition 5 is considerably less than adequate. The relationship claimed between life expectancy and income distribution has not been 'shown'. At best it has been more than somewhat speculatively suggested.

Proposition 6 is very curious indeed. 'What this means' can only be designed to suggest that what follows can be deduced from what precedes, but there seems to be no logical connection at all. The alleged linkage between life expectancy and income distribution has no implications whatsoever, even if it were true, for the size of the category of the population defined as poor. The two sets of alleged facts are wholly distinct the one from the other, logically, empirically and in any other conceivable way. One suspects an uncorrected printer's (or word-processor) error and the accidental omission of one or more sentences. But this may be too generous an interpretation. Logical bloomers of the same order recur throughout the introduction, throughout the book as a whole, and throughout the literature of socialist welfare apologetics in its entirety (Flew, 1992).

This illogicality perhaps serves Oakley usefully as a cloak to disguise the naked absurdity of the substance of Proposition 6. Only in unconsidered relativist terms has the number of 'poor' people increased during the period covered by the proposition, or indeed over any other period of British history since the processes of modernization and industrialization began. Throughout the past 150 years at least, the standard of living of the whole population and of each and every sub-group within it has continued, now more rapidly, now more slowly, to improve (see Chapter 3 above for a detailed analysis of the historical evidence). Proposition 6 is fashionable, but none the less entirely fallacious.

Proposition 7 is a mere extrapolation from Proposition 6, and shares all of its fundamental inadequacy. Except on the basis of the most ludicrous assumptions about the nature of poverty, it is a blatant falsehood. We have become so used over the past decade to reading headlines in the papers announcing the vast extent of poverty among children, and to seeing television presenters unthinkingly mouthing the latest 'discovery' by social researchers about the disadvantage and deprivation suffered by children right across the land, that we forget entirely about the continuing improvement in the quality of life of all our children. Real poverty among children is occasional and temporary. Its primary cause is nothing to do with welfare reform. The real mischief-maker is the splitting-up of families. This in turn is fuelled precisely by the *unreformed* character of welfare provision, and its tendency to encourage divorce and separation. Those who claim to be concerned about poverty among chidren should not align themselves with reactionary resistance to welfare reform. They should be among its most active supporters.

Proposition 8 is in part a corollary of Propositions 6 and 7, and to this extent it shares their logical and empirical inadequacies. It therefore fails because they fail, and should be rejected on this account alone. There are other difficulties with it, however, over and above this. The apparent scale of the increase should not be taken at face value. It does not mean – since the measure of poverty used is relative – that vastly more children have lower standards of living than they would have had ten years back. It does not mean, either, that vastly more children have inadequate standards of living compared with the situation ten years ago – on the contrary, the number in such conditions has, despite recession, markedly decreased. Nor can any demonstrable worsening of the living standards of children be attributed with any justice to the level of welfare provision, which has been upgraded more than adequately. Such increase in child poverty as there has been is attributable almost entirely to the remorseless increase in the number of one-parent families, a phenomenon which is unamenable to correction by any amount of benefits, which are indeed themselves a primary cause of its persistence and expansion.

Proposition 9 represents arbitrary relativism compounded with arbitrary relativism. Its function is purely rhetorical. Not only are things terrible in Britain, and getting progressively worse, Oakley would have her readers believe, but they are worse and getting even worse even faster than almost anywhere else. In fact the negativism of the comparison is almost entirely specious and ironically produced largely by relatively *positive* features of the British situation: our high standards of living and generous benefit levels by comparison with most other countries, the rate of improvement in our average standard of living over the relevant period, and the liberalism of our divorce laws, separation customs and enforcement procedures. One is almost surprised that Oakley fails to claim that child poverty is increasing faster in the UK than in Egypt or Peru.

The nine chapters of the book are all, with two partial exceptions, as obtusely tendentious as Oakley's introduction. The two commendable exceptions are by Chris Ham and colleagues on priority setting in the NHS, and by Jane Lewis on community care. Even Ham's relatively thoughtful and balanced analysis is based on somewhat shallow, sketchy research, and concludes by commending yet more 'protocols and guidelines' – as if we didn't have more than enough such already in the health service and right across the welfare system! Lewis manages to admit that Mrs Thatcher did at least one thing that wasn't mistaken or ill-intentioned (p. 147), which must be some kind of a record in the recent welfare literature. But even given this and a notable lack of prejudice compared with other chapters, she succeeds in the end in emphasizing the resource constraints and the practical difficulties affecting community care, rather than anything positive.

As for the rest of this book, it is an incoherent farrago of error, falsehood, and fantasy. I restrict my comments here to just the more blatantly tendentious welfare apologetics. Chapter 1 ('Interpretations of welfare and approaches to the state, 1870–1920') begins with the implausible, if hackneyed, claim that 'many of the welfare gains of the late 19th and early 20th centuries are being whittled away'. It sees Sheila Rowbotham busily digging up arbitrary chunks of 'women's history' with a remarkably blunt left-feminist spade in order to demonstrate, at least to her own satisfaction, that even the Welfare State which is supposedly being destroyed by Thatcherism was a long way short of adequately egalitarian. 'It is as necessary', she concludes, 'today as it was in those earlier decades to develop an effective and democratic strategy that will challenge the unequal distribution of resources and create new relations of freedom and equality, individual initiative and associative collectivity.' Press on, as it were, and we can have a Welfare State which truly works. She admits accurately, that is to say, that the real Welfare State has been and is authoritarian, but claims – with nothing but utopian wish-fulfilment to support her – that it might somehow have been otherwise.

Chapter 2, by Rodney Lowe, is another partisan *tour d'horizon* of the imaginary past. Focusing on the period 1945–76, it purports to learn 'lessons from the past' by exploring 'the rise and fall of the classic welfare state'. Lowe claims 'three potential strengths' for the Welfare State: its 'functional efficiency', its 'acceptance of the constructive complementarity of economic and social policy', and its 'underlying assumption that state intervention was compatible with and not inimical to individual initiative and freedom'. While he classifies these three features with deliberate care as '*potential* strengths' (my emphasis) – thus leaving scope for criticism from the left of the Welfare State's failure so far to deploy them effectively – it is plain that he views them, despite all the evidence to the contrary, as expressions of plausible and attractive objectives. His conclusion (p. 52) makes it unambiguously clear that his sole objection to the

Welfare State is that its 'potential advantages' have not to-date, as a result of 'managerial and political failure', been 'fully realized'. His prescription for correcting these failures would turn Britain into an outpost of Deng's China in short order.

In Chapter 3, Charles Webster includes at least some accurate analysis in his sweepingly revisionist critique of the idea that Conservatives were genuine participants in a national consensus concerning the NHS between 1951 and 1964. However, he protests altogether too much. The facts do not bear out his determination to read off an anticipation of Thatcherism from the unmitigatedly Butskellite record. In particular, he manages – by sleight of rhetoric and encouraged by over-credulous reliance on Richard Titmuss's jaundiced opinion – to make reductions in Conservative funding for the NHS which were only relative, proportional and slight, seem savage, while ignoring entirely the real, swingeing and absolute cuts made by Labour. (See Chapter 4 above for the real pattern of public expenditure since the War.) What he calls 'a more accurate reading' of the 1951–64 record 'is essential', he concludes, 'to an understanding of current predicaments in the NHS and the Welfare State more generally'. The implication of this proposition, as of his whole analysis, is transparent: increase public expenditure on health and welfare even more extravagantly, and all will be for the best in the best of all possible worlds.

Popay and Williams's examination in Chapter 4 of 'Local voices in the National Health Service' eschews altogether even the pseudo-objectivity of Lowe's and Webster's archivalism. It is a downright, unembroidered, wholesale critique of Government health policy, of the newly introduced and overdue focus on patients' rights as consumers, and on the discipline of epidemiology – on which the modernization of health care is, quite properly, increasingly reliant.

The purposes and tone of the chapter are more accurately indicated than the authors might imagine by its solitary illustration (p. 83). Captioned 'Playing in the Streets of London's East End 1990', it displays carefully selected Bangladeshi children posing, as it were, for an official Poverty Lobby photographer. Their overall conclusion is one-sidedly trenchant: 'To seek these views (of local people) is not necessarily to hear them, and to hear is not readily equated with understanding, involvement or participation.' And again 'fundamental changes in policy and practice within the service are required'.

They make much of the problem of sorting out the difference between on the one hand 'What the NHSME calls science' and on the other mere 'opinion', without themselves demonstrating much understanding of what this crucial distinction entails in the way of research skills and discipline.

Indeed, they challenge any disjuncture between belief and knowledge, and in pursuing the politically motivated objective of increased direct public participation in the administration of the NHS go so far as to demand an extent of 'lay participation in research' which would subvert entirely the objectivity of health research. 'In a very real sense', they claim, 'effective lay participation within the NHS will only be achieved when there is a more democratic structure within the health care system.'

Thus they are not in the business here merely of challenging the adequacy of current health research or of seeking an improvement in local democratic accountability in the NHS. What they really seem to be after is some bizarre kind of localized health soviet, with knowledge firmly under the control of political (or as they would say popular) forces and deployed resolutely on behalf of what Williams refers to in the title of another of his publications as 'the people's health'. Little wonder they are critical of epidemiology, since they think they know all there is to know about health, ill-health and its causes without the assistance of *any* merely bourgeois knowledge.

There is more in the book – although nothing quite so blatant as this – for those who seek to understand the role of intellectuals in preventing democracies from recognizing reality and from designing social policies to cope with it realistically and effectively. There is Whitty and his colleagues' remarkable reading (in Chapter 8) of the City Technology Colleges and the rest of the Government's efforts at improving educational standards as an exercise in malevolent class subjugation. There is Bartley's painstaking but ill-founded and implausible attempt (Chapter 9) to arraign the Government for suppressing what he supposes is the truth about the connections between unemployment and ill-health. And more besides. The whole book is a feast of socialist obscurantism.

There are four crucial questions which need to be asked about '*The Politics of the Welfare State*', and by extension about the whole huge and still-expanding literature of Welfare State apologetics. First we should ask where, despite its obvious one-sidedness and its manifest weaknesses, it would be reviewed other than entirely positively? Second, who is paying for the research reported in the book, and why? Third, what are the implications for the future of genuinely pluralist democracy if social policy analysis – from research, through teaching and the curricula of secondary and higher education, to publishing and reviewing – is thus monopolized by sectarian ideologists? And fourth, what can be done to rectify this anomalous and intolerable state of affairs?

These, it seems, are questions which must await an answer until we have a government more confident than any we have had for many years (indeed since the Welfare State was established) in its right to govern, in the benefits of freedom by comparison with state control, and in its duty of safeguarding the truth against the mistakes, exaggerations, and mendacity of irresponsible, unelected media and intellectuals.

The Politics of Welfare Reform

In the meantime, even if the analysis presented in this book were, as I trust it may be, substantially correct, it might not be very useful in practical and political terms. A manifesto commitment to radical reform of the Welfare State by the Conservatives might prove a more hysterical suicide note than even the Labour Party's re-run of tax and spend in 1992. So at least it is claimed by some Conservatives and some media pundits (Marr, 1993). The British people remain, it is alleged, fundamentally collectivist, even indeed mildly socialist, when it comes to welfare, and nervously anxious about their own capacity to look after themselves and their families out of their own financial and psychological resources. We still need 'Nanny', as it were.

I am not persuaded by this seemingly 'realistic' perspective. Some critics of welfare reform who use this ploy are themselves committed and less than impartial supporters of the Welfare State. Almost all the journalists, academics and researchers (including not least the opinion pollsters) who claim to find evidence of antipathy among the public to welfare reform are themselves fundamentalist ideologues of collectivism. We should treat their case, therefore, with scepticism.

As with trade union reform, the sale of council houses, and every privatization to-date, supposed opposition may very quickly be transformed into – or revealed as – enthusiastic support. There is, in my view, an electoral majority ready and waiting to have welfare reform put to them positively, explained to them clearly, and sold to them hard as the latest instalment in the ongoing restoration of their freedom.

Handled properly and construed positively as the primary mission of the Majorite succession to Margaret Thatcher, welfare reform is not at all – as the left pretends and the pragmatic centre nervously fears – an election loser for the Conservatives. On the contrary, it is the most significant large-scale, vote-winning platform available, along with law and order and the national interest, in the 1990s. At the same time, and more importantly, it is an essential step on the long journey towards the British nation's economic and moral renewal, and an indispensable means of restoring the social cohesion which four decades of Welfare State ideology have destroyed. It should be taken up vigorously by whichever political party has the courage and the moral honesty to risk it.

Sadly, however, reactions in the current brittle political climate to proposals for fundamental renewal of the whole system are muted and defensive. We could liberate upwards of 90 per cent of the population from malign, incompetent state domination of pensions, health care, education and all the rest within ten years, reducing taxes massively and improving efficiency out of all recognition at a stroke. We could simultaneously eliminate fraud, reduce dependency and provide improved assistance for the minority who need and deserve it. But nervous of upsetting its backbenchers, the media and the public, the Government appears to prefer for the time being piecemeal fine-tuning to radical reform.

This has entirely predictably opened a tempting space for Opposition spokesmen to lay claim to the role of welfare reformers. Acknowledging after decades of brazen denial that state welfare is less than perfect, the Labour Party is unashamedly promising, through its new leadership, the pig in a poke of a 'modernized Welfare State'. Of course the claim is implausible and specious – more so, indeed, even than Labour's parallel claims to have become all of a sudden the party of law and order, the family and dynamic market economics!

Every next word from the Party's think-tanks, from the so-called 'Commission on Social Justice', and from Mr Blair himself confirms one's suspicions that the result will not be reform, but extravagant enlargement – Beveridge-plus, as it were – with yet more fictitious rights, redoubled public expenditure, and a multiplication of bureaucracy. Would the trade unions allow 'their' Party to privatize one jot or tittle of the Welfare State? Would constituency activists permit Mr Blair to trade universal benefits for tax cuts? Would the Labour Party's tame intellectuals in the universities and the media tolerate for a moment any practical policy implementation of his – typically woolly – ideas for limiting the damage which state welfare does to the family? No, a Labour Government and European bureau-socialists would gleefully conspire to magnify the Welfare State – and drive Britain into permanent beggary.

Thus, tinkering adjustments to the old, failed Welfare State, whether they are shaped from the emboldened centre-left or the defensive centre, are inadequate, and in the last resort irrelevant. What we need is a new Welfare State which the silent majority can support as positively, enthusiastically and successfully as they supported, from the mid-1970s through the 1980s privatization, trade union reform and the right to buy.

Official estimates – which means gross under-estimates – have identified fraud in the welfare system of some five billion pounds every year. In my film *'Let's Kill Nanny'* (shown on BBC2 on 4 August 1994, after a delay from June 'in case it should influence the European elections'!), I interview a young welfare conman. He claims to draw three unjustified helpings of unemployment benefit, and, making use of further false identification papers, three lots of housing benefit. Three or four hundred pounds a week regularly and a BMW from your pocket and mine for nothing!

Besides massive fraud, the film also explores that even worse product of state welfare: incompetent dependency. It charts the explosive growth over the past five decades of a deviant underclass nourished on government hand-outs and false promises of fictitious rights. It outlines a programme of practical reform which would remedy these problems and restore the British people's traditional commitment to hard work, honesty, and enterprising initiative.

And how does the welfare establishment, the collective assembly of Mr Blair's natural allies, respond to the challenge of real welfare reform? How but with misrepresentation, feigned moral indignation, and obscurantist defence of the failed, destructive status quo. Thus, displaying a rather more enthusiastic commitment to balance than it usually manages, the BBC itself put up Polly Toynbee, its own Social Affairs Correspondent and a high priestess of the welfare orthodoxy, to answer our arguments at length in the *Radio Times before the film had even been shown!* Pre-emptive balance perhaps? Not content with the extravagantly privileged opportunities she already has every week to rubbish every serious attempt at genuine welfare reform, she feasted her readers with an account of the film so prejudicially inaccurate that it could only be calculated to distract them from watching it and from making up their own minds about it for themselves.

The manifest deficiencies and destructive impacts of state welfare are open secrets. We should be free to discuss them and debate them in public. The selfish defence of free health care – for themselves – by the wealthy. The pious resistance to rational targeting of child benefit by people whose children have two television sets, a computer and a half-share in a pony. The sanctimonious insistence of an outmoded élite on free libraries and subsidized opera tickets. The 'unemployed' working at two black-market jobs. The supposedly lone parents with live-in boyfriends housed free at the taxpayer's expense. Recipients of invalidity benefit who are fit enough to play football with a local club and astute enough to persuade socialist doctors they are dying.

One could go on. We *should* go on. We should insist on the truth about the great Welfare State Fraud, and put things straight urgently. Above all we should resist the continuing flood of specious claims about the contemporary condition of British society (Johnson, 1990; Jones, 1993; Law,

1993). Yet another influential example has been recently produced by Richard Wilkinson (1994), remarkably on behalf of Barnardo's, which has hitherto seemed the most sensible of our great charities.

'*Unfair Shares*' is in the long tradition of sentimental social policy analysis stretching back through Townsend, Titmuss and Tawney to Marx and Engels. Like its sadly influential antecedents:

- It conflates and confuses poverty and inequality.
- It exaggerates the extent of disadvantage by relativizing poverty and by focusing on extreme cases.
- It presumes that economic inequality is inherently wrong.
- It artificially privileges persisting inequalities in its description of social conditions over generally improving standards of living.
- It is rhetorically cavalier with complex facts.
- It contents itself with a superficial analysis of data which presumes that any correlate of poverty is caused by poverty. At the same time it displays naïve amazement in the face of entirely predictable correlates of income differences.
- When its primary explanations in terms of poverty fail, it turns unashamedly to contradictory explanations – here in terms of relative poverty, which are themselves wholly implausible.
- It announces its preordained conclusions in the voice of prophetic, missionary utopianism.
- Its policy programmes are unrealistic, impractical, and – since its diagnoses are mistaken – damagingly counter-productive.

This orthodox mode of social policy analysis has been dominant since the War. We cling to it despite its continuing failure. Instead, those genuinely concerned with the suffering and pain of disadvantaged children – and of any of our fellows who are in difficulty – should focus attention on quite different factors, which the policy orthodoxy dogmatically denies: the collapsing family, the decaying work ethic, and the spreading underclass culture.

Even where these factors *are* acknowledged in orthodox social policy analysis, they are typically blamed – in a complete reversal of the real causal link – on unemployment. Their origins lie rather in collectivist welfare policies and the dependency which they generate. The policies commended in '*Unfair Shares*' will not solve the problems: they will make them worse. Instead we need self-reliance all-round, plus sharply targeted 'tough love' assistance for the temporarily incapable. It is the ideology and structures of the Welfare State which are the primary and continuing cause of our malaise.

Conclusion: The Cancer of State Welfare

All over the free world, state welfare has expanded enormously throughout this century, and everywhere it has caused worse problems than those it was designed to remedy. Conceived by its proponents as an antidote and an alternative to socialism, in practice it has either served as a stepping-stone *towards* socialism (the United Kingdom, Scandinavia), or (as in the United States and Germany) it has brought in its train problems which had earlier seemed to be peculiar to socialist societies: big government, high taxes, bureaucracy and the destruction of individual autonomy. Intended by its largely benevolent founders as a means of providing help for the disadvantaged and the vulnerable, the Welfare State has proved to be the worst enemy its supposed beneficiaries could find. It has transformed them into a subjugated underclass of welfare dependents, excluded from mainstream society and incapable of exercising either their rights or their responsibilities as citizens of free societies. The history of welfare and the aetiology of the welfare disease make a strange and tragic tale.

The eighteenth century saw the demise of political absolutism and the establishment of democratic capitalism throughout much of the civilized world. A primary distinguishing mark of the new era was that the psychological needs and social functions which have come to be defined as 'welfare' were handled by individual self-reliance, by the family, by voluntary charitable agencies and through the market. The role of the government and the state was carefully restricted in order to prevent infringements of liberty either directly, as a result of political control of social life, or through the indirect impact of the increasing costs of big government and augmented taxation.

Alas, responses during the course of the nineteenth century to urbanization and industrialization and to the social problems associated incidentally with the triumphant progress of economic development increasingly took our societies in a dangerously different direction. By the late nineteenth century, more and more responsibilities – in housing, education, health care and the alleviation of poverty – were taken over by the state and the central authorities. More and more of the rights in these spheres of individuals, of families and of voluntary and market agencies were restricted and brought under governmental regulation and control.

The twentieth century has gradually seen this process of state appropriation of welfare carried further, particularly in response to the disruptive effects of world war and economic recession. As the Welfare State has inexorably expanded, its operations have increasingly been underpinned by an explicitly anti-capitalist welfare ideology, and supported by a swelling 'New Class' of local and central state employees, who depend for their very livelihood on continued expansion of the bureaucratic machinery of state welfare.

By the 1970s, societies throughout the free world were almost all equipped – or encumbered – by a fully developed Welfare State. Public expenditure as a proportion of GNP had increased wildly beyond the levels conceivable even fifty years earlier, and most of this was being spent on welfare. The state was heavily involved in every sphere of welfare, with state monopoly control increasingly normalized. More and more of the assistance originally provided on a temporary basis had come to be regarded as a right. This had detrimental effects both on its increasingly welfare-dependent recipients, and on the political process of democracy itself, as parties irresponsibly bid up their competing promises to greedy electorates.

The 1970s represented at the same time the zenith of welfare state development and a watershed in public attitudes throughout the free world to state welfare. By the start of the 1980s a process of retrenchment was underway. At first it was primarily the extravagant costs of state welfare which – in Reagan's America as in Thatcher's Britain – became subject to critical challenge. Within a short period, however – its beginning symbolized by the publication in 1984 of Charles Murray's 'Losing Ground' – other and much worse deficiencies in state welfare, particularly its destructive impact on the capacity of people for self-reliant autonomy and enterprising initiative, were brought to light and became issues in public policy debate.

By the 1990s it had become apparent even to liberals and social democrats that state welfare had been all along a Pandora's box, from which had sprung at least as much of evil as of good. In the United States President Clinton has taken on board much Republican rhetoric and seems intent on cutting back at least some of the worst excesses of state welfare. The new Republican majorities in Congress seem intent on trumping the President's hand, or at least nerving his arm.

In Britain, the new leadership of the Labour Party is at least promising, supposing it won power, wholesale 'modernization' of the Welfare State. Even in the European Community, which remains a largely unreconstructed champion of state welfare, growing awareness of the impact of welfare on wage costs and thus on competitive capacity in the global market is inducing a degree of reluctant realism.

The Welfare State has proved a cul-de-sac in social development. It has led us nowhere, save to the ultimate dead-end of subverting and contradicting the fundamental principles of the culture which permitted its development in the first place. Like a cancer in the body politic, it has spread its destructive influence through more and more of the organs of society. It is time to call the immune system of the free societies into action, and stop the cancer of state welfare in its tracks.

In a recent apologia for the Welfare State in America, David Stoese and Howard Karger (1994) propose that 'By the 1990s, social, political, and economic circumstances in the United States precluded new governmental initiatives, in so doing effectively stalemating the American Welfare State'. The implication of the analysis reported in this book is that, while we can be thankful for stalemate, it is not enough.

Stalemate provides a crucial window of opportunity for social imagination and political will to provide Britain, America and the rest of the free world with an alternative to state welfare more appropriate to the twenty-first century and less incompatible than the failed utopia of the Welfare State with the needs, capacities and varying preferences of free people. The last word on this essential project might be left with Madsen Pirie (1994, p. 29):

The privatized welfare state will end the psychology of dependence. Most people will provide for themselves and their families and will be proud and pleased to do so. They will, through the state, help those who cannot manage such provision for themselves. Our successors will live with a system that is more efficient, more humane, and which lacks the pathology of the present welfare state. Their reaction will be one of puzzled bemusement that society tolerated for so long the outrages perpetrated daily in the name of universal benefits.

Appendix 1
Briefing Notes to
Let's Kill Nanny

During 1994 I was offered the opportunity by BBC2 to make a film for its Open Space programme presenting, in terms appropriate for television, the analysis argued in *The End of the Welfare State* (Adam Smith Institute, 1994), of which I had been a co-author,

Making the film was hard work but enormously interesting and exciting. Images are a new language for a writer. It was pleasing to find all the BBC staff involved wholly professional, and more than ready to put all their various efforts into a programme whose line was quite distinct from the usual 'quality media' view of welfare. In my view, dissident social scientists should do all they can to get more involved in television. We have interesting, true stories to tell, and they should be told.

I prepared Briefing Notes to be sent to enquirers. They are reproduced here as an Appendix to this book so that readers can see what can be achieved in a short (half-hour) television film. Those interested might contact the BBC to enquire about using the film in education or as a basis for discussion and debate at local meetings.

Introduction

These Briefing Notes provide back-up information on the programme *Let's Kill Nanny* shown on BBC2 on 4 August 1994. The programme was based on *The End of the Welfare State* by Michael Bell, Eamonn Butler, David Marsland, and Madsen Pirie. The book, which spells out the practicalities of welfare reform, was published by the Adam Smith Institute in March 1994 and is available from ASI, 50 Westminster Mansions, Little Smith Street, London, SW1. Alternatively it should be available in libraries.

A comprehensive analysis of the deficiencies of state welfare and a practical plan for radical reform is offered in my new book *Welfare or Welfare State?*, which will be published by Macmillan.

This pack contains (with permission and thanks) a copy of a recent article from *The Sunday Times*, reading lists, and useful addresses.

The Collectivist Case

Of apologias for the status quo in welfare policy, there is no shortage. They are mostly quite well known already, since theirs is the orthodox line, figuring as if it were self-evidently true in educational curricula and the media. 'Defend the Welfare State at all costs' remains, alas, the unconsidered slogan of most academic social scientists, the bulk of social researchers, the Opposition parties in Parliament, and most social affairs correspondents in the quality press and on television.

Our list includes some of the best recent publications of this type. They are included here in order to locate them for once in a critical, comparative context. Readers are advised to consider them carefully alongside the alternative, dissident account of state welfare presented in *Let's Kill Nanny*.

Deakin, N. (1994), *The Politics of Welfare* (Harvester Wheatsheaf)

Hills, J., ed. (1990), *The State of Welfare: the Welfare State in Britain since 1974* (Clarendon Press)

Oppenheim, C. (1994), *The Welfare State: Putting the Record Straight* (Child Poverty Action Group)

Wicks, M. (1987), *A Future for All: Do We Need a Welfare State?* (Penguin)

Walker, A. and Walker, C., eds (1987), *The Growing Divide* (Child Poverty Action Group)

Many publications which defend the Welfare State rather uncritically are produced by the campaigning organizations and pressure groups which together make up what has come to be known as the 'Poverty Lobby' or even the 'Poverty Industry'. These include the Child Poverty Action Group, the Low Pay Unit, Shelter, the National Association of Citizens' Advice Bureaux, the Family Studies Centre, Oxfam, the Unemployment Unit, the Campaign for the Homeless and Roofless (CHAR), the National Council for One Parent Families, Christian Action, NACRO and the Howard League for Penal Reform.

Many of their publications are interesting and valuable. It should be noted, however, that although these organizations are indeed, as they claim, independent, they appear to be consistently negative about recent Government social policy initiatives, and predisposed against radical reform of state welfare.

In examining their material, readers might want to consider how far their authors seem genuinely open to the possible benefits – for the disadvantaged and vulnerable in particular – of reforming welfare. Are these organizations prepared even to contemplate a bigger role in welfare for private, independent and voluntary agencies? Or are they committed – out of habit, ideological inclination, or investment in the status quo – to resisting reform regardless of the benefits it would provide for those who most need help?

The Case for Welfare Reform

The orthodox side of the welfare argument is probably already well-known to most readers of these notes. Sources on the other side of the argument, which explore the advantages of greater freedom for everyone from state control, and better opportunities for people to look after themselves and their families independently, are less often allowed a hearing.

In addition to *The End of the Welfare State* and *Welfare or Welfare State?*, readers may find some of the following publications interesting and useful. The list includes some of the most important recent studies. In addition, some of my own work is included by way of back-up for the arguments presented in *Let's Kill Nanny*.

Anderson, D. C. (1981), *Breaking the Spell of the Welfare State* (Social Affairs Unit)

Berger, P. (1987), *The Capitalist Revolution* (Gower)

Dennis, N. (1993), *Rising Crime and the Dismembered Family* (Institute of Economic Affairs)

Gilder, G. (1981), *Wealth and Poverty* (Basic Books)

Gilder, G. (1988), *The Spirit of Enterprise* (Penguin)

Green, D. G. (1984), *Mutual Aid or Welfare State?* (Allen and Unwin)

Green, D. G. (1993), *Re-inventing Civil Society* (Institute of Economic Affairs)

Harris, R. and Seldon, A. (1987), *Welfare Without the State* (Institute of Economic Affairs)

Marsland, D. (1988), 'The Welfare State as Producer Monopoly' (*Salisbury Review*, Vol. 6, No. 4)

Marsland, D. (1988), *Seeds of Bankruptcy: Sociological Bias against Business and Freedom* (Claridge Press), especially chapters 9, 10 and 11 on poverty, inequality, and work

Marsland, D. (1991), 'Squalor: Problems of Housing and the Environment' (*Social Policy and Administration*, Special Beveridge Issue, Vol. 25, No. 1)

Marsland, D. (ed.) (1994), *Work and Employment in Liberal Democratic Societies* (Paragon House)

Marsland, D. (1994), 'Tales from the Dependency Culture' (*Salisbury Review*, Vol. 12, No. 4)

Murray, C. (1984), *Losing Ground: American Social Policy 1950–1980* (Basic Books)

Murray, C. (1990), *The Emerging British Underclass* (Institute of Economic Affairs)

Saunders, P. and Harris, C. (1989), *Popular Attitudes to State Welfare Provision* (Social Affairs Unit)

Segalman, R. (1986), *The Swiss Way of Welfare* (Praeger)
Segalman, R. & Marsland, D. (1989), *Cradle to Grave: Comparative Perspectives on the State of Welfare* (Macmillan)
Seldon, A. (1981), *Wither the Welfare State* (Institute of Economic Affairs)
Seldon, A. (1990), *Capitalism* (Blackwell)
Willetts, D. (1993), *The Age of Entitlement* (Social Market Foundation)

Useful Addresses

The organizations listed below regularly publish reports and articles which examine the Welfare State, and social policy as a whole, more genuinely critically than is usual. They also present accounts of the positive case for personal independence and self-reliance.

Adam Smith Institute
50 Westminster Mansions, Little Smith Street, London SW1.

Institute of Economic Affairs
2 Lord North Street, London, SW1.

Libertarian Alliance
25 Chapter Chambers, Esterbrooke Street, London SW1.

Salisbury Review
33 Canonbury Park South, London, N1.

Social Affairs Unit
Suite 5/6 1st Floor, Morley House, Regent Street, London W1.

Planning for Your Future

As prosperity grows, and as expectations in relation to welfare change, the need for us all to plan for our own and our families' future in the areas of life covered by the Welfare State will become more pressing. The following list includes organizations which provide professional advice on the services which we have been persuaded by history and habit to think of as 'welfare'. There are, of course, many competing alternatives to the organizations on the list. That is the whole point – outside the State monopoly, we all have choices.

GENERAL ADVICE
Adam Smith Institute, 50 Westminster Mansions, Little Smith Street, London SW1 (0171 222 4995).

EDUCATION
Independent Schools Information Service (ISIS), 56 Buckingham Gate, London SW1E 6AG (0171 630 8793).

HEALTH AND COMMUNITY CARE
Independent Healthcare Association, 22 Little Russell Street, London WC1A 2HT (0171 430 0537).
Independent Hospitals Association, Africa House, 64/78 Kingsway, London WC2B 6BD (0171 790 0990).

Third Age Initiative (Long-term care and nursing homes), Commercial Union, 69, Park Lane, Croydon, CR9 1BG (0171 283 7500).

INSURANCE
Association of British Insurers, 51 Gresham Street, London EC2V 7HQ (0171 600 3333).
PPP Lifetime, Elm Court, Stratford on Avon, Warwickshire CV37 6PA (01789 415 151).

HOUSING
Building Societies Association, 3 Savile Row, London W1X 1AF (0171 437 0655).

PENSIONS AND SAVINGS
Independent Financial Advisor Promotion Ltd, 4th Floor, 28 Greville Street, London EC1N 8SU (01483 461 461).
National Association of Pension Funds, 12-18 Grosvenor Gardens, London SW1 (0171 730 0585).
Society of Pension Consultants, Ludgate House, Ludgate Circus, Fleet Street, London EC4.
Association of Unit Trusts & Investment Funds, 65 Kingsway, London WC2 (0171 207 1361).

Appendix 2
Which Sociology? A Consumer's Charter for Students

To a very large extent the errors in social policy analysis which this book examines are caused by – and find their most powerful justification in – the concepts and theories of the discipline of sociology, my own professional discipline.

This saddening truth has occasioned me, over many years, to spend considerable time and effort in critical analysis of modern sociology. This work is represented primarily in my book *Seeds of Bankruptcy* (1988) and in my paper *Fact and Fancy in Social Analysis* (1992). Innumerable enquiries from school and college students and from other members of the public provoked by references to these publications in colleagues' work and in the media persuaded me to produce 'Which Sociology?', an innocent and enquiring consumer's view of the absurdities and the potential of the discipline.

It is reproduced as an Appendix here in order to help readers of this book who are not sociologists to begin to understand the intellectual infrastructure of the persisting folly of modern social policy.

Modern British sociology is an enemy of freedom. Most sociologists teaching and writing today in Britain are:

- Obsessed with inequality.
- Hypnotized by the concept of class.
- Fanatical supporters of the Welfare State.
- Naïvely trusting of state power.
- Opposed to capitalism and suspicious of business, enterprise, and individual initiative.
- Contemptuous of the capacity of individual men and women to run their own lives competently without the bossy interference of a Governmental Big Brother or the fussy ministrations of a Nanny State.

I have examined these collectivist, paternalist, and socialist inclinations of British sociologists in *Seeds of Bankruptcy* (Claridge Press, 1988), in *Cradle to Grave* (with Ralph Segalman, Macmillan, 1989), and in *Fact and Fancy in Social Analysis* (Libertarian Alliance, 1992). Parallel errors in American sociology are mercilessly investigated by Irving Louis Horowitz in his remarkable book *The Decomposition of Sociology* (Oxford University Press, 1993).

Students of sociology, especially students coming to the discipline for the first time at university, should not be surprised by these prejudices and distortions. Be warned, and read some of the references above as antidotes. Use them by way of support for your own natural, commonsensical inclinations, and as a stimulus to persevere with your own analysis of the truth about the nature of social life in Britain. Don't give up on sociology, or abandon it to the conformists. Stick with it. Don't let yourself be bullied or tricked into swallowing the orthodox line either. Read. Think. Sift the evidence. Seek out for yourself alternative concepts and more truthful theories.

Easter Parade

At Easter 1994 the British Sociological Association held its annual conference in Preston. The theme was 'Sexualities in Social Context'. It provided almost a week of gay liberationists and radical feminists sounding off about their peculiar and predictable hobby-horses.

Britain was condemned yet again as a 'patriarchal' society, as if it were here rather than in the Middle East that women have to wear veils, stay at home and stick to cooking, and avoid the polluting shadow of every man except their masterful husband. There were also the usual mendacious accusations about the 'oppressive' character of British society, about 'stereotypes', about 'prejudice', and about the supposed inadequacies of British democracy. All this in relation to one of the most genuinely free and most unusually tolerant societies in human history!

This annual festival of politically correct nonsense provides a suitable occasion for reviewing the contribution of sociology to life and progress in Britain. How much good and how much harm are sociologists doing, and how much does it matter? They all have at least one 'ology', so what exactly does that qualify them to do?

Corruption of a Proud Tradition

There is a long tradition in Britain of wise and scholarly social analysis. This includes brilliant figures from the Scottish Enlightenment such as Adam Smith, who identified and explained the benefits of capitalism and the market economy. It includes such careful observers of the temptations of modernity as Edmund Burke, who correctly predicted the dictatorial outcome of the French Revolution and celebrated the advantages of moderate British democracy by contrast with the extravagant utopianism of continental philosophers.

It includes the intelligent common sense of Herbert Spencer, who foresaw the destructive effects of state welfare right from the start. It includes remarkable contributions in the first half of this century by British statisticians, such as Fisher, and anthropologists, such as Fortes, to the development of research methods used all over the world in the study of societies and social relationships.

This proud tradition was gradually frittered away over the past fifty years as sociology became established as a large-scale enterprise in the universities. There were two strands to this process of intellectual decay. First it weakened commitment to scholarly standards and to the disciplines of scientific research. Secondly, it opened the flood-gates to politically inspired nonsense of all sorts.

This did not happen all at once. In the first post-war generation of sociology in the 1950s, people whose ideas had been shaped by re-constructionist socialism, many of them actual or fellow-travelling communists, moved into influential positions. They were people to whom equality mattered more than freedom, and who believed that society could be and should be planned in detail by so-called experts. They organized the expanding curriculum of sociology. They wrote the textbooks. They appointed their successors.

Modern Sociology: Anything Goes?

In the 1960s sociology rapidly expanded, in the old universities and the new, in the polytechnics, in the teacher training colleges and in the schools. Right across the board, this newly fashionable discipline began to disseminate socialism, radicalism, and straightforward, unabashed Marxism as if they were the fifth Gospel.

Anything less was dismissed as conservative – and therefore not sociology at all. Textbooks, lectures, and examination scripts were suddenly full of one-sided, dogmatic rediscoveries of 'poverty', implausible allegations about 'inequality', and ignorant critiques of the supposed injustice and inefficiency of 'capitalist Britain' by contrast with the Soviet Union, China and even Cuba.

In the 1970s and right through to the mid-1980s, as sociology grew bigger and bigger, all this hokum got worse and worse. As I have showed in *Seeds of Bankruptcy*, the textbooks and other teaching materials of sociology were by this period unself-critically anti-capitalist, thoroughly anti-democratic, and sweepingly anti-British. Students of sociology were being indoctrinated at the state's expense to undermine the state, and trained for nothing more useful than a subversive role as saboteurs of society as most ordinary people wanted it to be.

The 1980s saw continuous defeat for the Labour Party, successive electoral victories for Margaret Thatcher, and the gross world-wide failure – now manifest even to addicts – of the planners' paradise of socialism. This had some effect on sociology, but less than one might have hoped or expected. New left-wing fantasies sprang up to replace the old ones: instead of economic planning, ecology; instead of the anti-war movement, feminism and gay liberation; instead of international socialism, third-world campaigning; instead of attacks on business, defence at all costs of the Welfare State. The more sociology changed, the more it stayed dreadfully the same.

Indeed, the only new element so far in 1990s' sociology – enthusiastic incorporation of the fashionable gibberish of post-modernism – has made its incoherence and its systematic negativism even worse. This French pseudo-philosophy has been stirred in with the absurd fantasies of German socialism to render sociology almost entirely immune to the careful, commonsensical sifting of evidence which is fundamental to the traditional British approach to the advance of knowledge. Now anything, or almost anything, goes.

The Necessity of Sociology

This is a gross distortion of sociology. It doesn't have to be this way. It is an exciting and important discipline. Provided it works in co-operation, rather than in rivalrous conflict, with history, economics, political science, psychology and biology, it promises accurate, vivid descriptions of social life and powerful, cogent explanations of crucial social issues. Provided that social analysis and social research are shaped by rational concepts and disciplined methods, it can help significantly to advance the British people's understanding of the state of our society, and assist in finding genuine solutions to the real and difficult problems we face.

If we could begin to get some honesty and sense back into the discipline, young sociologists could very soon get on with the urgent business – in central and local government, in industry and commerce, and in the public services – of correcting the collectivist assumptions and utopian ideas which have dominated thinking in all these spheres since at least the Second World War. For example:

- How can we get a more competitive spirit in industry unless the key role of profit and incentives in a modern economy is properly understood?
- How can we bring the escalation of crime under control until the concept of punishment and the crucial importance of individual moral responsibility are acknowledged?
- How can we expect the decay of the family to be controlled and reversed while the negative effects of state welfare in creating a dependent underclass and in subverting parental responsibility are denied on sectarian ideological grounds?
- How can we improve the efficiency and responsiveness of our expensive educational and health-care systems without new understanding based on objective analysis of the damaging impacts of state monopoly and bureaucratic planning?
- How can we develop rational employment policies and reduce unemployment while social policy analysts are allowed to get away with incoherent, outmoded concepts of poverty?
- How can we secure British interests effectively with sensible foreign and defence policies until the mischievously influential prejudice of social scientists against nationalism and the nation state is exposed and refuted?

And so on. There are dozens of immensely important issues and problems where public understanding – or rather misunderstanding – is presently defined and controlled by phoney sociology. From the academics, these mistaken ideas are passed on to the media, and on again from the media to the politicians and the people. This vicious process, which magnifies nonsense, multiplies misunderstanding and perpetuates folly, cannot be reversed simply by ignoring or deriding the erroneous social science which feeds it. Instead, poor sociology has to be replaced by better sociology, utopian dreams by realistic analysis, wish-fulfilment by honest facts, and incoherent notions by lucid concepts.

Towards Higher Standards in Sociology

If all this is to be achieved, our best students have to try sociology and stick with it, to read hard and argue back, to wrest intellectual hegemony from the left orthodoxy and retrieve it for open-minded, liberal scholarship. You will have to win the discipline back to the pursuit of truth in that genuinely critical, objective spirit which Sir Karl Popper has so powerfully characterized and defended in *Objective Knowledge* (Clarendon Press, 1972).

There are sociologists who, on my reading of their work, can help you in this task. Assistance is also available from several organizations. For addresses, for names, and for bibliographies, write to me.

A new sociological analysis of the state of Britain, Brown and Crompton's *Economic Restructuring and Social Exclusion* (UCL, 1994), is described in advertisements as 'A timely reminder of persisting inequalities of class, race and gender'. Perhaps it is sociologists who need a timely reminder – of their privileged good fortune in living in modern Britain, and of their duty as teachers and researchers to sustain a balanced and objective approach in their work.

Appendix 3
State Welfare Destroys Honesty

When my BBC2 film *Let's Kill Nanny* was eventually shown (it was postponed for three months in case it influenced the outcome of the European elections! They didn't say in which direction...), it provoked a considerable postbag. Some of it was predictably poisonous, much of it proved very positive.

I was especially pleased to receive many letters thanking me for speaking out against evils which had seemed to have become entirely taken for granted. There were letters to this effect from men and from women, from people of all ages, and from all over the country. Many of them (the positive letters rather than the negative ones mainly) were beautifully written, in terms both of handwriting and of style. Many were extraordinarily moving, revealing injustices of all sorts.

One in particular struck me as so remarkable in every way that it should be published. With permission, I reproduce here a letter from a lady in her sixties. It tells the story of her disappointment and her pain in the face of her discovery that so many of her fellow pensioners have been driven into deceit and dishonesty by the Welfare State. It exposes the tip of what I believe may be a general and widespread iceberg of fraud. The whole issue should be thoroughly researched. In the meantime, she speaks for very many people who know that state welfare is corrupting the community around them, and dare not speak out for themselves. She deserves our thanks for the care and effort she put into writing, for agreeing to have her letter published, and above all for her truly British refusal to give in to powerful pressures to conform with values which are wrong. She has my thanks, at least.

Dear Professor Marsland,

I was unable to write sooner after watching your programme *Let's Kill Nanny* on BBC2 on 4th August, so I am hastening now to express my appreciation of such a timely spotlight on the Welfare State in its present critical condition.

Although only a brief mention was made then of the situation regarding pensioners, it was suggested towards the end that this was not as deprived as was commonly thought, and with that I am in wholehearted agreement. Because, though much is heard about 'fiddling' in younger age groups, dishonesty among the retired is successfully hidden by a strong conspiracy of silence.

I am a single woman who returned to my native Lancashire in the 1980s after many years in inner city bedsitters in the Bristol area and several different types of job. At that time I was wholly naïve about the situation of senior citizens. Though I had had experience with unscrupulous younger folk in the South West, I had assumed without question that pensioners – reared in a different era – were an honest section of the community.

I was granted the tenancy of a bungalow in an Old Folks' Quarter of a council estate (rather disconcerting, though I was glad to be housed) and given forms to fill in. Since I hadn't much in the way of savings and only one pension (the State) my rent at the very beginning with housing benefit was, I thought, reasonable. But after a short time I was notified about a legacy from a cousin for £10,000. Without hesitation I wrote to inform the Council at once about this. I had always taken honesty for granted and so lost no time in obeying the instructions displayed prominently in all the rent offices – i.e. to let the Council know immediately if changes occurred in your finances. Prosecution was threatened for any failure to report this, but I needed no such warning.

In my innocence I imagined that my action was the usual one, adhered to faithfully by all tenants as a matter of course. With hindsight, however, I can guess that Council staff must have been paralysed with shock when my letter arrived. At that time (before 1988) rent was calculated on pensions and the interest on your capital. On the next assessment my rent almost doubled. This seemed to me quite fair. I never took notice of the amounts paid by other tenants at rent offices. And so I lived in blissful ignorance for a year or two.

But then certain events began to strip away my naïveté. After paying rent one Monday, I called for a brief visit on a retired couple I knew. As I sat down, my rent card slipped out of my full shopping bag and was retrieved by the husband from the floor. He caught sight of the amount I was paying and and was thrown into consternation. 'Why the dickens are you paying all this? We only pay £X a week.' I explained about my cousin's legacy, which I had mentioned to them before. Their horror increased. 'Yes, we thought this very foolish of you. But you don't mean to say that you told the COUNCIL too?' Both were speechless at such stupidity, which was how they interpreted my behaviour. 'We thought you had some intelligence!'

This incident threw me into great turmoil. I knew that this couple had quite a decent lifestyle but it had never entered my head that any tenants lied about their means. Why, it was a serious offence and they would inevitably face prosecution sooner or later! So heavily did this conviction weigh upon me that in the end, after weeks of worry, I decided to share these fears with another neighbour, a man living alone. I had of course concluded that the couple were rare exceptions among the retired community and that they would run headlong into public disgrace when their deception came to light, as I was sure was bound to happen. So after swearing him to secrecy, I related my story to this man, never doubting that he would share my anxiety.

But to my bewilderment he remained unmoved and silent, his expression one of cynical disbelief at my agitation. And shortly afterwards he confided that his life savings were hidden away in a strong box in his home because he was 'supposed to be destitute'. He let me know very bluntly that he had not been taken in by what he saw as my pretending to play the innocent, adding – 'You've got a nice nest-egg tucked away somewhere too. Don't try to deny it. Everybody has.'

These two revelations had a devastating effect on me. I began to make enquiries among folks I knew in the nearby town. And at last reality hit me in the face. The pensioners whom I had put down as regrettable exceptions in a truthful world were only too normal. It was I who was the exception.

And so I finally learned the facts, so different from what I had imagined. The commonest device on retirement is to put capital in the name of a close relative – with the agreement of course that you retain full rights to possession of the account in your lifetime, after which it will pass without a hitch to the family. The next most popular ruse (already mentioned) is to keep large sums in secret places in the house or bungalow. There are other methods too.

This information shocked me to the core. But I soon realized that 'fiddling' was a long-established custom among working-class pensioners, looked upon as perfectly normal and carrying with it not the slightest suggestion of wrongdoing. In fact it is considered just obvious common sense to which no stigma could possibly be attached. And it is practised by those who claim to be 'religious' and regular churchgoers just as much as 'heathens'.

I made the mistake of showing my horror about this state of affairs to folk whom I assumed to be above reproach – only to discover after a while that they too had been less than truthful in their statements of means. In fact, fiddling is so woven into the fabric of pensioners' lives in areas such as this that few believe that anyone could be so self-destructive as to be frank with the Council. 'Pull the other leg' was the usual reaction I got until I realized the futility of saying anything. For my views on honesty seemed to others as fantastic and incomprehensible as though I were some strange visitant from outer space. And this incredulity speaks volumes about Welfare State morality.

Now it is true that the State pension in Britain compares unfavourably with that in most other countries. And this fact is made much of in the national press. What they do not say is that it is so easy to compensate in other ways that this alters the picture entirely. Life after 60 is rarely the gloomy existence that is usually painted by the media. In fact it can be very comfortable. Avaricious pensioners (by no means thin on the ground) can be very successful indeed in playing skilfully on the sympathies of compassionate people in authority to ensure that they live in what amounts to comparative luxury, paying the bare minimum in living expenses and collecting every available benefit without difficulty. Needless to say, they are almost invariably the least deserving.

Once I believed that I had found a kindred spirit in a widow who came to live in the area. She told me that her strict upbringing by religious parents had made any kind of dishonesty unthinkable to her. Thus encouraged, I confided in her the facts that had shaken me so profoundly. She reacted with horror. If she had lied on official forms, she declared, she would never have known a moment's peace thereafter. This gave me a tremendous boost. How reassuring to discover that someone else also saw such things as a matter of honour!

But dark days lay ahead. The 'targeting reforms' brought in by Mrs (or Lady) Thatcher in April 1988 brought home to me the full irony of my situation. My rent went up alarmingly, since I was now called upon to pay two-thirds of my State pension to the Council every week. I had always been careful with the legacy, because I thought that it had to last as long as possible. Feeling responsible for my own welfare, I viewed this as a moral obligation. But of course I had been forced to draw on it, even though being very strict with myself – forgoing holidays, making do without a telephone, new clothes, etc. I hadn't even replaced the old 12" black and white TV from bedsit days with a large colour model, such as all my neighbours had. And now all this counted against me, brought double penalties. For I had to suffer for trying to be thrifty as well as for being truthful.

The new rules now classified me as one of the 'better off' – whilst most pensioners around me were put in the category of the 'targeted poor'. So I was paying as much rent as 5 or 6 of them put together. Mrs Thatcher and her colleagues showed a frightening lack of knowledge of human nature, no conception of reality, when they assumed that all British pensioners were indisputably honest. And what they did, in fact, was to reward still further the unscrupulous majority and add immeasurably to the burden already borne by the small number with a conscience.

I was naturally depressed and resentful about this terrible injustice though my widow friend seemed unperturbed. I concluded that she was a better person than I, undismayed by these crippling losses because consciousness of virtue sustained her. And then one day my credulity was once again shattered. We were discussing an entirely different matter when she suddenly burst out – 'Haven't you been a foolish woman, though? Fancy handicapping yourself like that!' I assumed that she was referring to my caring for stray animals – a cat being on my knee at the time – but was speedily set right. 'No – I mean for telling the Council about the money your cousin left you.' I was flabbergasted. 'But you did the same. You told the truth too.' She flashed a shrewd look and then admitted: 'Well, no, I didn't. Nobody does. The Council doesn't expect it from pensioners. This is understood on both sides.' So her niece had drawn every penny she had out of the bank and opened a new account under her own name. She would oblige her aunt whenever withdrawals were requested, bring the book in for regular inspections and presumably be suitably recompensed for her part in the plot. The amount transferred must have been substantial, since this neighbour had worked throughout her married life as well as her husband and they had no family.

So the honest widow had turned out to be just another fiddler – and my disillusionment was complete. And I know now that the Housing Estate where I live is typical of thousands of others all over the country where the bulk of the nation's pensioners are found.

Since then I have discovered a few other rare pensioners in the area who share my dismay about the wholesale fiddling that goes on unchecked. They too have paid out huge sums to the Council but since they have much greater capital than I run no risk of being reduced to poverty. Nevertheless I sympathize fully with their resentment they feel at being punished for their folly in practising self-discipline when younger by budgeting and saving. Yet they were no better off than others who have extorted huge sums from the State by presenting themselves as impoverished victims in urgent need of help. Three years ago I read a pamphlet – The Saving Trap – by a Mr Brown, a Conservative MP, I believe. This sets out very plainly the disadvantages that fall to the lot of those misguided enough to try and make provision for their later years (i.e. those honest enough to make frank declarations about their means).

I also feel for people who entered private pensions schemes in earlier decades for security after retirement. Unlike savings, pensions cannot be concealed. And since it is improvidence, dependence and greed that the State rewards (not foresight and self-reliance) such attempts now turn out to be a major drawback. The only positive thing is that pensions are constantly renewed, whereas capital is gone forever.

It is obvious that the financial assistance you receive on retirement has little to do with money and everything to do with character. In fact I think that your behaviour at this milestone demonstrates more clearly than anything else what your real nature is. For it is the kind of person you are that decides how much aid you get from the State. Literal-minded people who see the 'destitute' as having lived on pitiful sums in their working lives and the 'better-off' as having been in receipt of much higher incomes lack all insight into the truth of the situation. Indeed, the facts are often the reverse. The reality is of course that some have been irresponsible and feckless and some with greater moral fibre (though with no more money) have practised self-denial and thrift. And if in addition to the former characteristics you are acquisitive and unscrupulous, you will be sure to get every hand-out available. But if in contrast you are proud, independent and above all have principles, you will learn very quickly that these qualities are not understood, still less admired, in Britain today and bring harsh penalties in their wake.

My position in the years 1988 and onwards was critical. A friend had advised me to take the legacy out of the Building Society and put it in Unit Trusts and Income Bonds for better returns. The former proved to be a disaster from the start, for steep falls on the Stock Market just after the purchase meant that I received only meagre sums and the good days to balance these that I was told to expect never materialized. When my rent went up again in 1989 I was thrown into a panic and obliged to draw out half the Income Bonds – though not realizing that I would have to wait three months for the cheque. I was in a terrible state, once or twice having to replace goods on supermarket shelves because I couldn't meet the bill at the check-out. I was too proud to borrow but saw to it that my pets didn't suffer. You may imagine the colour of my thoughts. All this hardship because I had not lied to the Council, whilst those who did had been handsomely recompensed and were now better off than ever. A clerk at the rent office, aghast at the amount I was paying, said to me one week – 'Why didn't you keep your money under the bed, as others do? Surely you must know by now that honesty is NOT the best policy!'

In despair, I wrote to a number of folk in authority (including Mrs Thatcher, who passed the letter on to the head DHSS office in London). But I was either ignored or told that I had been 'misinformed' – a strange word to use to someone living in an Old Folks' Quarter! One or two indignantly rejected the very idea that any British pensioners would resort to trickery when claiming benefit.

I have come to the conclusion therefore that this turning of a blind eye to the misdeeds of the retired working classes, who form the largest section of the pensioners in the land, is the result of powerful propaganda about their plight. For the media never ceases to present them as 'poor old dears', tragic as an Age Concern poster, struggling along bravely in abject poverty = cold, hungry and unable to afford the smallest treat. To add to the pathos, they are also portrayed as utterly guileless, often ignorant of all the benefits to which they are entitled or too timid or illiterate to claim.

On the radio recently I heard such assertions yet again. You may imagine my reaction after my very different experiences! I am not saying that no such people exist, though they certainly do not live on Council Estates! Those I know (a great many) are only too well aware of the benefits to be claimed – and so are their families. I have never come across any pensioners who remotely resemble the popular image, especially since they are usually pictured as living isolated lives with relations playing no part.

And this brings me to a very sore point. I think it is very unfair that no distinctions are made between the majority, who have families helping them all the time, and the few who have no such advantage. As you know, working-class folk are as a rule very clannish indeed: their whole lives are almost exclusively family-centered. In contrast, the percentage of the retired who manage alone on Council Estates is very small. Nearly all the pensioners I know have children giving constant financial assistance – paying for holidays, often buying clothes and groceries, doing indoor decorating free of charge, seeing to quarterly bills in whole or in part, providing furnishings, domestic appliances, etc, etc. All this amounts to a staggering sum per year, whilst the tiny number in my position are dependent on their own resources. Yet both categories are treated in exactly the same way by the authorities, who ignore family help as immaterial, as though it were a trivial thing of no consequence, instead of its being the equivalent of a giant-sized extra pension. And this is not to mention the importance of the psychological support it provides.

And when, as often happens, pensioners put their savings in the name of a son or daughter in order to qualify for maximum State benefits, their many advantages make this lumping together even more ludicrous. For they come off victorious from every angle: ample funds from benefits, constant family gifts – and concealed accounts to draw upon with no risk of detection. And thanks to the generosity of the Welfare State, this capital is saved from any danger of serious depletion for the children to take over after the parents' deaths – without the slightest suggestion that they are anything other than exemplary citizens. I think that the way in which the younger generation can benefit in such instances is one of the most deplorable consequences of the trust and magnanimity shown by benevolent 'Nanny'.

Two years ago, visiting a friend in a different area, I was shown a collection of letters from the readers' correspondence page of a local newspaper. A young unemployed man had written up some time before to protest about the way in which he was so often scorned and and labelled a sponger on the State. Then what about all the retired folk, he enquired, who had transferred sizeable bank accounts to their children – and now lived on State benefits in Council accommodation, immune from all censure and the jibes that were directed at younger folk?

To my surprise, only one man had written in support of this youth – obviously someone in the higher income groups who (like most people in such circumstances) had been influenced by years of media brainwashing and was shocked to realize that his former deep sympathy might have been misplaced, However, all the other correspondents were violently antagonistic towards the young man and fiercely protective of the older generation who had 'All suffered so much hardship and deserved all the help they could get'. He had dared to break the rigid taboo regarding criticism of pensioners – and did he get a bashing!

It was easy to see that fiddling by over-60s was well-known to some (no doubt collaborators in parental deception) and this made them all the more vicious. The message was plain: it was contemptible to cast aspersions at pensioners, by popular consensus of opinion sacrosanct, in this deplorable fashion. Their lives were harsh enough without these malicious charges of dishonesty – and could their detractor furnish any proof? No! One woman explained how this libel might have arisen. She said that while she was shocked at such allegations, she could understand that in rare instances pensioners might in good faith enter inaccurate information on official forms. But accusations of cheating were unpardonable: the old folk were simply confused. And in any case it was well known that at that time of life everyone was, to some extent, 'non compos mentis'!!

Up to 1993, to my surprise, no checks on declarations of means were ever undertaken. However, last year tenants were asked to take in bank/building society books, etc., to substantiate their statements to the Council. But since the majority use the successful devices already described, to make disclosure impossible ('They can't prove anything') such schemes are bound to be largely futile. Councils cannot investigate major frauds for which there is no evidence. So these measures are doomed to failure, since they check up only on the less culpable tenants and leave the countless thousands of offenders on a large scale untouched.

Mrs Thatcher's 'reforms' continued to cause me great distress long after 1988. The Unit Trusts, which had been such a dismal flop all along, became such a millstone that I decided to sell three-quarters of them three and a half years ago. And suffered another catastrophe. For I lost £482 on the sale. My cousin's gift, meant to provide a few extras, had been eroded away in high rents and later on poll tax too until I could no longer meet these demands. And this although I had long given up anything even mildly 'extravagant' – magazines, an occasional trip to the coast in summer, minor Bank Holiday treats. Clothes of course had to come from second-hand market stalls. Though my rent is now much reduced, my circumstances are bleak, for the damage was done in the years following 'targeting'.

It is ironical to think that I would have been better off without the legacy – and spared much anguish, too. And incomparably better off if I had followed the crowd and concealed it, when I would now be in clover and with no stain on my character either. An added irony is that I am one of the very rare women in an area like this who paid full NI stamps throughout my working life. The only solace I have is the knowledge that my cousin, the soul of honesty, would have applauded my behaviour, even though it had such disastrous consequences. And our background was as deprived as that of any family in the area.

The true situation of British pensioners seems to be one of the nation's best-kept secrets, to be divulged only at the cost of finding yourself an outcast, denounced as a heartless wretch by all decent folk. Many younger people fear growing older so much that they seem to expect some form of retribution later on if they don't look upon the older generation with an indulgent eye. And pensioners on the whole are keenly aware of this, accepting it as no more than their due. I have heard it said – 'The country has a duty to see that we end our days in comfort.' Being treated as a stereotyped 'old dear' (whatever your real nature) with your faults dismissed and safe from all criticism is a kind of trump card for many, to be used with great effect on anyone rash enough to disregard this unwritten law. But an attitude of pity, even if motivated by kindliness, is only another aspect of ageism and does not help people psychologically. In fact, it robs them of full humanity.

My experiences here (and I have omitted much that would sound far-fetched to those unfamiliar with life on Council Estates) have shown only too clearly that pensioners' benefits are a farce. Both sides act a part: the older folk pretending to supply correct details of their finances and the authorities pretending to believe them. Yet nothing can be allowed to leak out. Fiddling pensioners and their collaborating families are not likely to broadcast this outside their own circles in the working class, who are of course already in the know. And authorities seem more than anxious for this successful cover up to continue. The facts must be swept under the carpet, for it is essential that the myths be accepted unconditionally by the rest of the population.

So the question must be asked: is fiddling, which is unofficially condoned in the case of pensioners, also justifiable? I know retired people who seem decent enough in other ways yet who maintain stoutly that it is. And when cheating is so easy and brings such pleasant results, they judge it foolish not to jump on the bandwaggon along with most other senior citizens nationwide. Why punish yourself, they argue, for the sake of old-fashionend ideas on morality that no one cares cares a rap about any longer? Especially when that way leads to financial suicide while the other means that you can have your cake and eat it. I have heard a wag ask this riddle – 'What is a conscience?' ANSWER – 'Something that puts your rent up.' I have thought of another – 'When is a crime not a crime?' ANSWER – 'After your retirement birthday.'

After nearly half a century of the Welfare State, the old moral code which was generally thought to be observed more strictly in Britain than in any other nation has undergone a marked revision. So that pensioners can see nothing odd in being indignant about shoplifting and thieving of all kinds whilst remaining unperturbed about their own (often long-standing) dishonesty. No doubt this curious blindness arises from the belief that whilst robbing another human being might give them a few qualms, stealing from a huge impersonal organization like the State is quite legitimate, indeed fair game.

Whilst many are unconcerned about false claims, others consider themselves models of rectitude, any lingering twinges of guilt having been banished by years of successful unchallenged fiddling, now blotted out of consciousness. Amply cushioned by substantial benefits and involved relations, such pensioners can make pleasant and obliging neighbours. But I feel sure that if their rationalizations could be questioned and their misdeeds described in plain language, they would be outraged. Any reluctant admission wrung from them would undoubtedly be to sanctify their actions by claiming that this had been done 'for the family'. For 'family' is another hallowed word, almost as emotive as 'pensioner'. And equally powerful in converting serious offences into harmlessness or even virtue.

I confess that I often envy their elastic consciences and even wonder whether my ideas are now really outdated and ridiculous. A test I did on honesty in a newspaper classified high scorers as 'neurotic' and less conscientious ones as 'better balanced'!

It is very obvious of course that many of the retired retain bitter memories of early poverty. And this in their eyes justifies all attempts to compensate by wresting as much as possible from State coffers for themselves and ultimately their children. No one living in an Old Folks' area can fail to note the preoccupation with money that is so clearly evident, despite the many books I have read that state so convincingly that a growing detachment from earthly concerns is characteristic of later decades! Although I have suffered such severe financial losses, I find this concentration on money hard to understand. I have never been a materialist and it all seems very disturbing. For money is held to be the only thing that matters, with bigger pensions and fatter handouts the only needs. I have a feeling that this is probably a substititute for the lack of other interests and values in life and the real problem is spiritual poverty.

In the last year or two, additional amounts have been made available to the over-65s. Attendance Allowance DS 702 does not normally require a medical examination, is paid regardless of all other benefits and doesn't even need a carer to justify its name. This is worth over £30 a week and seems to be asking for exploitation.

In some ways this is a Britain even more bizarre than George Orwell's vision of 1984. The prizes go to the least worthy and responsible: virtue is punished and the lack of it rewarded. When you think of the passionate endeavours of idealists who fought to create the Welfare State earlier this century, it is all such a feast of irony. What would these ardent pioneers make of the consequences of their efforts to guarantee a better life for future generations? The corruption that has grown steadily since 1948 would have utterly destroyed their cherished dreams of a trans-formed Britain.

In a library book I read – 'The Welfare State, which is supposed to give individuals a better start in life by improving their material conditions, bred a generation which believed that the State was there to nurse them. The result was the precise opposite of what was intended and a net decrease in human enterprise.'

Not to mention the collapse of an ideal formerly held to be so worthwhile – the once admired goal of personal integrity.

Yours sincerely,

Bibliography

Abel Smith, B. and Townsend, P. (1965), *The Poor and the Poorest* (Bell).

Adams, J. (1995), *Risk* (UCL Press).

Allen, I. and Leat, D. (1994), *The Future of Social Services: Accountability, Planning, and the Market* (Policy Studies Institute).

Anderson, D. C. (1988), *The Megaphone Solution: Government Attempts to Cure Social Problems with Mass Media Campaigning* (Social Affairs Unit).

Anderson, D. C. (ed.) (1988 [2]), *Full Circle: Bringing Up Children in the Post-Permissive Society* (Social Affairs Unit).

Anderson, D. C. (ed.) (1992), *The Loss of Virtue* (Social Affairs Unit).

Anderson, D. C. (1993), 'The Wages of Sin' (*Sunday Telegraph*, 7 February).

Anderson, D. C., Lait, J., and Marsland, D. (1981), *Breaking the Spell of the Welfare State* (Social Affairs Unit).

Anderson, D. C. and Dawson, G. (1986), *Family Portraits* (Social Affairs Unit).

Ashford, N. (1993), *Dismantling the Welfare State: Why and How* (Libertarian Alliance).

Ashford, N. (1995), 'The Right after Reagan: Crack-up or Comeback?' (A. Grant, (ed.), *Contemporary American Politics*, Dartmouth).

Atkinson, A. B. (1989), *Poverty and Social Security* (Harvester Press).

Atkinson, A. B. and Mogenson, G. (1993), *Welfare and Work Incentives* (Clarendon Press).

Atkinson, R. (1989), *The Failure of the State* (Compuprint).

Audit Commission (1987), *Competitiveness and Contracting Out of Local Authorities' Services* (HMSO).

Bacon, R. and Eltis, W. (1976), *Britain's Economic Problem: Too Few Producers* (Macmillan).

Banfield, R. (1958), *The Moral Basis of a Backward Society* (Free Press).

Barnett, C. (1986), *The Audit of War* (Macmillan).

Barr, N. (1989), 'Social Insurance as an Efficiency Device' (*Journal of Public Policy*, 9, 1, pp. 59–82).

Barr, N. (1993), *The Economics of the Welfare State* (Oxford University Press).

Barr, N. (1994), *Labor Markets and Social Policy in Central and Eastern Europe* (Oxford University Press).

Barr, N. (Undated and out of print), *The Mirage of Private Unemployment Insurance* (STICERD, London School of Economics).

Barry, N. (1990), *Welfare* (Open University Press).

Bauman, Z. (1988), *Freedom* (Open University Press).

Beck, U. (1992), *Risk Society: Towards a New Modernity* (Sage).

Beenstock, M. (1994), 'Unemployment Insurance' (*Economic Affairs*, Vol. 14, No. 5).

Beenstock, M. and Brasse, V. (1986), *Insurance for Unemployment* (Allen and Unwin).

Bell, M. (1994), 'Privatizing Pensions' (Chapter 4 in M. Bell *et al.*, *The End of the Welfare State*, Adam Smith Institute).

Bell, M., Butler, E., Marsland, D., and Pirie, M. (1994), *The End of the Welfare State* (Adam Smith Institute).

Benson, J. (1983), *The Penny Capitalists: a Study of Nineteenth Century Working Class Entrepreneurs* (Gill and Macmillan).

Berger, B. (ed.) (1991), *The Entrepreneurial Revolution* (ICS Press).

Berger, B. and Berger, P. (1983), *The War Over the Family* (Hutchinson).

Berger, P. (1987), *The Capitalist Revolution* (Gower).

Berger, P. and Neuhaus, R. (1977), *To Empower People* (American Enterprise Institute).

Beveridge, W. (1942), *Social Insurance and Allied Services* (The Beveridge Report, Cmd 6404, HMSO).

Beveridge, W. (1948), *Voluntary Action* (Allen and Unwin).

Biddulph, G. (1990), 'South America's First Welfare State' (*Daily Telegraph*, 18 August).

Bishop, M. *et al.* (1995), *The Regulatory Challenge* (Oxford University Press).

Boyd, N. (1982), *Josephine Butler, Octavia Hill, Florence Nightingale: Three Victorian Women who Changed their World* (Macmillan).

Bracewell-Milnes, B. (1989), *The Wealth of Giving* (Institute of Economic Affairs).

Bradshaw, J. (1972), 'The Concept of Social Need' (*New Society* 19, 640–3, 30 March).

Breach, R. W. and Hartwell, R. M. (1972), *British Economy and Society 1870–1970* (Oxford University Press).

Brindle, D. and Mihill, C. (1991), 'Minister Blames Poor over Bad Diet' (*The Guardian*, 4 June).

Brittan, S. (1995), 'Redistribution, Yes: "Equality", No' (*Financial Times*, 16 February).

Buchanan, J. M. (1988), *The Political Economy of the Welfare State* (Industrial Institute for Economic and Social Research, Stockholm).

Burnett, J. (1979), *Plenty and Want: a Social History of Diet in England from 1815 to the Present Day* (Scolar Press).

Burrows, R. and Loader, B. (eds) (1994), *Towards a Post-Fordist Welfare State?* (Routledge).

Butler, E. (1994), 'From Problem to Solution' (Chapter 2 in M. Bell *et al.*, *The End of the Welfare State*, Adam Smith Institute).

Butler, E. and Pirie, M. (1989), *The Manual of Privatization* (Adam Smith Institute).

Bytheway, B. and Johnson, J. (eds) (1990), *Welfare and the Ageing Experience* (Avebury).

Cahill, M. (1994), *The New Social Policy* (Blackwell).

Caines, E. (1994), 'How Competition is Creating Winners' (*The Times*, 17 November).

Campbell, T. (1988), *Justice* (Macmillan).

Cannan, C. (1992), *Changing Families, Changing Welfare: Family Centres and the Welfare State* (Harvester Wheatsheaf).

Carlson, A. (1988), *The Swedish Experiment in Family Politics: the Myrdals and the Interwar Population Crisis* (Transaction Books, 1988).

Carlson, A. (1994), *Family Questions* (Transaction Books).

Central Council for Education and Training in Social Work (1991), 'Rules and Requirements for the Diploma in Social Work' (Paper 30, 2nd edition, CCETSW).

Central Council for Education and Training in Social Work (1995), 'The Statement of Requirements for Qualification in Social Work' (Revised).

Chaney, D. (1994), Review of *The Authority of the Consumer* (*Sociology*, Vol. 28, No. 4).

Cherry, G. E. (1981), *Pioneers in British Planning* (Architectural Press).

Cheung, S. N. S. (1981), *The Myth of Social Cost* (Institute of Economic Affairs).

Chodes, J. (1990), 'Friendly Societies: Voluntary Social Security and More' (*The Freeman*, March).

Clark, S. (1994), 'What the Hospital Boss Saw' (*Sunday Times*, 24 April).

Coad, P. (1990), *The Persistent Offender: Fact and Fiction* (Probation Service Fellowship).

Cochran, A. and Clarke, J. (1993), *Comparing Welfare States: Britain in International Context* (Sage).

Cockett, R. (1995), *Thinking the Unthinkable* (Harper Collins).

Coleman, A. (1985), *Utopia on Trial* (Hilary Shipman).

Commission on Social Justice (1994), *Social Justice: Strategies for National Renewal* (The Borrie Report, Viking).

Commission on the Urban Priority Areas (1985), *Faith in the City* (Church House Publishing).

Court, W. H. B. (1965), *British Economic History 1870–1914* (Cambridge University Press).

Cousins, M. (1993), 'EC Recommendations on Social Protection' (*Social Policy and Administration*, Vol. 27, No. 4, pp. 286–98).

Cowen, T. (ed.) (1992), *Public Goods and Market Failures* (Transaction Books).

Culpitt, I. (1992), *Welfare and Citizenship: Beyond the Crisis of the Welfare State* (Sage).

Dalrymple, T. (1994), *If Symptoms Persist* (André Deutsch).

Darley, G. (1990), *Octavia Hill: a Life* (Constable).

Davies, J. (ed.) (1993), *The Family: Is It Just Another Lifestyle Choice?* (Institute of Economic Affairs).

Deakin, N. (1994), *The Politics of Welfare: Continuities and Change* (Harvester Wheatsheaf).

Dennis, N. (1970), *People and Planning* (Faber).

Dennis, N. (1972), *Participation and Planners' Blight* (Faber).

Dennis, N. and Erdos, G. (1992, revised 1993), *Families without Fatherhood* (Institute of Economic Affairs).

Dennis, N. (1993), *Rising Crime and the Dismembered Family* (Institute of Economic Affairs).

Department of Health (1991), *The Patient's Charter* (Department of Health).

Department of Social Security (1993), *Households below Average Income 1979 to 1990–1* (HMSO).

Desai, M. (1995), 'Borrie is no Beveridge: Citizen's Income Now' (*Citizen's Income Bulletin*, No. 19, January).

Devlin, B. *et al.* (1990), *Medical Care: Is It a Consumer Good?* (Institute of Economic Affairs).

Diebold, J. (1987), *Private Enterprise and Public Policy* (Diebold Institute).

Directorate General for Employment, Industrial Relations & Social Affairs (1993), *Green Paper: European Social Policy* (Commission of the European Communities).

Donnison, D. (1994), *Why All Society's Accidents Become Housing Problems* (*Sunday Times*, 28 August).

Drover, G. and Hokenstad, M. (1994), 'Social Welfare Policy: Developments and Directions in North America' (Introduction to Special Issue, Vol. 28, No. 2, of *Social Policy and Administration*).

Douglas, J. (1990), *The Myth of the Welfare State* (Transaction).

Doyal, L. (1989), *A Theory of Human Needs: towards a Feasible Socialism* (Macmillan).

Eberstadt, N. (1989), *The Poverty of Communism* (Transaction Books).

Economist Intelligence Group (1991), *Business Comparisons* (EIG).

Edinburgh, HRH The Duke of (1994), 'Charity or Public Benefit' (11th Arnold Goodman Charity Lecture, Charities Aid Foundation, 9 June).

Eisenstadt, S. N. and Ahimeir, O. (1985), *The Welfare State and its Aftermath* (Croom Helm).

Enthoven, A. C. (1980), *Health Plan* (Addison Wesley).

Enthoven, A. C. (1985), *Reflection on the Management of the National Health Service* (Addison Wesley).

Erikson, E. H. (1956), *Childhood and Society* (Norton).

Erikson, E. H. (ed.) (1968), *Identity: Youth and Crisis* (Faber).

Esping-Andersen, G. (1990), *The Three Worlds of Welfare Capitalism* (Polity Press).

Etzioni, A. (1994), 'Who Should Pay for Care?' (*Sunday Times*, 9 October).

Farmer, R. and Miller, D. (1991), *Lecture Notes on Epidemiology and Public Health Medicine* (Blackwell).

Field, F. (1989), *Losing Out: the Emergence of Britain's Underclass* (Blackwell).

Field, F. (1994), *Let's Be a Friendlier Society* (*Observer*, 30 October).

Flew, A. (1981), *Thinking about Thinking* (Collins-Fontana).

Flew, A. (1991), 'Market Order or Commanded Chaos?' (*Public Affairs Quarterly*, Vol. 5, No. 1).

Flew, A. (1992), *Thinking about Social Thinking* (Fontana).

Flew, A. (1994), 'Minimum Government for Maximum Liberty' (*Human Affairs*, Vol. 4, No. 1, pp. 3–16).

Flew, A. *et al.* (1992), *Empowering the Parents* (Institute of Economic Affairs).

Floud, R. *et al.* (1990), *Height, Health and History* (Cambridge University Press).

Forsythe, M. (1986), *Re-servicing Britain* (Adam Smith Institute).

Frankland, M. (1994), 'Cruel Tide of History Drags Sweden from its Dreams of Utopia' (*Observer*, 11 September).

Fraser, D. (1981 and 1993), *The Evolution of the British Welfare State* (Macmillan).

Friedman, M. and Friedman, R. (1980), *Free to Choose* (Secker and Warburg).

Friedmann, R. R. *et al.* (eds) (1987), *Modern Welfare States: a Comparative View of Trends and Prospects* (Wheatsheaf).

Galbraith, J. K. (1993), *The Culture of Contentment* (Penguin).

Gammon, M. (1987), *Health, Security and You* (St Michael's Organization).

Gammon, M. (1992), 'Bureaucracy and Black Holes in the Economic Universe' (United States Army Health Services Command Conference, San Antonio, 28 October).

Garton-Ash, T. (1990), *We the People: the Revolution of 89 Witnessed in Warsaw, Budapest, Berlin, and Prague* (Granta Books).

Gash, N. (ed.) (1974), *The Long Debate on Poverty* (Institute of Economic Affairs).

Gedye, R. (1987), *Daily Telegraph*, 11 December.

Gellner, E. (1992), *Post-modernism, Reason, and Religion* (Routledge).

Gellner, E. (1994), *Civil Society and its Rivals* (Hamish Hamilton).

George, V. and Wilding, P. (1984), *Ideologies and Social Policy* (RKP).

George, V. and Wilding, P. (1994), *Welfare and Ideology* (Harvester Wheatsheaf).

Gewirth, A. (1982), *Human Rights* (University of Chicago Press).

Giddens, A. (1991), *Modernity and Self-Identity* (Polity Press).

Gilder, G. (1981), *Wealth and Poverty* (Buchan and Enright).

Gilder, G. (1988), *The Spirit of Enterprise* (Penguin).

Giles, C. and Webb, S. (1993), *Poverty Statistics: a Guide for the Perplexed* (Institute for Fiscal Studies).

Glennerster, H. (1992), *Paying for Welfare: the 1990s* (Harvester Wheatsheaf).

Glennerster, H. (1993), 'Paying for Welfare: Issues for the Nineties' (Chapter 1 in R. Page and N. Deakin (eds), *The Costs of Welfare*, Avebury).

Golding, P. and Middleton, S. (1981), *Images of Welfare: the Mass Media, Public Attitudes, and the Welfare State* (Blackwell).

Goldman, M. (1976), *The Spoils of Progress: Environmental Pollution in the USSR* (MIT Press).

Goldman, M. (1983), *USSR in Crisis: the Failure of an Economic System* (Norton).

Goldsmith, V. (1994), *Adieu to the Welfare State* (Independent on Sunday, 2 January).

Goodin, R. (1985), *Protecting the Vulnerable* (University of Chicago Press).

Goodin, R. (1988), *Reasons for Welfare: the Political Theory of the Welfare State* (Princeton University Press).

Goodin, R. and Le Grand, J. (eds) (1987), *Not Only the Poor: the Middle Classes and the Welfare State* (Unwin Hyman).

Goodin, R. and Le Grand, J. (1987 [2]), 'The Middle Class Infiltration of the Welfare State' (Chapter 6 in Goodin and Le Grand).

Gordon, C. and Winter, D. (1989), *The Welfare State in the United States; Data on Federal Expenditures, Needs and Distribution 1977–85* (STICERD, London School of Economics).

Gough, I. (1979), *The Political Economy of the Welfare State* (Macmillan).

Green, D. G. (1982), *The Welfare State: for Rich or for Poor?* (Institute of Economic Affairs).

Green, D. G. (1984), *Mutual Aid or Welfare State?* (Allen & Unwin).

Green, D. G. (1985), *Working Class Patients and the Medical Establishment* (St Martin's Press).

Green, D. G. (1986), *Challenge to the NHS* (Institute of Economic Affairs).

Green, D. G. (1990), *The NHS Reforms: Whatever Happened to Consumer Choice?* (Institute of Economic Affairs).

Green, D. G. (1991), *Empowering the Parents: How to Break the Schools Monopoly* (Institute of Economic Affairs).

Green, D. G. (1993), *Reinventing Civil Society* (Institute of Economic Affairs).

Green, D. G. (1994), 'Medical Care before the NHS' (*Economic Affairs*, Vol. 14, No. 5).

Green, D. G. and Lucas, D. A. (1993), *Medicard: a Better Way to Pay for Medicines* (Institute of Economic Affairs).

Greenslade, R. (1994), 'No Place like Home' (*Sunday Times*, 5 June).

Gray, J. (1989), *Limited Government: a Positive Agenda* (Institute of Economic Affairs).

Gray, J. (1992), *The Moral Foundations of Market Institutions* (Institute of Economic Affairs).

Gray, J. (1993), *Beyond the New Right* (Routledge).

Grice, A. and Nelson, F. (1993), 'Lilley to Curb Doctors' Abuse of Sick Notes' (*Sunday Times*, 21 February).

Grosse, E. (1987), *Welfare without the State* (Institute of Economic Affairs).

Halsey, A. H. and Dennis, N. (1988), *English Ethical Socialism* (Clarendon).

Hammond, J. L. and Hammond, B. (1947), *The Bleak Age* (Revised Edition, Pelican Books).

Hamnett, C. *et al.* (1989), *The Changing Social Structure* (Sage).

Hanson, C. (1974), 'Welfare before the Welfare State' (In N. Gash (ed.), *The Long Debate on Poverty,* Institute of Economic Affairs).

Hanson, C. (1994), 'Self-Help: an Idea whose Time has Come' (*Economic Affairs*, Vol. 14, No. 5).

Harris, D. (1987), *Justifying State Welfare* (Blackwell).

Harris, J. (1977), *William Beveridge* (Clarendon Press).

Harris, R. (1988), *Beyond the Welfare State* (Institute of Economic Affairs).

Harris, R. and Seldon, A. (1977), *Not from Benevolence: Twenty Years of Economic Dissent* (Institute of Economic Affairs).

Harris, R. & Seldon, A. (1987), *Welfare without the State: a Quarter Century of Suppressed Public Choice* (Institute of Economic Affairs).

Harrison, B. (1994), *Lean and Mean* (Basic Books).

Harrison, P. (1983), *Inside the Inner City* (Pelican).

Harrison, R. (1968), *Samuel Smiles' Self-Help* (1859) (Sphere).

Hasenfeld, Y. and Zald, M. N. (1985), *The Welfare State in America: Trends and Prospects* (Sage).

Hayek, F. A. (ed.) (1975), *Collectivist Economic Planning* (Kelley).

Hayek, F. A. (1982), 'The Impossibility of Socialist Calculation' (*Journal of Economic Affairs*, Vol. 2, No. 3).

Hayek, F. A. (1988), *The Fatal Conceit* (Routledge).

Heller, R. (1993), *The Fate of IBM* (Little Brown).

Heller, R. (1994), 'The Dubious Economics of Scale' (*Management Today*, November).

Hennessy, P. and Seldon, A. (eds) (1987), *Ruling Performance: British Governments from Attlee to Thatcher* (Blackwell).

Hennessy, P. (1992), *Never Again: Britain 1945–51* (Cape).

Hennessy, P. (1993), 'How Benefit Cheats Con Britain out of Billions Every Year' (*Daily Express*, 27 October).

250   *Bibliography*

Her Majesty's Government (1993), *Financial Statement and Budget Report 1994–95* (HMSO).

Higgins, J. (1988), *The Business of Medicine* (Macmillan).

Hill, C. P. (1989), *British Economic and Social History 1700–1982* (Edward Arnold).

Hill, D. (1992), 'The American Philosophy of Welfare' (*Social Policy and Administration*, Vol. 26, No. 2).

Hill, Octavia (1883), *Homes of the London Poor* (Macmillan).

Hills, J. (ed.) (1990), *The State of Welfare: the Welfare State in Britain since 1974* (Clarendon Press).

Hills, J. (1993), *The Future of Welfare: a Guide to the Debate* (Joseph Rowntree Foundation).

Hills, J. (1994), 'What Future for Welfare?' (*LSE Magazine*, Spring).

Hilton, I. (1991), 'Trouble in Paradise' (*Independent*, 19 April).

Himmelfarb, G. (1987), *The Idea of Poverty: England in the Early Industrial Age* (Knopf).

Himmelfarb, G. (1991), *Poverty and Compassion: the Moral Imagination of the Late Victorians* (Knopf)

Himmelfarb, G. (1994), *On Looking into the Abyss* (Knopf).

Himmelfarb, G. (1994 [2]), 'Will America's Shame Become Britain's Fate?' (*Sunday Times*, 11 September).

Himmelfarb, G. (1995), *The De-moralization of Society: from Victorian Virtues to Modern Values* (Knopf).

Hirschman, A. (1970), *Exit, Voice, and Loyalty* (Harvard University Press).

Horowitz, I. L. (1993), *The De-composition of Sociology* (Oxford University Press).

House of Commons Social Security Committee (1993), Review of Expenditure on Social Security, Minutes of Evidence, 15 December (HMSO).

Howell, R. (1985), *Why Unemployment* (Adam Smith Institute).

Howell, R. (1991), *Why not Work: A Radical Solution to Unemployment* (Adam Smith Institute).

Huhne, C. (1993), 'Tory Choice that Hurts the Poorest' (*Independent on Sunday*, 4 July).

Huhne, C. (1993 [2]), 'Public Sector Must Change its Culture' (*Independent on Sunday*, 6 June).

Hussey, M. (1994), Chief's Girl is Jailed for £1m Benefit Swindle' (*Daily Express*, 11 August).

Hutton, W. (1995), 'Why Public Ownership Must not be Derailed' (*Guardian*, 9 January).

Ignatieff, M. (1984), *The Needs of Strangers* (Chatto and Windus).

International Expert Meeting (1989), Common Goals and Different Roles for Social Welfare Policies in the European UN-Region (Bonn, January 25–27)'

Jackson, P. M. and Palmer, R. (1993), *Developing Peformance Monitoring in Public Sector Organizations* (Management Centre, Leicester University).

Jacques, M. (1994), 'The Future of the Welfare State' (Lead paper presented to a conference organized by the 21st Century Trust, 21–29 January).

Jallade, J. P. (1987), *The Crisis in Redistribution in European Welfare States* (Manchester University Press).

Jamieson, B. (1994), 'Borrie's Panacea is a Suicide Pill' (*Sunday Telegraph*, 30 October).

Johnson, N. (1990), 'Reconstructing the Welfare State: 1980–1990' (Wheatsheaf).

Jones, C. (ed.) (1993), *New Perspectives on the Welfare State in Europe* (Routledge).

Jones, T. (1991), 'British Workers among World's Wealthiest' (*The Times*, 29 March).

Jordan, G. and Ashford, N. (1993), *Public Policy and the Impact of the New Right* (Pinter).

Keat, R. *et al.* (1993), *The Authority of the Consumer* (Routledge).

Kellner, P. (1994), 'Don't Blame the Underclass: the Trouble Starts at the Top' (*Sunday Times*, 29 May).

Kiernan, K. and Estaugh, V. (1993), *Extra-marital Childbearing and Social Policy* (Family Studies Centre, Occasional Paper 17).

Klein, R. *et al.* (1988), *Acceptable Inequalities: Essays on the Pursuit of Equality in Health Care* (Institute of Economic Affairs).

Kleinman, M. and Piachaud, D. (1993), 'European Social Policy: Models and Rationales' (*Journal of European Social Policy*, 3, 1).

Lal, Deepak (1995), *The Minimum Wage: No Way to Help the Poor* (Institute of Economic Affairs).

Lane, G. (1994), 'Responsabilité et Assurance ou A-Sécurité Sociale' (*Revue des Etudes Humaines*, No. 14).

Lansley, S. (1994), *After the Gold Rush* (Century/Henley Centre).

Lansley, S. and Mack, J. (1985), *Poor Britain* (Allen and Unwin).

Law, R. (1993), *Social Welfare and Social Work: the Welfare State in Britain since 1945* (Macmillan).

Leat, D. (1993), *Managing Across Sectors: Similarities and Differences between For-Profit and Voluntary Non-Profit Organizations* (Centre for Voluntary Sector Management, City University).

Leat, D. (1993 [2]), *The Development of Community Care by the Independent Sector* (Policy Studies Institute).

Lee, P. and Raban, C. (1988), *Welfare Theory and Social Policy: Reform or Revolution* (Sage).

Le Grand, J. (1982), *The Strategy of Equality* (Allen and Unwin).

Le Grand, J. and Estrin, S. (1989), *Market Socialism* (Oxford University Press).

Le Grand, J. (1991), *Equity and Choice* (Routledge).

Leira, A. (1992), *Welfare States and Working Mothers* (Cambridge University Press).

Li, Zhisui (1994), *The Private Life of Chairman Mao: the Inside Story of the Man who Made Modern China* (Chatto and Windus).

Lightfoot, W. (1994), 'Cut State's Role to Ease Public Spending Burden' (*Sunday Times*, 21 August).

Loney, M. (1986), *Greed: the New Right and the Welfare State* (Pluto Press).

Macfarlane, A. and Chambers, M. (1994), *Department of Health Hospital League Tables* (Radical Statistics Health Group).

Machan, T. R. (1990), *Capitalism and Individualism* (St Martin's Press).

Mackaay, E. (1993), 'Assurances Sociales et Responsabilité' (*Revue des Etudes Humaines*, No. 12, October).

Macnicol, J. (1994), 'Is there an "Underclass": The Lessons from America' (Chapter in M. White (ed.), *Unemployment in Focus*, Policy Studies Institute).

Macrae, N. (1994), '*Is Newt Giving the Right a Bad Name*' (*Sunday Times*, 15 January).

Macrae, N. (1995), 'America Gets Sensible about Welfare' (*Sunday Times*, 5 February).

Magnet, M. (1993), *The Dream and the Nightmare: the Sixties' Legacy to the Underclass* (Morrow).

Marquit, E. (1978), *The Socialist Countries* (Minneapolis, Marxist Educational Press, Studies in Marxism 3).

Marr, A. (1993), 'Icicles at the Heart of the Welfare State' (*Independent*, 23 November).

Marshall, T. (1994), 'The Welfare Costs that are Dragging Down Europe' (*Los Angeles Times*, 15 February).

Marsland, D. (1980), 'Three Fallacies: Ideological Error in Local Government Thinking' (Chapter 5 in A. Seldon (ed.), *Town Hall Power or Whitehall Pawn?*, (Institute of Economic Affairs).

Marsland, D. (1981), 'Education: Vast Horizons, Meagre Visions' (Chapter 4 in D. C. Anderson *et al.*, *Breaking the Spell of the Welfare State*, Social Affairs Unit).

Marsland, D. (1984), 'Public Opinion and the Welfare State' (*Sociology*, Vol. 18, No. 1).

Marsland, D. (1988), 'The Welfare State as Producer Monopoly' (*Salisbury Review*, Vol. 6, No. 4).

Marsland, D. (1989), 'An Appreciation of the NHS Review' (*Salisbury Review*, Vol. 8, No. 1).

Marsland, D. (1989 [2]), 'Changes in Education: Rescue and Reform' (In M. Pirie (ed.), *A Decade of Revolution*, Adam Smith Institute).

Marsland, D. (1989 [3]), 'Social Policies for a Free Society' (*Crossbow*, Summer).

Marsland, D. (1989 [4]), 'Progress in Health Care' (*Medical Sociology News*, Vol. 14, No. 2).

Marsland, D. (1989 [5]), 'Universal Welfare Provision and Dependency' (*Social Studies Review*, Vol. 5, No. 2).

Marsland, D. (1989 [6]), 'Reform or Reaction in Health Care' (*Medical Sociology News*, Vol. 15, No. 1).

Marsland, D. (1990), 'The Social View' (*Transportation*, Vol. 17, No. 4).

Marsland, D. (1990 [2]), 'Poverty' (*Salisbury Review*, Vol. 8, No. 3).

Marsland, D. (1990 [3]), 'Beyond Welfare' (In A. B. Cooke (ed.), *British Society in the 1990s*, Conservative Political Centre).

Marsland, D. (1990 [4]), 'Research into Health Care' (*Medical Sociology News*, Vol. 15, No. 3)

Marsland, D. (1990 [5]), 'Help for the Helpless and Self-help for All' (*Ethnic Enterprise*, Vol. 1, No. 1).

Marsland, D. (1991), 'Socialist Planning' (*Socialist Organiser*, No. 508, 21 November).

Marsland, D. (1991 [2]), 'The Bedrock of Freedom' (*Salisbury Review*, Vol. 10, No. 1).

Marsland, D. (1991 [3]), '*Beyond the Welfare State*' (Libertarian Alliance, 1991).

Marsland, D. (1991 [4]), 'Reform and Reaction in Health Care' (*Free Life*, No. 15).

Marsland, D. (1991 [5]), 'Squalor: Problems of Housing and the Environment' (*Social Policy and Administration*, Vol. 25, No. 1).

Marsland, D. (1992), 'Enemies of Promise: the Folly of Resistance to Health Care Reform' (*The Reformer*, February).

Marsland, D. (1992 [2]), 'The Consequences of Paternalist Collectivism' (*Social Policy and Administration*, Vol. 25, No. 2).

Marsland, D. (1992 [3]), *Towards the Renewal of British Education* (CRE).

Marsland, D. (1992 [4]), 'Beveridge, Collectivism, and the Environment' (*Salisbury Review*, Vol. 10, No. 4).

Marsland, D. (1992 [5]), 'Educational Reform, the World of Work, and Britain's Future' (*Modern Management*, Vol. 6, No. 3).

Marsland, D. (1992 [6]), *Fact and Fancy in Social Analysis* (Libertarian Alliance).

Marsland, D. (1993), 'Implementing Health Care Reform: from Policy to Practice' (*Medical Sociology News*, Vol. 10, No. 1).

Marsland, D. (1993 [2]), 'Let's Replace Self-Pity with Self-Reliance' (*Sunday Times*, 31 October).

Marsland, D. (1993 [3]), 'Social Engineering in the European Community: a Comment' (*Economic Affairs*, Vol. 13, No. 5).

Marsland, D. (1993 [4], 'Bureaucracy or Enterprise' (*Modern Management*, Vol. 7, No, 4).

Marsland, D. (1993 [5]), *A Deadly Embrace: the Socialist Appropriation of Sociology* (Libertarian Alliance).

Marsland, D. (1994), *Freedom, Self-Reliance, and Welfare Reform* (Radical Society).

Marsland, D. (1994 [2]), 'Liberating Welfare' (Chapter 1 in M. Bell *et al.*, *The End of the Welfare State*, Adam Smith Institute).

Marsland, D. (1994 [3]), 'Artful Beggars: a Comment on Arts Subsidies' (*Economic Affairs*, Vol. 14, No. 2).

Marsland, D. (ed.) (1994 [4]), *Work and Employment in Liberal Democratic Societies* (Paragon House).

Marsland, D. (1994 [5]), 'Samuel Smiles is Frowning: the Work Ethic Today' (*Work and Employment*, 1994).

Marsland, D. (1994 [6]), 'Not Quite the Fifth Gospel: the Failed Analysis of the Commission on Social Justice' (*Parliamentary Brief*, Vol. 3, No. 2).

Marsland, D. (ed.) (1995), *Self-Reliant: Reforming Welfare in the Advanced Societies* (Transaction Publishing).

Marsland, D. and Seaton, N. (1993), *The Empire Strikes Back: the 'Creative Subversion' of the National Curriculum* (CRE).

Marsland, D. and Leoussi, A. (1995), 'Epidemiology' (Chapter in V. Aitken, G. Jordan and H. Jellicoe (eds), *Behavioural Science for Health Care Professionals*, W. B. Saunders).

Marsland, D. and Emly, G. (1996), *Quality in Health Care* (forthcoming).

Matthews, M. (1987), *Poverty in the USSR* (Cambridge University Press).

McKinstry, L. (1995), *Forget Mr Blair, Look at the Record* (Spectator, 21 January).

Mead, L. M. (1986), *Beyond Entitlement: the Social Obligations of Citizenship* (Collier Macmillan).

Mead, L. M. (1992), *The New Politics of Poverty: the Non-working Poor in America* (Basic Books).

Miller, D. (1976), *Social Justice* (Clarendon Press).

Minford, P., *et al.* (1988), *The Housing Morass* (Institute of Economic Affairs).

Minogue, K. (1989), *The Egalitarian Conceit* (Centre for Policy Studies).

Mishra, R. (1990), *The Welfare State in Capitalist Society* (Wheatsheaf).

Mitchell, B. (1989), *Why Social Policy Can't be Morally Neutral: the Current Confusion about Pluralism* (Social Affairs Unit).

Mitchell, D. (1991), *Income Transfers in Ten Welfare States* (Avebury).

Morgan, Patricia (1995), *Farewell to the Family* (Institute of Economic Afffairs).

Morgan, Peter (1991), 'The Morality of Wealth Creation: a Business View' (*Institute of Economic Affairs/Institute of Directors Conference*, 4 July).

Morgan, Peter (ed.) (1994), *New Zealand: the Turnaround Economy* (Institute of Directors).

Moynihan, D. P. (1986), *Family and Nation* (Harcourt Brace Jovanovich).

Moynihan, D. P. (ed.) (1969), *On Understanding Poverty* (Basic Books).

Murray, C. (1984), *Losing Ground: American Social Policy 1950–1980* (Basic Books).

Murray, C. (1990), *The Emerging British Underclass* (Institute of Economic Affairs).

Murray, C. (1994), *The Underclass: the Crisis Deepens* (Institute of Economic Affairs).

Myrdal, G. (1960), *Beyond the Welfare State* (Duckworth).

National Consumer Council (1993), *Paying the Price: a Consumer View of Water, Gas, Electricity, and Telephone Regulation* (HMSO).

National Health Service and Community Care Act (1990, HMSO).

National Opinion Polls (1994), *Care in the Community* (PPP Lifetime).

Norridge, J. (1995), 'Consuming Passion' (*InterCity*, February).

Novak, M. (1982), *The Spirit of Democratic Capitalism* (Madison Books).

Novak, M. (1991), *The Spirit of Democratic Capitalism* (Institute of Economic Affairs).

Nozick, R. (1974), *Anarchy, State, and Utopia* (Basic Books).

Nozick, R. (1981), *Philosophical Explanations* (Oxford University Press).

Nozick, R. (1994), *The Nature of Rationality* (Princeton University Press).

Oakley, A. and Williams, S. (eds) (1994), *The Politics of the Welfare State* (UCL Press).

Oakley, A. and Popay, J. (eds) (1995), *Welfare Research: a Critique of Theory and Method* (UCL Press).

Oakeshott, M. (1991), *Rationalism in Politics and Other Essays* (Liberty Press, 2nd edition).

Offer, J. (ed.) (1993), *Spencer: Political Writings* (Cambridge University Press).

O'Keeffe, D. (1985), *The Wayward Curriculum* (Social Affairs Unit).

O'Keeffe, D. (1994), 'Charity and the State' (*Economic Affairs*, Vol. 14, No. 5).

O'Keeffe, D. (1995), 'Capitalism and Corruption: the Anatomy of a Myth' (Chapter in E. Butler and M. Pirie (eds.), *Markets and Morality*, Adam Smith Institute).

O'Keeffe, D. and Stoll, P. (1995), *School Attendance and Truancy: Understanding and Managing the Problem* (Pitman).

Olaski, M. (1992), *The Tragedy of American Compassion* (Regnery Gateway).

Olsson, S. E. (1990), *Social Policy and the Welfare State in Sweden* (Archiv Forlag).

Oppenheim, C. (1994), *The Welfare State: Putting the Record Straight* (Child Poverty Action Group).

Osborne, D. and Gaebler, T. (1993), *Reinventing Government: How the Entrepreneurial Spirit is Transforming the Public Sector* (Addison-Wesley).

Oyen, E. (1986), *Comparing Welfare States and their Futures* (Avebury).

Page, R. (1971), *The Benefits Racket* (Tom Stacey Ltd).

Page, R. (1993), *Altruism and Social Policy* (Avebury).

Page, R. and Deakin, N. (eds) (1993), *The Costs of Welfare* (Avebury).

Parker, H. (1982), *The Moral Hazards of Social Benefits* (Institute of Economic Affairs).

Peacock, A. T. and Wiseman, J. (1967), *The Growth of Public Expenditure in the UK* (Unwin).

Peters, T. (1993), 'The Performance Imperative' (*Independent on Sunday*, 22 January).

Peters, T. (1994), 'Travel the Independent Road' (*Independent on Sunday*, 2 January).

Phillips, M. (1994), 'The Wrongs of Standing up for Rights' (*Observer*, 19 June).

Phillips, M. (1994 [2]), 'Nit-picking Nightmare for BBC Baby' (*Observer*, 11 September).

Pierson, C. (1991), *Beyond the Welfare State* (Polity Press).

Pirie, M. (1988), *Privatization: Theory, Practice, and Choice* (Adam Smith Institute).

Pirie, M. (1994), 'Reforming the Welfare State' (Chapter 3 in M. Bell *et al.*, *The End of the Welfare State*, Adam Smith Institute).

Plant, R. *et al.* (1980), *Political Philosophy and Social Welfare* (Routledge Kegan Paul).

Plant, R. and Barry, N. (1990), *Citizenship and Rights* (Institute of Economic Affairs).

Pliatzky, L. (1982), *Getting and Spending* (Blackwell).

Pollard, S. (1983), *The Development of the British Economy 1914–80* (3rd edition, Edward Arnold; 4th edition 1992).

Pope, R., Pratt, A., and Hoyle, B. (eds) (1986), *Social Welfare in Britain 1885–1985* (Croom Helm).

Popenoe, D. (1988), *Disturbing the Nest: Family Change and Decline in Modern Society* (Aldine de Gruyter).

Power, A. (1993), *Hovels to High Rise: State Housing in Europe since 1850* (Routledge).

Quest, C. (ed.) (1992), *Equal Opportunities: A Feminist Fallacy* (Institute of Economic Affairs).

Randall, G. and Brown, S. (1994), *Falling Out: a Research Study of Homeless Ex-Service People* (Crisis).

Rawls, J. (1972), *A Theory of Justice* (Oxford University Press).

Reagan, R. (1971), *Meeting the Challenge: a Responsible Program for Welfare and Medical Reform* (Office of the Governor of California).

Rector, R. (1992), 'Requiem for the War on Poverty', *Policy Review* (No. 61, Summer, pp. 40–6).

Redwood, J. (1983), *Public Enterprise in Crisis* (Blackwell).

Reece, D. (1994), 'Trouble Ahead as State Care Fails the Masses' (*Sunday Telegraph*, 20 November).

256   *Bibliography*

Ricketts, M. (1994), 'Housing without the State' (*Economic Affairs*, Vol. 14, No. 5).
Rigby, R. (1995), 'A Perspective on Property's Past' (*Management Today*, May).
Robinson, C. *et al.* (1994), *Regulating the Utilities: the Way Forward* (Institute of Economic Affairs).
Robinson, I. (1983), 'Subsidizing Stigma: Social Consequences of Council Housing Policies' (In D. C. Anderson and D. Marsland (eds), *Home Truths*, Social Affairs Unit).
Roepke, W. (1992), *The Social Crisis of our Time* (Transaction Books).
Rose, R. and Shiratori, R. (1987), *The Welfare State East and West* (Oxford University Press).
Roth, G. and Wittich, C. (eds) (1978), *Max Weber – Economy and Society* (University of California Press).
Rowntree Foundation (1995), *Inquiry into Income and Wealth*, Volume 1 (Joseph Rowntree Foundation).
Salter, B. and Tapper, T. (1994), *The State and Higher Education* (Woburn Press).
Saunders, P. (1990), *Social Class and Stratification* (Routledge).
Saunders, P. (1990 [2]), *A Nation of Home Owners* (Unwin Hyman).
Saunders, P. (1994), 'Social Mobility and Meritocracy' (Chapter 4 in D. Marsland (ed.), *Work and Employment in Liberal Democratic Societies*).
Saunders, P. (1995), 'Might Britain be a Meritocracy?' (*Sociology*, Vol. 29, No. 1).
Saunders, P. and Harris, C. (1989), *Popular Attitudes to State Welfare Provision* (Social Affairs Unit).
Saunders, P. and Harris, C. (1990), 'Privatization and the Consumer' (*Sociology*, Vol. 24, No. 1).
Savas, E. S. (1982), *Privatizing the Public Sector* (Chatham House).
Savas, E. S. (1987), *Privatization: the Key to Better Government* (Chatham House).
Schmahl, W. (ed.) (1991), *The Future of Basic and Supplementary Pension Schemes in the European Community* (Nomos Verlagsgesellschaft).
Scrivens, E. (1991),'Disease' (*Social Policy and Administration*, Vol. 25, No. 1).
Scrivens, E. (1993), *Widening Consumer Choice in Social Welfare* (Avebury).
Segalman, R. (1978), *Dynamics of Social Behaviour and Development* (University Press of America).
Segalman, R. (1986), *The Swiss Way of Welfare* (Praeger).
Segalman, R. (1994), 'The Underclass Revisited: Causes and Solutions' (Chapter 5 in D. Marsland (ed.), *Work and Employment in Liberal Democratic Societies*).
Segalman, R. and Basu, A. (1981), *Poverty in America* (Greenwood).
Segalman, R. and Marsland, D. (1989), *Cradle to Grave: Comparative Perspectives on the State of Welfare* (Macmillan).
Segalman, R. and Himelson, A. (1994), 'The Family: Past, Present and Future' (Paper presented to a PWPA Conference, 28 April–2 May, Seoul, Korea).
Seldon, A. (1981), *Wither the Welfare State* (Institute of Economic Affairs).
Seldon, A. (1990), *Capitalism* (Blackwell).
Seldon, A. (ed.) (1994), 'Welfare: the Lost Century' (Special Issue, Vol. 14, No. 5, of *Economic Affairs*).
Seldon, A. (1994 [2]), 'Saving for Life-time Risks' (*Economic Affairs*, Vol. 14, No. 5).
Seldon, A. (1994 [3]), *The State is Rolling Back* (Institute of Economic Affairs).

Sen, A. (1987), *The Standard of Living* (Cambridge University Press).

Sen, A. and Williams, B. (eds) (1987), *Utilitarianism and Beyond* (Cambridge University Press).

Shand, A. H. (1989), *Free Market Morality: the Political Economy of the Austrian School* (Routledge).

Shaw, B. (1983), *Comprehensive Schooling: the Impossible Dream* (Blackwell).

Shepherd, D. (1983), *Bias to the Poor* (Hodder and Stoughton).

Shils, E. A. (1982), *The Constitution of Society* (University of Chicago Press).

Shrimsley, R. (1995), 'Lilley Studies Plan for Local Benefit Levels' (*Daily Telegraph*, 10 January).

Sillen, B. (1990), *The Rise and Decline of the Swedish Welfare State* (Foretagareforbundets Rapporter).

Sirico, R. (1994), *A Moral Basis for Liberty* (Institute of Economic Affairs).

Sissons, M. and French, P. (eds) (1963), *The Age of Austerity 1945–51* (Hodder and Stoughton).

Smiles, S. (1860), *Self-help* (John Murray).

Smiles, S. (1986), *Self-help: with Illustrations of Conduct and Perseverance* (abridged by G. Bull, with an introduction by Sir Keith Joseph, Penguin).

Smith, G. (1980), *Social Need* (RKP).

Soto, H. de (1990), *The Other Path: the Invisible Revolution in the Third World* (Harper and Row).

Sowell, T. (1981), *Markets and Minorities* (Blackwell).

Sowell, T. (1989), 'Affirmative Action: a Worldwide Disaster' (*Commentary*, Vol. 88, No. 6).

Spencer, H. (1873), *The Study of Sociology* (Henry King).

Spencer, H. (1908), *The Man Versus the State* (Appleton).

Spencer, H. (1910), *The Principles of Ethics* (Appleton).

Spiro, S. E. and Yuchtman-Yaar, E. (1983), *Evaluating the Welfare State* (Academic Press).

Stein, P. (1990), 'The Swedish Model' (*Institute of Humane Studies Network Newsletter*, Spring).

Stelzer, I. (1994), 'Runaway Welfare Costs Stoke Fears of Inflation' (*Sunday Times*, 28 August).

Stelzer, I. (1995), 'Clinton Swept to the Right by Republican Tidal Wave' (*Sunday Times*, 15 January).

Stigler, G. J. (1946), 'The Economics of Minimum Wage Legislation' (*American Economic Review*, Vol. 36, June, pp. 358–65).

Stoese, D. and Karger, H. (1994), 'The Decline of the American Welfare State' (*Social Policy and Administration*, Vol. 26, No. 1, Pages 3–17).

Sullivan, M. (1994), *Modern Social Policy* (Harvester).

Swaan, A. de (1988), *In Care of the State: Health, Education and Welfare in Europe and the USA in the Modern Era* (Polity Press).

Taverne, R. (1994), *Pensions Time-bomb in Europe* (The Federal Trust).

Taylor, P. J. and Burridge, J. (1982), 'Trends in Death, Disablement, and Sickness Absence in the British Post Office since 1891' (*British Journal of Industrial Medicine*, 39, 1–10).

Taylor-Gooby, P. (1986), 'Privatization, Power, and the Welfare State' (*Sociology*, Vol. 20, No. 2).

Thane, P. (1982), *Foundations of the Welfare State* (Longman).

The Times (1993), First Leader: 'The Benefit Calculus' (2 December).

Thurnham, P. (1993), *Choose Your Landlord: Best Choice for Tenants – Private Landlords* (Conservative Political Centre).

Titmuss, R. (1958), *Essays on the Welfare State* (Allen and Unwin).

Titmuss, R. (1968), *Commitment to Welfare* (Allen and Unwin).

Titmuss, R. (1970), *The Gift Relationship* (Allen and Unwin).

Townsend, P. (1979), *Poverty in the UK* (Penguin).

Transport and General Workers Union (1994), *In Place of Fear* (Transport and General Workers Union, Child Poverty Action Group, Low Pay Unit and Family Welfare Association).

USDAW (1994), *Social and Economic Policy for the Future.*

Vinson, N. (1994), 'Can the Nation Afford Pensions' (*Economic Affairs*, Vol. 14, No. 5).

Waldegrave, W. (1993), Speech to the Institute of Directors' Annual Convention.

Walker, A. and Walker, C. (eds) (1987), *The Growing Divide* (Child Poverty Action Group).

Walker, C. (1993), *Managing Poverty: the Limits of Social Assistance* (Routledge).

Walker, P. (1994), 'What Happens When you Scrap the Welfare State' (*Independent on Sunday*, 13 March).

Wann, Mai (1995), *Building Social Capital: Self Help in the Twenty-first Century Welfare State* (Institute for Public Policy Research).

Warde, A. ((1994), 'Consumption, Identity-formation and Uncertainty' (*Sociology*, Vol. 28, No. 4).

West, E. G. (1970), *Education and the State* (Institute of Economic Affairs).

West, E. G. (1990), 'Restoring Family Autonomy in Education' (*Chronicles*, Vol. 14, No. 10, pp. 16–21).

West, E. G. (1994), '*Education without the State*' (*Economic Affairs*, Vol, 14, No. 5).

Whelan, R. (1989), *Mounting Greenery* (Institute of Economic Affairs).

Whelan, R. (1994), *Broken Homes and Battered Children* (Family Education Trust).

White Paper on Health (1989), *Working for Patients* (HMSO).

Whitney, R. (1988), *National Health Crisis* (Shepeard-Walwyn).

Wicks, M. (1987), *A Future for All: Do We Need a Welfare State?* (Penguin).

Wildavsky, A. (1987), *Searching for Safety* (Transaction Books).

Wilding, P. (ed.) (1986), *In Defence of the Welfare State* (Manchester University Press).

Wilding, P. (1992), 'Social Policy in the 1980s' (*Social Policy and Administration*, Vol. 26, No. 2).

Wilkinson, R. (1990), 'Income Distribution and Mortality: a "Natural" Experiment' (*Sociology of Health and Illness*, 12 (4) pp. 391–412).

Wilkinson, R. (1994), *Unfair Shares* (Barnardos).

Willetts, D. (1993), *The Age of Entitlement* (Social Market Foundation).

Williams, C. (1994), 'Diagnosing the Cost of Private Health Plans' (*Sunday Times*, 18 September).

Williams, K. and Williams, J. (eds.) (1987), *A Beveridge Reader* (Allen and Unwin).

Williams, W. (1982), *The State against Blacks* (McGraw Hill).

Williams, W. (1994), 'Ethnic Minorities and Work' (Chapter 7 in D. Marsland (ed.), *Work and Employment in Liberal Democratic Societies*).

Wilson, J. Q. (1994), *The Moral Sense* (Free Press).

Wilson, T. and Wilson, D. (eds) (1991), *The State and Social Welfare* (Longman).

Wilson, W. J. (1987), *The Truly Disadvantaged* (Chicago University Press).

Wiseman, J. (1983), 'The Economics of Social Policy' (Proceedings of the International Institute of Public Finance, Wayne State University Press, 1983).

Wiseman, J. and Marsland, D. (1985), 'The Social Welfare Programme of the Republic of China' (Economists' Advisory Group for the Council for Economic Planning and Development of the ROC, 1985).

Wood, J. B. (1975), *How Little Unemployment? A Micro-economic Examination* (Institute of Economic Affairs).

Yarrow, G. (1994), 'The Friendly Societies' (*Economic Affairs*, Vol. 14, No. 5).

Yarrow, G. and Lawton Smith, H. (1993), *Social Security and Friendly Societies: Options for the Future* (National Conference of Friendly Societies).

Index

Abel-Smith, Titmus, 31
Adam Smith Institute, 201, 207, 225, 228
Affordability of state welfare, 64ff.
Anderson, D. C., 6, 12, 120, 186, 196
Assistance for the helpless, 175
Austerity and affluence, 26
  centralised control, 28

BBC Advice Shop, 24
Bacon and Eltis, 67
Barnett, C., 67
Barry, N., 19, 21, 36
Bell, M., 66, 203
Benefits: conditional upon behaviour, 25, 181
Benefit system fraud, 9, 83, 123, 124, 126, 183, 235–43
Beveridge, W., confusion in welfare thinking, 32, 33, 171
Black Report, 51, 212
'blaming the victim', 115
Borrie Report, 197, 199, 219
Bosanquet, N., 155, 156
British left, 197, 198
British people, trust in, 158
Bureaucracy, 1, 3, 95–101

Caines, E., 98
Capitation, 57
'cardboard city', 43
Cassam, E., 106
Cathy Come Home, 8
Central planning, failures, 101ff., 166
Charities, traditional role, 205
Cheung, S., 144
Child benefit, 73, 122
Child Poverty Action Group, 45, 48, 127
Child Support Agency, 167
Church Action for Poverty, Jihad, 42
Commission on Social Justice, 197, 219

Commitment to self-reliance sabotaged, 130
Consumer, 133ff., 152
Council house sales, 22, 171
Culture of entrepreneurship, 153

Delors, J., 8
Dennis, N., 119
Dependency culture, 120, 188
Discretionary welfare, 186
Donnison, D., 43

Enthoven, A., 167
Equality, 21ff., 221
  -mongering, 43
Esping-Anderson, G., 14

Family, 114, 119, 127, 194, 231
Field, F., 113, 118, 131, 192
Flew, A., 20, 24, 26, 170, 292

Gammon, M., 139
Gigantism, 100
Gilder, G., 14, 33, 152
Gingrich, N., 18
Glennerster, H., 98, 186
Grant Maintained Schools, 97
Greedy envy, 28
Green, D., 21, 48, 90, 142, 159, 201
Green movement, 145

Ham, C., 208, 214
Hampstead catechism, 120
Harris, R., 141
Hayek, F., 93, 102
Health care re-structuring, 4, 170, 207ff.
Higgins, J., 12, 13, 14
Hills, J., 75ff.
Himmelfarb, G., 131
Home-ownership, 27
Horowitz, I. L., 46
Housing rights, 4, 125
Howard, M., 135